AMERICAN GOTHIC:

The Mind and Art of
Ralph Adams Cram

Robert Muccigrosso

University Press
of America™

Copyright © 1980 by

University Press of America, Inc.™

4710 Auth Place, S.E., Washington, D.C. 20023

All rights reserved
Printed in the United States of America

ISBN: 0-8191-0884-7
Library of Congress Number: 79-5436

Copyright 1979 by Robert Muccigrosso

Quotations from My Life in Architecture by Ralph Adams Cram, Copyright 1936 by Ralph Adams Cram, by permission of Little, Brown and Company.

Portions of the book have appeared in "American Gothic: Ralph Adams Cram," Thought, 47 (Spring, 1972) 102-118, Copyright by Fordham University Press, and "Ralph Adams Cram: The Architect as Communitarian," Prospects, I (1975), 165-178, Copyright by Burt Franklin & Co., Inc. & Jack Salzman, and are reprinted by permission of the publishers.

FRONTISPIECE

Ralph Adams Cram - Courtesy of the Boston Public Library, Print
Department, and Hoyle, Doran and Berry

4403

To my mother

CONTENTS

Illustrations follow page 100

ACKNOWLEDGMENTS

It is a pleasure to acknowledge the generous
assistance I have received from various individuals
in the preparation of this book. Special thanks are
due to several members of the Cram family. Mrs. Mary
Carrington Nicholas, daughter of Ralph Adams Cram,
graciously granted me permission to quote from her
father's unpublished writings; Mr. Ralph Adams Cram II
provided me with several photographs of his grandfather; Mrs. Shirley Wall shared with me some reminiscences of her uncle. I also would like to acknowledge the truly delightful interview given me by
the late Ralph Wentworth Cram, the architect's son.
Mr. John T. Doran of Hoyle, Doran and Berry, successors to Cram, has aided me in diverse ways--permit-
ting access to his firm's papers, providing photographs, offering recollections--and I wish to thank
him for his kindness and patience. Colleagues at
Brooklyn College have been supportive of my work and
helpful with their suggestions. Among them, I particularly would like to thank Abraham S. Eisenstadt
for some early useful criticisms. I am also indebted
to scholars elsewhere, especially to Edward A.
Gosselin for his penetrating questions and assorted
suggestions, and to Douglass Shand Tucci for several
stimulating discussions. Too numerous to individuate,
the staffs of the following have my gratitude for
their unfailing courtesy and helpfulness: the Boston
Public Library, the New York Public Library, the
American Academy and Institute of Arts and Letters,
Hoyle, Doran and Berry, and the various libraries of
the Massachusetts Institute of Technology, Brown University, Yale University, Columbia University, and
the College of the Holy Cross.
Mrs. Marian Nock has generously granted permission to quote from the unpublished letters of Albert
Jay Nock, as has the Mercantile-Safe Deposit and
Trust Company of Baltimore, Maryland, Trustee under
the Will of Henry Louis Mencken, with regard to the
unpublished letters of Henry L. Mencken. Fordham
University Press and Burt Franklin & Co., Inc. & Jack
Salzman have given their kind permission to reprint
material which previously appeared in their publica-
tions. My thanks to Little, Brown and Company for
their permission to quote from My Life in Architec-

ture by Ralph Adams Cram, Copyright 1936 By Ralph Adams Cram.

As my typist, Nevah Assang has my thanks for all the assistance she rendered so cheerfully.

Finally, my greatest debt is to my friend of many years, Elizabeth Brunoski, for her warm encouragement and invaluable editorial suggestions.

New York, 1979   Robert Muccigrosso

INTRODUCTION

While he lived, Ralph Adams Cram was most renowned for his work as an architect. Devoting his
talents primarily to the design of churches and
schools, he was almost singlehandedly responsible for
a major Gothic revival in American architecture. Indeed, in speaking of his achievements as a designer
of churches, one modern critic believes that his work
"persuaded the land to an almost complete revolution
in the visual image of American Christianity."[1] His
principal efforts--the uncompleted Cathedral of St.
John the Divine, splendid churches like St. Thomas'
(New York), and a number of buildings at West Point,
Princeton, and Rice Institute--made his a household
name among architects and knowledgeable laymen alike,
winning for him a reputation as the finest Gothicist
in the nation's history and as the man "who could
justify the flying buttress in the age of Bryan."[2]

Yet Cram steadfastly refused to think of himself
only as a builder. Architecture, in his opinion,
constituted a touchstone for civilization to which it
both gave and reflected values. In the long run, art
could be no better (or worse) than the milieu from
which it sprang. Consequently, he was fully as concerned for the quality of those elements which comprised civilization as he was for architecture as
pure art. Author of numerous books and nearly one
hundred articles, as well as poems and plays, in literary terms he has been America's most prolific architect. That most of these works deal either with
architecture in its larger relation to society or
directly with political, socioeconomic, and religious
questions, underscores his commitment to the quest
for a better society. There exists, moreover, a
striking parallel between his architecture and his
social views. A Gothicist in his artistic prefer-
ences, he looked to the Middle Ages for a model of
what society could and should be like.

As a social critic, however, Cram has exerted
a diffuse rather than concentrated influence, a fact
which may account for the scant attention he has received from modern scholars. A few of these scholars
have remarked on the strange neglect into which he
has fallen; few have offered any extended analysis of
his ideas.[3] While all have agreed that these ideas
form part of the twentieth-century American conserva-

vative tradition, they have differed as to exactly why he is a conservative. At various times his elitism, anti-democratic prejudices, Anglo-Saxonism, and medievalism have been cited, but in each instance the treatment has been too meager to be of much assistance. To say, as Clinton Rossiter did, that his "love for the 'High Democracy' of the Middle Ages was the zenith of intellectual reaction in the United States,"[4] and to say virtually nothing else, is to miss the richer complexity of his thought.

Given the confusions which have surrounded the tradition, the student of intellectual history might do well to rephrase Crèvecoeur's two-century-old question to ask: "What then is the Conservative, this new man man?" To be sure, there are certain general characteristics which tend to set apart persons of this ideological persuasion: a propensity to look backward to some imagined Golden Age, a distrust of liberals and radicals, a strain of elitism and anti-democratic prejudice, and a repugnance for what loosely may be termed modernism. Yet heated disagreement among conservatives themselves compounds the problem of definition. Not every conservative, for example, readily admits to looking backwards, and for those who do, the foci are disparate. Nor would all accept the label "anti-democratic." Citing Jefferson or other suitable figures, some believe themselves to be staunch champions of democracy, asking only that the term be properly understood. Further, while most have deplored the conditions of their contemporary age, who, to one extent or another, has not? Turning to other areas-- education, the arts, business, religion, science--one again looks in vain for a definite consensus of conservative thought. Patterns exist, but not a precise definition. The whole simply does not equal the sum of its parts: the American conservative is both more and less than the sum of his characteristics.

Nor is defining the conservative simply as a defender of tradition particularly useful. What tradition? Whose tradition? Besides, as Louis Hartz has argued, there may be precious little in the way of a conservative tradition to defend.[5] At heart, so his argument runs, the vast majority of Americans have been Lockean liberals. Hartz may have overstated his case, but the fact remains that, lacking a medieval past, the United States has provided neither plentiful nor fertile soil for sowing and sustaining the seeds of a feudal-based Old World conservatism.

What sets apart Cram from other conservative intellectual figures in the nation's history--with the exceptions of some slavery and plantation system apologists in the antebellum South and a few twentieth-century conservatives such as Robert Nisbet and Richard Weaver[6]--is his adamant refusal to accept the implications of Hartz's thesis. Agreeing that the country offered a poor setting for the traditional European brand of conservatism, he nevertheless toiled as assiduously to evoke a medieval revival as he did to achieve a Gothic revival. Criticism to the contrary, he never meant for his medievalism to be construed literally. Though he did believe that some select practices and institutions of the Middle Ages could in modified form be resuscitated, it was the spirit of that era which most impressed him and which he thought could serve as symbolic and paradigmatic models for the modern world.

A second feature which distinguishes Cram's thought from that of many other conservatives is his conception of art as a force for social change. Recently, a few scholars have concluded that the essential importance of modern American conservatism has resided in its basically aesthetic efforts to restrain the worst of the effusions generated by democracy.[7] This seems to be another way of saying that the best conservatism can offer is largely negative in nature. Cram disagreed. Viewing art as "the most reliable history of a time,"[8] he saw the artistic effort as a means for attaining the summum bonum of society. Practicing what he persistently preached, he demanded that artists should act as guides by producing positive, yea-saying works. For his part, he proposed a congeries of changes which, if implemented, would amount to no less than a radical restructuring of his own society. A philosophical conservative he might be; a conserver of contemporary values and institutions he assuredly was not.

Cram's example strengthens the argument that American conservatism, a coat of many colors, defies neat definition. It is as though it were a kaleidoscope. Turned one way and then another, its variegated ingredients become first highlighted and then distorted as one looks in vain for T.S. Eliot's "stillpoint of the turning world." Frederick Jackson Turner once perceptively suggested that each generation tends to rewrite history in the light of its own values and experiences. A corollary of this observation might be that each age singles out those elements of a tradition which most pertain to its

3

current problems. This ultimately may be the fate of conservative thought. Cumbersome and diffuse when taken as a totality, it becomes most useful only when its diverse elements are disentangled and singled out for consideration and possible application. The same may be said for the views held by Ralph Adams Cram.

Books which explore more fully the prodigious body and technical virtuosity of Cram's architecture or which fit his ideas in greater detail into the American conservative tradition remain to be written. This book is a general consideration of Cram's achievements as both architect and social critic. It is a beginning, a study, to use Stewart Holbrook's phrase, of one of the "lost men of American history."

NOTES

1. Douglass Shand Tucci, Church Building in Boston: 1720-1970 (Concord, Mass., 1974), p. 85.
2. Oliver W. Larkin, Art and Life in America, 2nd ed., rev. (New York, 1960), p. 339.
3. For citations of Cram as a conservative, see Russell Kirk, The Conservative Mind: From Burke to Santayana (Chicago, 1953); Clinton Rossiter, Conservatism in America (New York, 1955); David Spitz, Patterns of Anti-Democratic Thought, 2nd ed., rev. (New York, 1965); Allen Guttmann, The Conservative Tradition in America (New York, 1967); Ronald Lora, Conservative Minds in America (New York, 1971); Michael Wreszin, The Superfluous Anarchist: Albert Jay Nock (Providence, R.I., 1972); Robert M. Crunden, The Mind and Art of Albert Jay Nock (Chicago, 1964) and From Self to Society: 1919-1941 (Englewood Cliffs, N.J., 1972). While Wreszin does devote the better part of a chapter to Cram, it basically (and understandably) examines the influence which he exerted on Nock.
4. Rossiter, Conservatism, p. 168.
5. Louis Hartz, The Liberal Tradition in America: An Interpretation of American Political Thought since the Revolution (New York, 1955).
6. Though Nisbet and the late Richard Weaver are not, strictly speaking, medievalists, their attacks on modern liberalism and the omnipotent state derive in part from their appreciation for certain aspects of the Middle Ages, notably its decentralization and communitarianism. For other modern conservatives who have been influenced by the medieval example, see George H. Nash, The Conservative Intellectual Movement in America: Since 1945 (New York, 1979), passim.
7. See especially the previously cited works of Guttmann and Lora.
8. Ralph Adams Cram, The Substance of Gothic (Boston, 1917), p. 15.

CHAPTER 1

THE EARLY YEARS: FAMILY AND APPRENTICESHIP

Until more recent times it has not been exceptional for Americans who have achieved considerable success and fame to have been born and raised in small towns. On the contrary, it probably has been closer to the rule that most of these men and women did have their roots in obscure, provincial habitations. Certainly this was the case for Ralph Adams Cram, who on December 16, 1863, was born in Hampton Falls, New Hampshire.

Situated in the extreme southeastern part of the state and bordering the ocean, Rockingham County, New Hampshire, contains the important coastal city of Portsmouth as well as the small totality of the state's beaches. It also encompasses a host of tiny hamlets and rural areas whose inhabitants since colonial days have struggled to earn a precarious living from the craggy soil of the region. Hampton Falls, only a few miles from the Massachusetts border and not to be confused with nearby Hampton, North Hampton, or Hampton Beach, is one such hamlet. In the mid-nineteenth century it possessed only a few thousand residents, most of whom were farmers, as had been their ancestors since the seventeenth century. Nor did they appear to have welcomed change. Perhaps it was the Puritan legacy with its albatross of Original Sin; perhaps it was nothing more than ingrained skepticism hardened by painfully raw winters. Or perhaps it was the determination to safeguard traditional values in the unmistakably threatening face of industrial change. Whatever the reason, when the Eastern Railroad, one of New England's most important burgeoning lines during the early years of the Iron Horse, proposed to extend a trunkline through the town, the residents summarily declined the offer. They preferred, instead, the secure, if harsh, life-as-is to the then uncertain prospects of change wrought by this revolutionary form of transportation. As a result, the line was forced to detour through marshland a mile outside the community.[1] The Eastern Railroad had been inconvenienced; Hampton Falls proverbially had signed its own death warrant in terms of any possible future growth. Today the township contains less than one thousand inhabitants.

If Ralph Adams Cram was less than fortunate to have a stagnant, backwater birthplace, he fared considerably better with respect to parentage. In fact, he fared quite well.

William Augustine Cram (1837-1908), Ralph's father, was able to trace his lineage approximately one thousand years back to a certain Ludolf von Cramm, a Teutonic knight living in the Duchy of Brunswick at the time of Louis the Pious. After several centuries, one of his descendants, a baron, migrated with family and soldiers to England, just in time to fight for Henry VIII against the Scots. Settling there, the von Cramms anglicized their name by dropping both the "von" and the final "m."

At least one of the baron's scions, however, apparently did not find the country congenial. John Cram (1596 or 1597-1682) from Bilsby (Lincolnshire), along with his wife Hester and their four children, set sail for the New World in 1634, reaching Boston the following year.[2] Five years later he and a small group of other malcontents who chafed under Puritan rule forsook the Massachusetts Bay Colony, traveled northward, and founded Exeter, New Hamshire, where he was allotted eight acres for himself and his family in the original distribution of land. When New Hampshire voluntarily became part of the Massachusetts Bay Colony in 1642 he joined the "Combination," the small party which continued to oppose domination by the Puritans. After he moved to nearby Hampton in 1650 and subsequently to Hampton Falls (part of old Hampton), little is known of him, however. At the time of his death the public record simply stated: "Good old John Cram, one just in his generation."[3]

If John Cram did nothing in his lifetime that was of lasting historical note, by coming to the New World he was responsible for a proliferation of subsequent Crams throughout the New England countryside. The Census of 1790, the nation's first, for example, indicates that there were fifty-eight of them as heads of families in New Hampshire, six in Maine, and cne in Massachusetts.[4] Occasionally, one of his descendants, either lineal or collateral, achieved national recognition, usually for martial successes. Both General Henry Dearborn (1751-1829), who served with distinction during the Revolutionary War and as Secretary of War under President Jefferson, and General Thomas Jefferson Cram (1805-1883), who was a professor of mathematics and of natural and experimental philosophy at West Point, and later served as an engineer during the Civil War, are cases in point. For the most part, however, they remained obscure. Ralph Adams Cram, for example, noted that his direct forbears--without exception--were simple tillers of the soil. "Simple" is perhaps misleading, at least when applied to his grandfather, who, though remaining a farmer, also became a staunch abolitionist. Much influenced by the moral views of Emerson and Thoreau, this "simple" man converted his farmhouse into a temporary haven for runaway slaves.[5]

Fewer details are available concerning the ancestry of Ralph Adams Cram's mother, Sarah Elizabeth Blake (1840-1927), although it is known that her first American progenitor was one John Blake, who came from Norfolk, England sometime in the 1630's.[6] There is information, however, pertaining to her father, Ira Blake, who, from all accounts, appears to have been an impressive man. The "Squire," as the family invariably referred to him, lived near Hampton Falls in Kensington on his small estate, "The Old Place," in a style akin to that of an impoverished but proud seventeenth-century English gentryman. The food which the family ate came entirely from the premises; even the rugs were braided at home. More than that, it was claimed that everything at "The Old Place" was done in the mid-nineteenth century exactly as it had been done at the time of William and Mary. In his politics the Squire had been an Adams Federalist, retaining that party's principles long after its demise. For his grandson, who was a constant visitor during school holidays, Blake and his life-style were to remain as cherished memories and also as reminders of a vestigial quasi-feudalism, whose European roots could not survive the transplantation to American soil.[7]

William Cram and Sara Blake were married in 1862, and the following year witnessed the birth of Ralph, the first of their three children. At this time a serious crisis of conscience confronted William. The Union, badly in need of additional man-

9

power to fight the Confederacy, had invoked con-
scription in 1863 and had called him into service.
Passionately hating slavery but believing that war
was ignoble except in clear-cut cases of self-de-
fense, he refused induction. Taken to Concord for
a hearing, he informed the governor that he was
willing to don a uniform but would never fire a gun.
As a matter of principle he refused to resort to the
common practice of hiring a substitute, preferring,
instead, to suffer imprisonment. Without his knowledge and much to his chagrin, however, his brother
hastily procured a willing substitute. William Cram
never forgave this brother for his well-intentioned
but misconceived assistance. [8]

Soon after the birth of his son, Cram decided
that to remain a farmer--and only a farmer--for the
rest of his life, though faithful to the familial
tradition, would be personally insufficient. Consequently, following his religious bent, he studied
theology and in 1866 was ordained in Boston as a Unitarian minister by one of New England's most eminent
divines, the Reverend Edward Everett Hale. Though
not yet three at the time of his father's ordination,
Ralph later could recall the occasion and the family's subsequent celebration, which included attending a theatrical performance of Harriet Beecher
Stowe's still popular Uncle Tom's Cabin. For some
reason not altogether clear, William's new vocation
aroused bitter resentment in his parents, who exact-
ed a promise from their son that wherever his duties
might carry him, he would return to Hampton Falls to
care for them when they became aged. [9]

For the next dozen years the family, which had
come to include another son, William Everett, and a
daughter, Marion,[10] lived first in Augusta, Maine
until 1872 and then in Westford, Massachusetts. Of
the two, Westford, near Lowell and not too distant
from Boston, seems to have provided the greater sense
of fulfillment. There, though he had earned a reputation for radicalism and mysticism, the minister was
extremely popular. In addition, the community, while
small, seemed almost cosmopolitan in comparison with
the more isolated Hampton Falls. If nothing else,
the Crams were intellectually oriented and were able
to find more like-minded persons in Westford. Moreover, they entertained dreams of sending their children to college, a possibility made distinct by
Mr. Cram's growing congregation and his hard work as
a farmer six days of the week. In 1878, however, the

10

dream was destroyed as the minister's parents, reminding their son of his earlier promise, summoned him and his family back to Hampton Falls. A man of his word, he complied, though by Ralph's later account the parents by no means needed care. The decision to return to Hampton Falls came as a particularly cruel blow to Sara Cram, who chafed at the intellectual provincialism.[11] Worse, the New Hampshire hamlet could not support another Unitarian minister, even though he be a native son. William perforce would have to return as a full-time farmer. And the children? College had become, figuratively speaking, an academic question.

Of all the discernible formative influences wrought by his parents, what stands out most clearly in the case of Ralph Adams Cram is the respect for learning which they inculcated in him. For the American living in the second half of the twentieth century when a college education has become all but de rigueur, it is somewhat of a marvel to reflect upon the large number of those who lived during the preceding century and who, bereft of higher formal education, taught themselves what is today taught by others. The Crams, in this instance, are exemplary. The son saw in his parents two complementary opposites. His mother, despite her poetic avocations, remained basically a confirmed rationalist; his father, despite the sobriety of his Unitarian religion, was, at heart, a "mystical philosopher."[12] Yet they shared a catholicity of intellectual interests. Both were, for example, gifted amateur linguists, who nearly every evening read to one another in French and/or German, as well as in English. Appropriately, young Ralph learned Latin from his father rather than from any formal instruction. According to the son, moreover, the Crams possessed an extensive library. Spinoza, Kant, Hegel, Arnold, Ruskin, and Emerson were among William Cram's favorite authors, as were Swedenborg, Blake, and the German mystics. More and more, William and Sara were forced to rely upon themselves for intellectual stimulation. Admittedly, the Reverend Cram, now involuntarily but permanently retired from the ministry, had set up a shoe repair shop in his garden where he did his best to discourse on arcane subjects to those--and they were fairly numerous--who visited him. Nevertheless, the bulk of the townspeople, while "bright," simply lacked his breadth of knowledge and interests.[13]

11

For Ralph, there was a certain sense of tragic non-fulfillment in his father's life. Writing almost incessantly during his last twenty-five years, the minister published virtually nothing. Yet in the adoring eyes and mind of his son he could have been famous in literature, philosophy, or science. In later years Ralph concluded that his father's lack of public achievements had been by choice, a case of a gifted man having limited, almost nonexistent personal ambitions. Questioning whether or not men who, like his father, spent their time in quiet meditation rather than in spirited accomplishment were not really better off, he wrote: "The material things--yes, even time, space, personality--may be but Maya, illusion, but thought is the abiding reality behind the show."[14] Still, one wonders. William Cram may genuinely have been a man of limited personal expectations. On the other hand, he--and, for that matter, his wife--may have been among those whom Thoreau so perceptibly characterized as having led "lives of quiet desperation."

As he grew up amid this familial reverence for learning, Ralph became an omnivorous reader, biting off and sometimes ingesting every book in his father's library. Much interested in works of science, his appetite--and tenacity--extended even as far as the seven volumes of Herbert Spencer's Synthetic Philosophy. In addition, he had a special interest in books pertaining to literature and, more important for the future, art. Of all the authors he read, Matthew Arnold and John Ruskin were his favorites.[15]

William Cram noticed more than his son's literary interest in art. Watching Ralph paint and sketch, he convinced himself that his eldest child had been endowed with genuine artistic talent. Since Ralph was now a teenager, the question of career had become both dominant and vexatious. If the father could not afford to send his intelligent, inquisitive son to college, just as surely he would not allow him to become a farmer. The son manifested a decided interest in acting, but the thought of a career in the theater was doubtlessly anathema, even for a "radical" minister. Nor did the ministry itself seem suitable. Ralph had evinced little enthusiasm for formal religion; the parents had never counseled otherwise.[16] With high hopes, Cram took a selection of his son's artistic works to Boston to obtain a professional evaluation. He never did tell him the exact details of the subsequent appraisal, but as Ralph later noted: "I took notice of the fact that an artist's career was not thereafter referred to by him or my mother with any degree either of confidence or enthusiasm."[17]

At approximately the age of fourteen, Ralph began to take an unusual interest in cutting out pictures of houses and public buildings from magazines and then arranging them to form an integrated town. Sometimes he would build cardboard houses, fill them with dried weeds, and then burn them. His parents were not quite sure whether he would become an arsonist or an architect, but, hoping for the latter, they encouraged his enthusiasm.[18] For his fifteenth birthday they presented him with a copy of C.J. Richardson's House Building (1873), a book which very quickly captivated his fancy. As he studied and restudied this work, along with Ruskin's The Seven Lamps of Architecture (1849) and The Stones of Venice (1851), Ralph's impulses gradually became less diffuse, and he moved toward the definition of a future career. Influenced by these readings, he later avowed: "I had three full years in close contact with good architecture and inspiring artistic theory before being plunged in the infusion of false principles, horrid methods, and shocking bad taste that marked American architecture and architectural practice in the year 1881."[19]

For William Cram, his son's future vocation now became a settled matter: a painter he might not be; an architect he certainly would be. In 1880 the former minister took Ralph and an assortment of his architectural sketches again to Boston for the purpose of an interview with the distinguished architect, William R. Ware (1832-1915). Himself the son of a Unitarian minister, Ware in 1865 had organized the Massachusetts Institute of Technology's Department of Architecture, the first of its kind in the United States, and had become the first professor of architecture in the nation's history. Having served as that department's chairman since its inception, he was about to leave for Columbia University, where in 1881 he would establish its School of Architecture. At their meeting, he took an immediate liking to both father and son and, as a result, promised to try to find a position for Ralph as an apprentice with his friends Arthur Rotch and George Tilden, who were soon to open a firm in Boston.[20]

One can imagine without much difficulty the mixed feelings Ralph must have experienced when the letter confirming his apprenticeship arrived. To accept the position meant leaving a loved and loving mother, a positively revered father, and the security of small-town life, howsoever one might have fretted at its dullness. On the other hand, though William Dean Howells' migration to New York in 1881 symbolized the triumph of that city as the nation's most vital cultural center, Boston, in all likelihood, still must have seemed to young Cram to be the literal and figurative hub of national life. The expectation of adventure was too strong to be denied. On New Year's Day, 1881, having just turned seventeen years of age, he boarded the Eastern Railroad for the journey to Boston and his forthcoming venture into architecture. The Crams' two-hundred-year unbroken skein as farmers had come to an end.

Soon after securing lodgings in Boston's South End, Cram, filled with "exultation tempered by a latent dismay," made his way to the office of Rotch and Tilden. Located in a five-story building (then one of Boston's tallest) at 85 Devonshire Street, it was a large firm for its time, employing ten draftsmen. Yet with neither telephone, typewriters, nor even blueprints, it utilized methods which were, as Cram later recalled, "primitive in the extreme." All drawings were traced by hand; all letters and specifications were "laboriously copied on flimsy paper by use of water, blotting paper, and a hand press."21 Still, the firm did provide the only distinctly professional training he would ever receive as an architectural tyro. Unlike virtually every other major architect of his time, Cram never attended either an American college or the world's then most prestigious school of architecture, the École des Beaux-Arts.

For five years, from 1881 to 1886, the young novice labored and studied, but, as he noted, "with no appreciable results." From the very beginning of his novitiate he rebelled against some of the work produced by Rotch and Tilden and began experimenting with his own style, which, since he was still under Ruskin's powerful influence, in substance was largely Gothic (at least as he then understood the term).22 Throughout this period he longed to visit Europe to see for himself those great works of art which the English critic had so vividly described. At one point it seemed as though the wish were to

become reality. Arthur Rotch had established a
two-year traveling fellowship to Europe for aspiring architects, the first such award in the United
States. Cram, who believed Rotch wanted him to win,
passed the preliminary exam and waited anxiously
for the competitive design itself to begin. Quite
fortuitously, however, he learned beforehand of the
subject for the contest. He apprised Rotch of the
situation, but his mentor was still willing to let
him compete, provided he promise to give no further
thought to the design until the competition actually commenced. A jealous co-apprentice, learning of
the matter, protested so vigorously that Cram was
forced to withdraw, but not without a great deal of
disappointment.[23]

If Cram had any doubts at this point in his
life as to his fidelity to architecture, they were
assuredly reinforced by a brief affair he had with
journalism. Not too long after arriving in Boston,
he wrote an impassioned letter to the Boston Transcript to save Henry Hobson Richardson's Trinity
Church, considered then--and now--something of an
architectural masterpiece, from the blight of a proposed four-story apartment house to be built directly in front of the church. Ultimately, the residential dwelling was not erected, and the Transcript's
editor, E.H. Clement, asked, concerning the letter,
"Have We a Ruskin Among Us?" Flattered by the editor's rhetorical query, Cram soon sent another letter, this one in praise of a recent exhibition of
Pre-Raphaelite water colors and photographs. Unde-
terred by not having received any further effusive
praise for his latest effort, he continued to bom-
bard the Transcript regularly for the next two
years with a barrage of letters, mostly pertaining
to matters of art. Clement, very likely, was highly impressed with these, and/or perhaps he may have
wanted gracefully to put an end to Cram's epistolary activities. In any case, in 1886 he offered
him the position of art critic for the newspaper.[24]

The young draftsman now faced a dilemma:
should he continue as a neophyte architect, already
having had five years of training and experience, or
should he turn to journalism? He chose the latter.
Certainly the prospect of earning a salary--any sal-
ary--was an enticement, for as an apprentice he had
drawn no pay, but only a weekly stipend of eight
dollars from a benevolent father.[25] But there were
probably other reasons as well for his decision.

He no doubt felt discouraged by his recent failure to secure the Rotch Scholarship. Also, he may have weighed the as yet invisible results of his five years as a draftsman against Clement's flattering Ruskinian comparison and found the former wanting. After all, for a devotee of Ruskin what could seem more apt than to follow in his footsteps as an art critic?

Happily for Cram (and for those who subsequently have appreciated his work), his decision to abandon architecture coincided with the announcement of an open competition for the building of a new Courthouse for Suffolk County (Massachusetts). His enthusiasm for architecture rekindled--particularly by the thought of the one-thousand-dollar first prize-- he hurriedly drew up and submitted his design, which was, interestingly enough, Richardsonian rather than Gothic in conception. He won the competition and in fulfillment of his hitherto thwarted desire immediately laid plans for visiting Europe. At the same time, he was able to get his new employer, the Transcript, to agree to publish forthcoming accounts of his pilgrimage.26

Cram's trip to Europe appears to have been an unqualified success. After taking in a number of churches, abbeys, and manor houses in England, he crossed to the Continent for visits to Paris and Chartres, the great Italian cities of art, and the Wagnerian Festival at Bayreuth before heading homeward. While in London at the outset of his journey, he had received news of the death of Richardson, probably the foremost American architect at this time and his own personal favorite. He mourned "the lost leader," but soon thereafter, under the weighty influence of English and Continental building, came to realize that Richardson's was not the last word in architecture--a revelation painful but altogether necessary for his own artistic emancipation. Indeed, the entire trip had served to broaden his artistic consciousness immeasurably. Having left his native land, "where the evidences of art and their manifestations were few, rudimentary, and, in addition, disappearing fast, such a journey was not only apprenticeship, but revelation." He added: "If anything could coordinate the random and chaotic impressions of youth, give reality to the literary transcriptions of old art, reveal through this art something of the culture that created it and the nature of the history that lay behind, it would be such a trip as this."[27]

Despite the fascination European architecture had held, once he returned to the United States, Cram resolved even more firmly than before to abandon architecture in favor of journalism. This somewhat puzzling decision possibly stemmed from the favorable reception accorded those articles which he had sent from Europe to the Transcript. Whatever the basis for his resolve, his newly determined vocation lasted but briefly. First of all, he was paid considerably less than he had anticipated. Secondly, he defied Mammon by stubbornly, if honestly, refusing to praise certain exhibitions of art featured in galleries which were prime advertisers for the Transcript. The interplay of these two factors led him to quarrel with the paper's editor and abruptly to resign his position.[28]

For the next year or two he kept himself together with a variety of odd jobs such as designing wallpaper, contributing occasional articles for Decorator and Furnisher, and serving as a decorating consultant for art-conscious women. None of these were especially gratifying, but they did permit him to tread water, with his feet occasionally touching bottom. At one point Cram--with journalism still very much in the front of his mind--and several friends were on the verge of founding a new monthly magazine dedicated to the several arts. They had even induced the well-known Harvard professor of literature, Barrett Wendell, as well as the still obscure art critic, Bernard Berenson, to contribute future articles. At the last moment, however, their prospective financial support collapsed, and the nation was forced to do without one more art magazine. The degree of disappointment experienced by his friends as a result of their abortive undertaking remains unknown; for Cram, however, coming after his several recent frustrations, the situation was exasperating. Shortly afterwards, with only two days' notice, he accepted a generous offer to go once more to Europe, this time as a tutor to a friend's stepson.[29] This second trip was to prove considerably more significant than the first.

At first the trip was sorely disappointing. By his own admission, he lacked adequate skill as a tutor, and, possibly for this reason, a strain quickly developed between him and the friend who had engaged his services. The Roman fall of 1888, moreover, was depressing with frequent rain spoiling the city's an-

17

ticipated autumnal brilliance. Then, quite by chance,
he met T. Henry Randall, an American traveler who was
also a student of architecture and who became and remained a close friend until his death a few short
years later. In fact, Cram would count this young
man as one of the handful of persons who had exerted
"an evocative and formative influence" on his development.[30] The influence took both a religious and vocational direction.

Cram, despite or perhaps because of a minister-
father, had never developed any appreciable feeling
for organized religion. Nevertheless, while unmoved
by what he considered the aridity of liberal Protestantism, he was appalled when visiting Europe in 1886
to see firsthand the vast destruction and desecration
of Catholic churches and works of art which had been
perpetrated during the Reformation. Further, on one
occasion he found himself, though unable to pray, in-
explicably kneeling at Assisi before the tomb of St.
Francis. This newly acquired religious sensibility,
while real, was not terribly profound; he returned
home and gave little further thought to the matter.
Yet his second European sojourn occasioned quite different results. For one thing, his friend Randall, an
Episcopalian, was devoutly religious. With a bit of
prodding, Randall managed to persuade him to attend
Christmas Eve services at Rome's Church of San Luigi
dei Francesi. What followed was nothing short of an
epiphany for Cram, overwhelmed by the pomp and pageantry of the Latin rites. He later professed of this
occasion: "I did not understand all of this with my
mind, but I understood." The next morning, Christmas
Day, he voluntarily accompanied Randall to an Anglican church. Immediately after returning to Boston he
was instructed and baptized in the Episcopalian
faith.[31] With his father's approval he had forsaken
his nominal Unitarianism for what he considered the
"real Catholicism of Christianity."[32] From that moment until his death there is no evidence whatsoever
to indicate that his religious convictions ever wa-
vered.

While Randall's role in Cram's religious conversion was, to some extent, coincidental, his influence on the latter's vocational future seems decidedly more direct. Shortly after their initial
meeting they began daily to sketch Rome's many extraordinary churches. In this respect, it was Randall
(along with the churches, of course) who acted as a
catalyst in rekindling Cram's flagging enthusiasm for

architecture. As the appreciative Cram noted: "It is quite possible that...had I not met him by accident in the cold gloom and the natural depression of that Roman winter, I might perfectly well have drifted off into some other undesignated activity--the theatre, perhaps, or writing or teaching--and so missed the chance of participation in what is, I honestly believe, one of the noblest professions open to man."[33] In early 1889 he severed his relationship as tutor and, with Randall, went to Sicily, where he continued to sketch, immersing himself in that island's hybrid heritage of Greek, Roman, Byzantine, and Moorish art. After three months the two men returned to Rome for Easter and then traveled northward for visits to Orvieto, Assisi, Perugia, Siena, Florence, and, finally, Venice.

As Venice was to convey death to Thomas Mann's fulfilled Gustav Aschenbach, conversely, it now brought life to Hampton Fall's artist manqué. Though he had cherished Ruskin's depictions and had even visited the city in 1886, it was only on this occasion that Cram was able fully to experience the overpowering grandeur of Venice. Renaissance masters, Ducal Palace, Grand Canal--its art, architecture, and natural beauty taken together--comprised "the most consistent and concentrated synthesis of beauty in the world." The brief trip which he then took to Austria before returning to the United States was pleasant but anti-climactic;for it was the once-proud Queen of the Adriatic which had "really settled the matter so far as an architectural career was concerned."[34]

To say that Venice determined his future career is to say, at once, everything--and nothing. While the statement is literally true, it offers no explanation for what kind of architecture he was most steadfastly to pursue. Cram would become a Gothicist par excellence; yet Venice is a mélange, howsoever exquisite, of styles. To understand more fully the roots of his passion for and dedication to the Gothic, one must look beyond Venice, beyond even the spectacular cathedrals he saw in other parts of Europe. One must look to two other significant factors: his religious conversion, already cited, and the cultural influence of the Aesthetic Movement.

NOTES

1. William Everett Cram, Time and Change (Boston,
   1927), p. 77. The acceleration of industrial
   change in the mid-nineteenth century, symbolized
   by the railroad, was traumatic for numerous Americans. For a most perceptive study of the impact
   of technology on a rural America, see Leo Marx,
   The Machine in the Garden: Technology and the
   Pastoral Ideal in America (New York, 1964). Com-
   menting upon Nathaniel Hawthorne's vision of a
   railroad disturbing the tranquility of an idyllic
   countryside, Marx notes: "In truth, the 'little
   event' is a miniature of a great--in many ways
   the greatest--event in our history" (p. 27).
2. While Ralph Adams Cram believed that John Cram
   had come from Newcastle-upon-Tyne in Northumber-
   land, two genealogists of the family more conclusively have traced this same person to Bilsby in
   Sinnett, "Ancestor John Cram and His Descendants,"
   typescript (Fertile, Minnesota, 1925?), p. 1, and
   Charles M. Cram, Genealogical Outline of the
   Cram, Walker, and Weekes Families, (Boston, 1934),
   p. 7. I am indebted to these two works for the
   background on Cram's ancestry.
3. Cram, Genealogical Outline, p. 8.
4. Ibid., p. 7.
5. Ralph Adams Cram, "Fulfillment," The American Review, IV (March, 1935), 514-515, 517.
6. Cram himself wrote very little about his private
   life or the lives of his family. His autobio-
   graphical My Life in Architecture, concerned as
   it is with his public career and views, contains
   only scattered references to his parents, wife
   and children. Two articles--"Fulfillment" and
   "The Last of the Squires"--plus an enlightening
   interview (August 9, 1972) with his son, Ralph
   Wentworth Cram, have provided me with much of the
   material for his family background and early
   years.
7. Ralph Adams Cram, "The Last of the Squires," The
   Atlantic Monthly, CLXV (January, 1930) 80-85.
8. Cram, "Fulfillment," 516-517, 519.
9. Ibid.,
10. William Everett Cram (1871-1947) was a farmer
    and naturalist whose writings and illustrations
    achieved some repute. Among his better known

works are <u>Little Beasts of Field and Wood</u> (1899),
<u>American Animals</u> (1902), and <u>More Little Beasts</u>
<u>of Field and Wood</u> (1912). A fine hunter, he
stands, in this respect, in marked contrast to
his older brother, who abhorred hunting. Interview with Ralph Wentworth Cram. There may have
been other striking dissimilarities, but the
author has not found a single allusion whatsoever
on the part of Ralph Adams Cram either to his
brother or to his sister, Marion Blake Cram Brown.

11. Cram, "Fulfillment," 519, 523.
12. Ralph Adams Cram, <u>My Life in Architecture</u>
    (Boston, 1936), p. 58.
13. Cram, "Fulfillment," 520, 525-527.
14. Ibid., 513, 522, 525-527.
15. Ibid., 521. As an art critic, Ruskin (1819-1900)
    won earlier and, like Spencer, greater apprecia-
    tion in the United States than in his native
    England, despite the fact that he had the Tory's
    detestation of industrialism, progress, and mod-
    ern democracy. One American critic has noted
    that his influence in this country was to be per-
    ceived "...in a hundred-odd byways and dead ends
    of upper-class neuroses and frustrations." James
    Marston Fitch, <u>American Building. 1: The His-</u>
    <u>torical Forces That Shaped It</u>. 2nd ed., rev.
    (Boston, 1966), p. 127. For a perceptive assess-
    ment of this influence, see Roger B. Stein, <u>John</u>
    <u>Ruskin and Aesthetic Thought in America, 1840-</u>
    <u>1900</u> (Cambridge, Mass., 1967).
16. Cram, <u>My Life</u>, p. 58.
17. Ibid., pp. 23-24.
18. The parents' fear that Ralph might be a potential
    arsonist was quite real, according to the archi-
    tect's son. Interview with Ralph Wentworth Cram.
19. Cram, <u>My Life</u>, pp. 24-27. On another occasion
    he wrote that his early reading of Ruskin was
    the single most instrumental factor in solidify-
    ing his interest in architecture. Ralph Adams
    Cram, untitled and unpaginated manuscript in the
    office of Hoyle, Doran and Berry, Boston.
20. Cram, <u>My Life</u>, pp. 40-41. The present architec-
    tural library of M.I.T. is named for Rotch.
21. Ibid., p. 41.
22. At this time Cram experienced his first encoun-
    ter with Gothic ecclesiastical architecture,
    preparing two sketches for Dorchester's Church
    of the Holy Spirit. Douglas Shand Tucci, <u>The</u>
    <u>Gothic Churches of Dorchester: Readings in Mod-</u>

ern Boston History (Boston, 1972), p. 14.

23. Cram, My Life, pp. 45-48. Cram admitted, however, that a more qualified apprentice, Clarence Blackall, deservedly won the competition and became the first Rotch Scholar.
24. Ibid., pp. 10-11.
25. Interview with Ralph Wentworth Cram.
26. Cram, My Life, pp. 49-50. Though the Courthouse was eventually built, Cram, after submitting his design, apparently played no further role in its creation.
27. Ibid., pp. 50-52.
28. Ibid., pp. 11-12.
29. Ibid., pp. 53-55.
30. Ibid., pp. 55-57.
31. Ibid., pp. 57-60.
32. Cram, "Fulfillment," 524.
33. Cram, My Life, p. 63.
34. Ibid., pp. 65, 63.

CHAPTER II

CRAM AND THE AESTHETIC MOVEMENT

During most of the nineteenth century Europe sported a facade of stability. The concluding of the Napoleonic Wars had ushered in nearly a century of general international peace; the Industrial Revolution had made manifest the fruits of material prosperity. Masked behind this equilibrium, however, were seething discontents and incipient revolts. By the middle of the century it had become all too apparent that the blessings conferred by the Industrial Revolution were mixed. Marching pari passu with a general proliferation of consumer goods and assorted benefits had come an army of sufferings for the individual and the community. For many, progress simply had not been worth its high price reckoned in class warfare, grinding poverty, and human degradation. The wonder is not so much that there was actual or threatened violence to upset the social balances--the Paris Commune, the assasinations and bomb throwings of the anarchists, the nationalist and imperialist frictions with their attendant armaments race--but that it remained more potential than kinetic for so long a period.

The revolt against dominant nineteenth-century ideas and institutions, however, was fully as much artistic and cultural as it was political and economic. For every Marx there was a William Morris, for every Bakunin an Aubrey Beardsley, and for every Narodnik a Friedrich Nietzsche. Almost without exception, the earliest rebels, the Romantics, chafed under the restrictions imposed by the eighteenth century's narrow formalism: its rigid adherence to the Aristotelian unities in drama, its dry neo-classicism in painting, sculpture, and architecture, and the implications deriving from Newtonian cosmogony. Moved by certain ideas of the Enlightenment and by the liberating energies set loose by the French Revolution, they posed artistic and personal self-expression as their highest desideratum. Denouncing conventional society as artificial and inhibiting, they extolled the natural and raised the rude, half-clad but noble savage to a position of preeminence at the expense of the urbane,

23

bewigged aristocrat. It was an age for unbound
Prometheuses, adventurous Renés, swashbuckling Herna-
nis--in short, for Byronic heroes. It was an age
moreover, when artists, such as Byron, sometimes
loomed larger than their creations. Or as Jean-Paul
Sartre quipped: "No one was Victor Hugo. Not even
Victor Hugo."
     In attacking nineteenth-century society, however,
not all artists placed a premium on an unrestrained
concept of self which bordered on anarchy. Indeed,
finding their own society suffering from an excess of
individualism, some looked back for an inspiring model
of communal organization. Almost invariably, those
who did focused on the Middle Ages.
     Ever since the flowering of the Renaissance, the
Middle Ages had begun to fall into disrepute. Its immediate ancestors tended to regard it either as an em-
barrassment or as a once powerful historical epoch
whose withered institutions and spirit had outlived
their usefulness. By the eighteenth century, however,
au courant Europeans had come to view the Middle Ages
with undisguised contempt as having been darkness
and obscurantism personified, a painful obstruction
to human progress which the Enlightenment was only
now setting aright.[1] The term "Gothic," with its
connotation of murderous hordes of barbarians pillag-
ing and ultimately destroying the Roman Empire, had
become the facile synecdochic pejorative for describing the era in toto as devoid of any saving features.
     Despite or perhaps even because of this fero-
cious prejudice, medievalism began to experience a revival in the second half of the eighteenth century.
Gloomy castles with ghost-ridden corridors emanated
from the pages of the popular Gothic horror novels of
Horace Walpole, Anne Radcliffe, and Matthew Lewis.
Walpole, getting, so to speak, into the spirit of
things, actually had remodeled a mansion into the
veritable Gothic fortress of Strawberry Hill. But it
was the Romantics of the early nineteenth century who
were chiefly responsible for the recrudescence of
medievalism. Sir Walter Scott, churning out what
seemed to be an endless profusion of his Waverley
novels, made the age come alive as no writer, before
or since, has done; Lord Byron saw fit to have his
Childe Harold wandering through the Europe of the
Middle Ages. On the Continent various peoples, particularly those whose nationalistic sensibilities had
been fired by Napoleon and his armies, suddenly discovered that they, too, had a medieval past and began

to divert their literary and artistic efforts accordingly. The Romantic movement, appropriately, also kindled a Gothic revival in architecture. Mutatis mutandis, medievalism, at least in its art forms, lived again, not barely, but as a fashionable alternative to an ebbing classicism.

Explicitly or implicitly, the medieval-minded were seeking an escape from their present. Faced with materialism, mammonism, and a merchant-class morality and mentality, they lauded the supposed medieval virtues of bold knights, distressed damsels and heroic feats. They were, in short, searching for mystery and romance. It was not surprising that many therefore turned to Catholic Christianity, the common faith of the Middle Ages, as a substitute for the simpler rites and practices of the various Protestant sects. As a half-way measure, the Reverend John Henry Newman and others formed the Oxford Movement during the 1830's in an attempt to push the Church of England closer to Roman Catholicism by accepting a High Anglican service and theology. Generally frustrated in his endeavors, Newman converted to Catholicism in 1845, ultimately donning the cardinal's red hat. Others, Catholic by birth, felt compelled to return to the Church after a period of self-imposed excommunication. As Chateaubriand, the French poet and erstwhile exalter of the noble savage, would say on his deathbed: "As for me, I am a Christian."

The actual fusion of medieval religion and medieval art, the sacred and the profane, had to await the mid-century advent of the Pre-Raphaelite Brotherhood.[2] An English movement, it was indebted to the German Nazarenes of the early nineteenth century who, influenced by Friedrich Schlegel among others, concluded that religion had been responsible for great art. Founded by Dante Gabriel Rossetti, William Holman Hunt, and John Everett Millais in 1848, the year of pandemic political convulsions throughout Europe, the Brotherhood remained for its decade or so of existence a small but elite group with staunch allies who included Edward Burne-Jones, Ford Madox Brown, and John Ruskin. The Pre-Raphaelites, while admiring Raphael himself, protested the perversion of his work into stale mannerism by subsequent academic schools of painting, notably the British Royal Academy. They proposed to return to the spirit of those late medieval and early Renaissance Italian painters who had preceded him. While none of the Brotherhood's originators had actually visited Italy, all had seen engravings done in

the early nineteenth century after Italian masters and
were familiar with the work of the Nazarenes. With
their love for precise details and the content of
ideas, they attacked the flabbiness and aridity of
contemporary painting. Yet Pre-Raphaelitism was never an art-for-art's-sake movement. Its adherents seem
to have deprecated the Renaissance less for its works
of art than for its humanist learning that had "bred
a Neo-pagan spirit which favoured and strengthened a
growing indifference to moral principles and religious
beliefs."[3] A stress on religious feeling, which sometimes lapsed into religiosity, became one of the most
salient characteristics of Pre-Raphaelite painting and
poetry.

In the nineteenth century--indeed, until more recent times when the process has increasingly become
reversed--the United States tended to take its cultural cues from England and, to a lesser extent, other
European countries. Pre-Raphaelitism presented no exception to this general rule. With an occasional artist of genuine talent and some stature, such as
William J. Stillman, and with several energetic organizations, primarily the Society for the Advancement
of Truth in Art, the American movement flowered briefly during mid-century. While supporting the various
principles and predilections held by its English counterpart, it never waxed as enthusiastic as when defending Gothic architecture. "It is necessary,
times when true Art is little practiced or understood," the American Pre-Raphaelites argued, "to look
back to other periods for instruction and inspiration.
That, in seeking for a system of Architecture suitable
for study, we shall find it only in that of the Middle
Ages, of which the most perfect development is known
as Gothic Architecture...." They were hoping, naïvely,
that a Gothic revival would bring "complete and permanent success" to art.[4]

A Gothic revival in architecture did take place
in the United States during the Civil War era, but it
proved to be neither complete nor permanent. In fact,
it was but one of three such revivals which occurred
during the century and, in many respects, the least
successful one at that (see Chapter III). Of course,
it was not wholly lacking aesthetically in pleasing
works. William R. Ware, Cram's early benefactor, was
a skillful utilizer of the Gothic until his premature
retirement from practice in 1881, as was his partner
Henry Van Brunt until his apostasy in favor of the
Romanesque and Classical. Nevertheless, the overall

quality of Gothic building at this time was considerably less than awesome. When the Pre-Raphaelite influence spread to ancillary art forms the results could be more encouraging. "Superb" is not too strong a word to describe the stained glass windows of John La Farge.

One of the most successful offshoots of Pre-Raphaelitism, both in its British and American phases, was the arts and crafts movement of the latter nineteenth century. Unable to come to terms with growing industrial technology, individuals such as Ruskin, William Morris, and Thomas Carlyle bitterly denounced the machine. No longer an artificer, the modern worker, so they argued at length, was in danger of losing his sense of self-value and identity. The only recourse seemed to lie in a return to the medieval ideal and practice of craftsmanship. While the arts and crafts movement achieved its most noteworthy successes in England, it also attained some minor success in the United States. Led by spirited polemicists like Elbert Hubbard and the United Crafts organization, it was responsible for an increased awareness of just how much technology had separated man from, as Thorstein Veblen called it, his "instinct of workmanship." In 1893, moreover, Hubbard, best known today for his story, "A Message to Garcia," founded the Roycroft arts and crafts colony in East Aurora, New York. Influenced by the efforts of William Morris, the Roycrofters were responsible for some fine work, particularly their furniture and book printing. The Ruskin Commonwealth, a similar association of artists and artisans, was established in 1894 in Tennessee. Though neither utopian venture lasted long, both served as dramatic examples of man in revolt against the machine and laissez-faire capitalism.

It would be a mistake, however, to attribute any undue importance to the American Pre-Raphaelite movement or its direct effects. At best, it was a limited movement which attained limited success. Russell Sturgis, the architect and noted critic, thought that the arts and crafts movement (of which he approved) had been destroyed because "medievalism became a pose, a fad."[5] More generous to would-be medievalists, Peter Bonnett Wight applauded and fought for the Gothic revival in architecture, but lamented that it had been wasted on an unappreciative and unsympathetic public.[6] It was Henry Adams' close friend, Clarence King, however, who may have captured most perceptively the fatal weakness of Pre-Raphaelitism and its atten-

27

dant Gothicism: "It seems to the writer that this is neither the age nor the people to meddle with Gothic art. To do Gothic requires a Gothic heart, a Gothic head, and a Gothic hand. We are sophisticated, blasé, indifferent to nature, and conventional to the last degree. The men who awoke from the sleep of the Dark ages [sic] and suddenly broke loose from monastic authority, prerogative, and precedent, and within fifty years created a style and carried it to the consummate flower of its whole life, were simple, direct, and religious."[7]

For King, then, it made little sense to superimpose Gothic art on a distinctly non-medieval people. Such a cultural grafting, even if successful, would only result in a strange hybrid, pleasing to neither the scion nor the tree. What, however, if one were to nurture a kind of social tree more conducive to the grafting of Gothic art branches? One might then have a satisfactory organism from root to branch. This literally, as well as symbolically, would entail a process of total, radical restructuring. The possibility, however remote, had begun to play upon the mind and imagination of young Ralph Adams Cram.

If Cram had any regrets about leaving Hampton Falls, he appears to have kept them to himself. Nowhere in his writings is there to be found any real nostalgia for his birthplace. Life in Boston in the 1880's, on the other hand, more than satisfied his expectations of adventure, and if he had not as yet definitely settled upon a career, his role as a cultural dilettante and general bon vivant around town more than compensated. For the exhilarated Cram, still with his illusions intact, these years, though possibly "a false dawn," marked an age of "high adventure" and "buoyant optimism," a "golden age, with the promise of high fulfillment." And was it any wonder? There were, he argued, more great artists and writers (almost all of whom were Europeans) at this time than in any other era, save perhaps that of Periclean Athens or the High Renaissance.[8] In a statement redolent of Henry Adams, he noted that "life began to widen out and take on a certain consistency and unity through multiplicity."[9] His options for a personal ethos still seemed very much open as he began to explore more fully the dominant ideas and art of his age.

One of those dominant ideas which he quickly and categorically rejected was scientism. Having been nurtured as a youth on the works of Darwin, Spencer,

Tyndall, and Huxley, he began seriously to question the doctrine of evolution. Eventually, he came to regard the latter as not only inherently false, but also as the unwitting source of much of the modern world's problems. "The ancient doctrine of progressive evolution which became dominant during the last half of the nineteenth century," he wrote, "was, I suspect, next to the philosophical dogmas of Dr. Calvin and the political and social doctrines of M. Rousseau, the most calamitous happening of the last millenium." By his own admission, he had been saved in his early years from succumbing to its deleterious influence only by having read the humanizing works of Emerson, Carlyle, Arnold, and Ruskin.[10] Though inconsistently he was later to develop a pseudo-scientific theory of history (see Chapter V) and to cloak at least one of his pet theories in the authoritarian garb of science (see Chapter IX), his distrust became profound. True, science provided the basis for some human material comforts, but the price came too high. Who but someone deeply disillusioned with science and technology could seriously rank the printing press and the internal combustion machine, along with gunpowder, as "the greatest calamity that has afflicted the world of man"?[11]

Rejecting contemporary science, Cram turned to those individuals or groups who struggled against the powerful scientism of the age. Increasingly, he was attracted to the non-rational features of the human mind although, surprisingly, he would never have a charitable word to say about Freud. For example, while some of the particulars of her Christian Science religion were repugnant to him, he appreciated the fervent faith of Mrs. Mary Baker Eddy. Likewise, conveniently overlooking the fact that he was a noted psychologist and physiologist, he extolled the "open universe" belief of William James which would pragmatically and rationally accept the possibility of spiritual experiences.[12] Even more seductive, however, was the philosophy of the Frenchman Henri Bergson, whom Cram exuberantly called "the greatest figure, perhaps, since St. Thomas Aquinas." In his Creative Evolution, Bergson, a friend of James, had posited his concept of the élan vital, that mystical force which flew so squarely into the granite face of nineteenth-century science. Having argued that man's intellect, by its very nature, was unable fully to apprehend reality, Bergson had provided support for the irrational and non-rational. In so doing, he had also enhanced religion's stature in a generation of materialism.[13] Along with Mrs. Eddy and William James he had provided Cram with strong arguments against the determinism and rationality of science. Nonetheless, important as these were for solidifying prejudices, the young architect was seeking something more positive during these formative years, something into which he could channel his own talents. By the late 1880's, "the balance between speculative and philosophical science on the one hand, and aesthetics of every sort on the other, was definitely inclined in the latter direction."[14] The search stopped when he discovered the Aesthetic Movement.

The Aesthetic Movement was a revolutionary cultural force in Europe during the last quarter of the nineteenth century.[15] While it had its artistic exponents in every country, it flowered most luxuriantly in England and France. The English Aesthetes built upon the achievement of the Pre-Raphaelites; the French artists owed much of their inspiration to the poetic genius of Charles Baudelaire and the Symbolists, particularly Mallarmé, as well as to Edgar Allan Poe, whom Baudelaire had translated. Regarding England, it is impossible to say whether the movement's greatest creativity was expressed in literature, painting, or drawings; for France, the creativity was largely literary in nature. Which had the greater artists? England with Pater, Burne-Jones, Morris, Wilde, Beardsley, and Beerbohm, or France with Verlaine, La Forgue, Huysmans, Nerval, Louÿs, and Villiers de L'Isle Adam? It is a question of taste. More tangible is the malaise, the mal du siecle, which artists of both nations experienced in common. Deploring the period's materialism, industrialism, and scientism, they stood in open rebellion against the loss of taste and/or faith. Many adopted a stance of perversion or "decadence," sometimes real, sometimes feigned. In any case, probably at no other earlier time in the history of Europe had as many artists felt so genuinely alienated from their contemporary society. Their example quickly spread to the United States.

Three diverse yet interrelated cultural events which took place in Boston during the 1880's first brought Cram into actual contact with the Aesthetic Movement: the first performance of Wagner's operas, given at Mechanics Hall; the first production of Gilbert and Sullivan's Patience, offered at the Boston Museum; and the first public exhibition of Pre-

30

Raphaelite art, displayed at the Art Museum in Copley Square.[16] Whether it was the heavy seriousness of the Ring Cycle or the lighter froth of Die Meistersinger, Wagner's operas, suffused with the glow of the German Middle Ages, appealed to both European and American audiences eager to escape the squalor and commonplace of the present. Cram almost immediately became a "besotted Wagnerite," and when he took his first trip to Europe in 1886, Bayreuth, along with Venice, was the chief attraction.[17] With regard to the Pre-Raphaelite exhibit, little elaboration is needed. Soon after seeing it, he wrote his enthusiastic letter (cited in Chapter I) to the Transcript. Finally, intoxicated as he was with the Pre-Raphaelites, he also was able to enjoy its more ludicrous side, appreciating, as he did, the foppish and effete posings of Gilbert and Sullivan's character, Bunthorne.

More than these events, it was meeting like-minded persons which was most responsible for Cram's wholehearted immersion in the Aesthetic Movement. In the 1880's and 1890's he befriended a number of talented young men (and at least one woman) who shared his artistic sensibilities. Almost all of them, Cram included, became fanatic converts to the Decadent movement, particularly as it was manifesting itself in England. Though they may or may not have agreed with Max Beerbohm's observation that while beauty had existed prior to 1880, "it was Mr. Oscar Wilde who managed her debut," they were greatly impressed by the achievements of their kindred spirits across the Atlantic. Wilde, Aubrey Beardsley, those splendid little magazines, The Yellow Book and The Savoy, the meticulously crafted books published by the Kelmscott and Vale presses--all pointed toward an artistic renaissance. As Arthur Symons, the most articulate interpreter of the movement, had declared: "To fix the last fine shade, the quintessence of things; to fix it fleetingly; to be a disembodied voice, and yet the voice of a human soul; that is the ideal of Decadence."[18]

For many years during the late nineteenth century this coterie of Boston Aesthetes informally met--sometimes at Cram's bachelor apartment, first on Dwight Street and then on Pinckney Street--to discuss their work as well as the work of other artists. As painters, architects, musicians, and writers, they were forever organizing social and artistic clubs: the Pewter Mugs, the Visionists, the Procrastinatorium.

From all accounts, the conversation and lectures at
their meetings were never disappointing. Although
most in the group never rose above minor status, a
few, such as Cram and his partner in architecture,
Bertram Grosvenor Goodhue, were to achieve real fame.
Two poets from the group, the Canadian-born Bliss
Carman and, more especially, Richard Hovey, also won
a certain renown.[19] Another promising artist,
Frederick Field Bullard, the musician who was most
famed for his "Stein Song," died at a relatively early
age (forty), while Louise Imogen Guiney, though fairly
well known as a poet, never received, according to
Cram, who considered her the most vital member of the
group, the just recognition merited by her talents.[20]
One of the members, who Cram thought looked like a
young John Keats, constantly but amicably quarreled
with him over the respective merits of Renaissance and
medieval art. On one occasion the two argued pre-
sumptuously as to which of them should succeed Charles
Eliot Norton as Professor Fine Arts at Harvard.[21]
Neither did, of course, but both Cram and Bernard
Berenson went on to distinguished careers anyway.
    In his autobiography Cram recalled this _fin de
siècle_ milieu with nostalgia, as well as with a certain degree of self-mockery:

> Of course it was quite the thing, at
> this time, to proclaim the era as one of
> decadence....This did not disturb us in
> the least or blur our optimism. Instead
> we rather gloated over the fact. If the
> world was indeed decadent, so much louder
> was the call for crusading. Besides, it
> was rather fun to envisage a crumbling
> society in which we could look on our-
> selves as superior beings. We rather rev-
> elled in Oscar Wilde and the brilliant and
> epicene drawings of Aubrey Beardsley. We
> accented our optimism with the vivacious
> but really most mistaken idea that we were
> quite wicked....We savoured the varied
> flowers of the cultural menu with relish,
> and altogether thought of ourselves as
> monstrously clever fellows--a conception
> notably lacking in validity.[22]

It was only in retrospect, however, that he made light
of his years as an Aesthete. At the time, both he and
his friends were quite in earnest with their endeav-

ors, most of which were of a literary bent.
The literary work produced during this period by
Cram's clique largely has been forgotten. The prose
and verse efforts of its more productive members--
Hovey, Carman, and Guiney--today hold their appeal
mostly as curiosities for the literary historian.
Nonetheless, one should remember that they--especial-
ly Hovey[23]--were popular with their own generation,
and on one occasion they pooled their talents to produce a fine, if short-lived, quarterly.

Established in 1892, Knight Errant devoted itself to the publication of verse and articles dealing
with contemporary thought, and exhibited in its for-
mat the skilled crafts so recently revived in England
by Morris and others. Lasting but a year, it was not
without distinguished contributors. Both Charles
Eliot Norton and Brander Matthews, the drama critic,
wrote pieces for the first issue; Berenson and Ernest
Fenollosa, the Orientalist who was then curator of
Oriental art at the Boston Museum and a convert to
Buddhism, offered later contributions. Cram's contribution to its first issue was a rather bombastic
article, "Concerning the Restoration of Idealism and
the Raising To Honour Once More of the Imagination."[24] Eschewing both advertisements and profits,
the journal's organizers had selected Boston as its
home since, in their opinion, it "would no doubt be
free...from the vulgar commercialism which permeates
the very stones of New York, the coarse effrontery of
'popular enterprise' which whirls through most things
emanating from Chicago, the unfathomable progress of
Philadelphia." Knight Errant, as befitted its name,
stood for "the resuscitated Medievalism of recent
years." In its fight against both mammonism and realism in the arts, it was decidedly out of step with
dominant trends and was attempting to launch what at
present would be called a counterculture movement.
The Architectural Record agreed with a critic who had
derided Knight Errant as "a luny, Quixotic champion,"
and predicted that should it survive at all, it would
survive only as "the organ of a coterie." The Record
admitted, however, that it had provided the useful
function of bringing the past into better perspective, "the service which all reactionaries tend to
perform."[25] Reactionaries or no, the Knight Errant
band were by no means alone in rejecting the present.

For all the seriousness of the Gilded Age's re-
formers and proposed reforms, much of the literature
of the age is conspicuously escapist in nature and,

as such, is a gauge of the general perplexity and
sense of loss experienced by a society in the throes
of upheaval. One manifestation of this literature of
escape was the reappearance of the utopian novel, a
recrudescence common to both Western Europe, particularly England, and the United States. This was the
age for England of Samuel Butler's Erewhon and News
from Nowhere, William Morris' response to Butler. In
the United States there was a simultaneous outpouring
of utopian literature, unparalleled, as Alfred Kazin
has noted, either in other epochs or literatures.[26]
Leading American works of this genre included Edward
Bellamy's Looking Backward, Ignatius Donnelly's ter-
ror-filled Caesar's Column, and two novels--A Traveler from Altruria and Through the Eye of the Needle
--by that period's doyen of letters, William Dean
Howells. These writers, much to their credit, could
conceive of a better society. Yet it was one generally far removed in time and/or space from their own.
    A second main expression of this literature of
escape was the artistic flight to the known past.
While it, too, was a form of reaction against the
present, it sought redress not through some future
utopia, but through a return to a specific historical
era, particularly the Middle Ages. For obvious reasons, this literary neo-medievalism never really took
root in the United States, which lacked both a feudal
and strong Catholic tradition. There was simply
nothing to revive. With the minor (and debatable)
exceptions of Mark Twain's occasional and ambiguous
forays into the world of the Middle Ages--A Connecticut Yankee, The Prince and the Pauper, and his biography of Joan of Arc--and Howard Pyle's fine medieval books and illustrations for youngsters, the
movement, quite strong in England and on the Continent, nearly bypassed the United States. It did not,
however, bypass Ralph Adams Cram, who espoused it
with enthusiasm.
    Judged artistically, Cram's literary use of me-
dieval themes and elements, principally in short stories and verse, was no better--and not infrequently
worse--than that of his friends. The fiction is
stylized and manneristic; the poetry, mawkish and
pretentious. From a purely aesthetic point of view,
one would do well to pass over these efforts hastily
and without fanfare. From the larger perspective,
however, one must pause, for the general themes,
spirit, and point of view conveyed did not pass with
the waning of the century. On the contrary, they be-

came foci for more serious thought. An integral part of his immersion in the Aesthetic Movement, they formed a point d'appui for his later attempts to reconstruct society.

In a lighter vein, Cram wrote Black Spirits and White, a series of six ghost stories which were published in 1895.[27] The inspiration for the stories seems to have come from his European trip on which he met T. Henry Randall. Indeed, he included Randall in these tales by fictionalizing him as "Tom Rendel," the narrator's traveling companion. Haunted houses and castles, heinous crimes, the terrors of the supernatural--in short, the whole psychopathology of the Middle Ages fairly leaps from the pages at the reader. In one story, an eerie French house, aptly called "La Bouche d'Enfer" ("The Mouth of Hell"), ultimately burns. The fictitious Kropfsberg Castle, scene for another macabre narrative, proves to be the former residence of a mad and debauched Count Albert, who had burned part of the castle with a group of friends trapped inside and then hanged himself after putting on his great-great grandfather's suit of armour. Medieval churches provided other settings. One fairly innocuous recital, for example, is set in a Breton church; a more lurid one takes place in a Sicilian convent in which the narrator and his wide-eyed companion (Rendel) are shown the body of a young girl who, like Poe's victim in The Cask of Amontillado, was immured while yet alive. Positively reveling in ghostly and ghastly lore, Cram, as narrator, jumps to Sweden for his final offering. Once there, he travels with great difficulty through a dense white fog in what was cheerfully called the Dead Valley, and for his efforts is rewarded with the sight of a skeleton tree, decorated with the heads of humans and animals. Horrified, our narrator hears piercing cries in the distance as the tale ends. What concerns us most about these ghost stories is not so much whether Walpole, Lewis or Mrs. Radcliffe would have been writhing in literary envy, nor what Freud might have said about the man who authored them. The point is simply that, whatever else might be said, they evidence a committed Gothic imagination.

Cram's literary medievalism, fortunately, was not confined to Gothic ghost stories. Throughout the 1880's and 1890's he dabbled in verse dealing with chivalry, romance, and occasionally, the more prosaic aspects of medieval life. As an illustration of how seriously the poetic muse had affected him, one might

consider a letter which he wrote to an editor of The
Century in early 1895.[28] In this letter, he: (1)
thanked the editor for having published "The Nottingham Hunt" in the magazine's February edition and for
his kind words concerning "The White Ladye," a poem
which had been rejected; (2) informed him that he was
currently writing "The Wave Song" as part of a "long
series of songs written for music"; (3) expressed his
anticipation of having "The Angelus," a one-act play
written in blank verse, performed in prose verse; and
(4) promised to send him future poems.
    Sometimes Cram and his friend Bullard joined
forces respectively as lyricist and composer. Their
"Royalist Songs" (which included "The Nottingham
Hunt") were quite popular, at least as Cram tells it,
but paled in quality before their secular cantata,
The Boat of Love.[29] Although the cantata itself was
never produced, two years before his death Cram published its lyrics, subtitling them, A Masque for Music.[30] An ambitious work, this intensely romantic
poem contained a variety of rhyme schemes and a motley cast of medieval characters, including a merchant,
a monk, several crusaders, four warriors, a spate of
sea-spirits, a girl, a lover, a narrator and a chorus
of friars. The following brief selection is fairly
representative of the poem as a whole:

> Wavering, wandering waves,
> We who hold in our hands
>   The Crystal sphere,
>   Alpha, Omega,
>   Secret of timeless time:
> Out of the swallowing sea, out of Eternity,
> We call the Wonder of Life.
> Unto the silent deep, into its infinite sleep,
> We yield the Wonder of Death.[31]

One wonders what his poet friends must have said.
    The Aesthetic Movement witnessed a quickening
of the religious impulse among its members, a number
of whom were or became Catholics and/or mystics. A
large part of its "wickedness" or "perversity" can in
fact be explained as a painful search for salvation
on the part of those who considered a purely rational
religion and conventional morality to be ineffective
and stunting. Like the poet Francis Thompson, one of
their confreres, the Decadents might admit: "I fled
Him down the nights and down the days; /I fled Him
down the arches of the years." Still, they tended to

36

conclude as Thompson did: "Yet ever and anon a trumpet sounds /From the hid battlements of Eternity."[32] The example of Joris Karl Huysmans, although extreme, perhaps best testifies to the symbiotic and bizarre relationship which existed between religion and Decadence. Born a Catholic, he became a Satanist, but then reconverted to Catholicism.[33]

Medieval Christianity provided still another literary theme for Cram, also a religious convert. His most noteworthy effort along this line was Excalibur, written in 1893 but not published until 1909. Subtitled An Arthurian Drama, this work in blank verse represented the first of a projected but unrealized trilogy concerning the Arthurian legends.[34] Forced and bombastic, the drama did very little to advance the state of the arts. What interest it did generate resulted from his avowed purpose to create an epic for "our race," comparable to what Wagner had done for Germans with his Ring Cycle. As a staunch Anglo-Saxonist, Cram, not unnaturally, had selected the heroic saga of Camelot. Yet it was not essentially for purposes of intoning the praises of the Anglo-Saxon that he chose his subject. Of primary importance, the Arthurian legends conveyed "the perfect embodiment of the spirit and impulse of the greatest Christian epoch we call Medievalism."[35] Nearly half a century after having written Excalibur, he was to claim that "it is the best thing I ever wrote and some day it may be discovered."[36]

The single work, however, which best expresses Cram's commitment to the Aesthetic Movement was The Decadent, a work written in 1893 which, along with Black Spirits and White, he later characterized as "early indiscretions."[37] A derivative work, it owes a great deal for its central character and general tone to Huysmans' masterpiece, À rebours, sometimes called "the breviary of the Decadents." For all its flaws--stylistic, structural, and substantive--this didactic composition of less than fifty pages remains more than a period piece, Cram's self-criticism notwithstanding. Unremarkable as fiction, The Decadent contains some genuinely serious reflections.

As the narrative begins, Malcolm McCann, a dour socialist, is en route to visit Aurelian Blake in order to ascertain the reason for the latter's apostasy from socialism. Having passed through a squalid industrial town, he finally reaches Blake's home and is stupefied at its sumptuousness. Vita Nuova, its name conjuring up associations with Dante, scarcely

seems a fitting abode for one who had strong socialist sympathies. But as McCann soon will see, the
story's protagonist had indeed assumed a "new life."
Aurelian Blake's very name suggests a certain
dissatisfaction with modern life and a penchant for
the past: Marcus Aurelius, the heroic Stoic exemplar;
William Blake, the eighteenth-century mystic in artistic rebellion against society. Or perhaps "Blake"
more properly alludes to Cram's grandfather, the
"Squire," who was also, in a sense, in revolt against
his society. In any case, McCann's initial shock
quickly turns to consternation and disgust when he
enters Vita Nuova only to find Blake and a few
friends[38] freely indulging in drugs and alcohol.
Like Des Esseintes, the decadent hero of Huysmans'
À rebours, Blake has clearly yielded to self-indul-
gence and the seductions of la dolce far niente. Our
puritanical socialist, who has rejected his host's
offer of some hashish in favor of his own briar bull
dog tobacco, is further startled by the arrival of a
beautiful Japanese servant "with flesh like firelight
on ivory, clad in translucent silk of a dusky purple
that made no sound as she came," and who was called
"the Honourable White Dew." The subsequent entrance
of a black male servant wearing a red fez convinces
McCann that the rumors of his friend's renunciation
of socialism had been well-founded.[39]
     The appalled McCann, described by Cram as a
"red-bearded agitator," pleads in vain with his erstwhile disciple to repent his folly. Blake, who has
already praised philistinism for having brought forth
Decadence, however, claims to despise materialism--
this, in the midst of his palatial residence--and de-
sires "only absolute individuality and the triumph of
idealism." Inferentially, socialism is neither sufficiently individualistic nor idealistic to suit him.
Besides, it was too late for revolution, and even if
it were not, to what avail would it be? The French
Revolution had led only to capitalism and the Third
Republic. Revolution--any revolution--is only part
of a larger, cyclical historical pattern and, as such,
yields successively to tyranny, chaos, counterrevolu-
tion, and finally, still another revolution. As for
the present world, the great artists--Turner, Rossetti, and Wagner--are dead; those remaining--Arnold,
Pater, Burne-Jones--will die soon enough. Blake, in
a phrase Cram often was to use, informs the dejected
McCann that "art is a result, not an accident," and
that for him, both art and chivalry were dead, leav-

ing the field of battle to materialism and degeneration. Speaking frankly, hashish notwithstanding, he
confesses to being numbed with "that despair which
kills all effort."[40]
It is, then, a sober aesthete who discloses to
McCann that he has been forced reluctantly to turn to
decadence out of utter revulsion against modernism.
Democracy, freedom of the press, and public opinion--
"the idolatrous tritheism of a corrupt generation"--
has alienated our hero. "The whole world," he com-
plains, "kneels before them, confessing their dominion.
So long as this is so, so long will reform be impossible." Meanwhile, supported by a well-meaning but
foolish populace, we have a system "which is the government of the best, by the worst, for the few." Add
to this the decline of religion and the ascendency of
an irresponsible press which supplies us with our demagogues and destroys canons of beauty and truth, and
you have a composite picture of late nineteenth-century Western European and American ills. As a result,
Blake has decided to isolate and insulate himself at
Vita Nuova, "the world of the past and the future,"
and literally and figuratively look down upon the
pitiful industrial town through which McCann had passed. Ultimately, he has resigned himself to a hermetic
life, "for the night has come when man may no longer
work."[41] If Cram (as Blake) seems unduly pessimistic,
one must remember that he, too, was faced with what
one student of the period has called, "the stunting
social shock" of the 1890's. In his own way, he, like
the outstanding literary figures of that decade--James,
Howells, Twain, Garland, Crane, Norris, and others--
was trying "to habituate America to the fact that internal divisiveness was more than geographical, that a
civilization which pursued commerce and technology
constructed for itself a morality drawn from commerce
and technology...."[42]
Two further elements need mentioning to complete
the portrait of Cram as Aesthete: his socialism and
his monarchism. As to the former, it was scarcely of
the virulent variety. Not only did he not consider
himself a communist, he had never, and doubted whether
his friends had ever, read anything by Karl Marx. Nor
could he be considered a Fabian or even municipal socialist. Speaking for himself and his like-minded
associates, he confessed: "We were socialists because
we were young enough to have generous impulses. We
were William Morris enough to hate industrialism, and
were rebellious enough to want to attach ourselves to

something new and not as yet accorded that popular fa-
vour that was so soon to follow in more fashionable
circles."[43] In other words, his socialism was part
sentimental, part pour épater les bourgeois. He later
described socialism as merely "a rather insecure and
blundering revolt against the whole economic theory
and practice of the last epoch of history."[44] Nevertheless, the scathing diatribes against capitalism and
some of the suggested panaceas of his mature years do
mark him as a socialist in spirit, if not name.

In the closing years of the nineteenth century
few people this side of mental asylums thought of socialism and monarchism as anything but mutually exclusive terms. Cram, however, saw no ideological incom-
patibility in the juxtaposition of the two. Neither,
apparently, did some of his friends, who joined with
him in 1896 to form the Order of the White Rose, an
organization long in existence in England and dedicated to that grand old cause of Jacobinism. As Cram
describes it, the Order (or at least its Boston version) held "services of mourning and expiation on the
Feast of Charles the Martyr and on other Loyalist days,
drank our seditious toasts, sang our Jacobite songs,
and even indulged in complimentary (but limited) correspondence with Queen Mary of Bavaria, the 'legiti-
mist' King of Spain, and other deposed monarchs."[45]

Three years later, having been elected Prior of
this North American Cycle of the Order of the White
Rose, Cram issued an encyclical in which he emphasized
the necessity of enhancing the organization's membership, even to the point of including women. Not content with memorializing the regicide of Charles I or
celebrating St. George's Day, he further recommended
that the Order be "Americanized." He confessed to his
brethren that although he firmly believed in the divine right of monarchy and deplored "the heresy of
popular sovereignty," he realized that the nation was
not about to opt for monarchy. "The revolution of
1775," he avowed, "whether or no we may hold it to be
unavoidable, is yet an accomplished fact." While the
United States might not be ready for salvation by monarchy, however, it might be amenable to a healthy
transfusion of Hamiltonianism. For Cram, Alexander
Hamilton was "perhaps the greatest man this continent
has ever known." The nation, he argued, must reject
the "democratic follies" of Jefferson and accept
Hamilton's proposed but inoperative constitution. If
this were done, the people could at last receive the
benefits of a wise and honest government. They could,

in sum, enjoy the substance of constitutional monarchy.
Having blindly chosen Jefferson rather than Hamilton
for their political guide, Americans now must be eman-
cipated from the "dark ages of the eighteenth century."[46]

Not all the venerable Prior's associates approved
of his reactionary advice. Louise Guiney, who had referred to him at various times as "a mad agitator for
'dead issues,'" "a Dear thing," "lunatic angel," and
"Sir Ralph, the false knight,"[47] was appalled. As she
wrote to one of their mutual friends: "I am sorry you
didn't accept the office, so as to save a decent historical society from inevitable ridicule. Nor can I
understand how R. A. von C. ever came to maunder like
that. All our gang is howling with laughter."[48] A
month and a half later she was still complaining that
"poor old R. Cram had been making a DONK of himself...."[49] The general mirth and derision probably
proved too much for the unfortunate Prior, who quickly decided to keep his monarchical views to himself.
The silence lasted for more than thirty years. During
the Great Depression, however, he once again suggested
the desirability of monarchy, and this time there was
to be no doubt as to his seriousness.

The Aesthetic Movement in Europe proved to be as
evanescent as it had been pervasive. By the early
years of the twentieth century, with its leading figures dead, soon to die, or, like Huysmans, having re-
canted their work, its major force had been spent.
Even its "decadence" was soon to become more or less
respectable in Edwardian England and the France of la
belle époque. In Boston, perhaps the heart of the
movement in the United States, there was also a corresponding demise. Richard Hovey died in 1900; Fred-
eric Bullard died in 1904. Louise Guiney became an expatriate in 1901. Others, like Cram, simply became ab-
sorbed in different interests. What had it all meant?

For Cram, involvement in the movement had brought
the joys of human relationships, the memories of which
remained vivid throughout his life. Equally as important, involvement presaged more mature attitudes
and convictions. Virtually every element which was to
form his future intellectual baggage--Christianity,
Gothicism, monarchism, socialism (or at least anti-
capitalism), craftsmanship, and detestation of modern
democracy--found its early expression during his participation in the Aesthetic Movement. Though seemingly inchoate, these elements were soon to solidify from
an attitude of discontent to a credo of neo-medieval-

ism. Nowhere did this transformation begin to express itself so tangibly as in his work as a Gothic architect.

NOTES

1. Not every scholar, of course, has accepted the notion that the Enlightenment and Middle Ages represent systems of value almost diametrically opposed to one anther. Indeed, in what has become a minor classic, The Heavenly City of the Eighteenth Century Philosophers (New Haven, Connecticut, 1932), Carl Becker cogently argued that the two shared much in common. More recent scholarship, however, has weakened this American historian's position.

2. The literature of and on the movement, as might be expected, is profuse. Some of the more interesting and helpful works include: William Holman Hunt, Pre-Raphaelitism and the Pre-Raphaelite Brotherhood, 2 vols. (New York, 1905); Ford Madox Ford, The Pre-Raphaelite Brotherhood (London, 1907); Esther Wood, Dante Rosetti and the Pre-Raphaelite Movement (New York, 1894); and Dennis Welland, The Pre-Raphaelites in Literature and Art (London, 1953). For a description of the movement in the United States, see David Howard Dickason, The Daring Young Men: The Story of the American Pre-Raphaelites (Bloomington, Indiana, 1953).

3. Dickason, The Daring Young Men, p. 123.
4. Ibid., pp. 79-80.
5. Ibid., p. 163.
6. Ibid., pp. 103-104.
7. Ibid., p. 98. Dickason has perceived the American Pre-Raphaelites' influence as extensive, however, extending to Art Nouveau, Christian Socialism, and a variety of literary figures, including Van Wyck Brooks, Sidney Lanier, Charles Eliot Norton, Richard Hovey, Sara Teasdale, Edward Arlington Robinson, and Ezra Pound (pp. 216-249, passim). He further sees Pre-Raphaelitism and the arts and crafts movement as having affected such twentieth-century social projects as the "City Beautiful," "Garden Cities," and "Greenbelts" (pp. 168-169). Dickason also considers Cram to have been "of vital importance" in the regeneration of Gothic architecture (p. 109).

8. Cram listed forty celebrated persons whose total achievements, he thought, comprised an age of greatness. Of the forty, one (Grover Cleveland)

was in politics, two (Cardinal Newman and Pope Leo XIII) were religious figures, and the rest were prominent in the arts. Ralph Adams Cram, My Life in Architecture (Boston, 1936), pp. 6-7.

9. Ibid., p. 5.
10. Ralph Adams Cram, "Why We Do Not Behave Like Human Beings," The American Mercury, XXVII (September, 1932), 41.
11. Cram, My Life, p. 65. He considered the internal combustion machine as the worst of the lot and, appropriately, refused to learn how to operate an automobile. As for his denunciation of the printing press, one wonders at this, especially in light of the many books and nearly one hundred articles that he wrote.
12. Ralph Adams Cram, The Gothic Quest (New York, 1907), p. 341. Cram, however, would not have approved of James' acceptance of the possible "truth" of any or all religious experiences. His devotion to Anglican and Catholic Christianity was much too strong. James, nonetheless, had offered an intelligent argument for the general belief in miracles and mysticism.
13. Ralph Adasm Cram, The Ministry of Art (Boston, 1914), pp. 50-51; Ralph Adams Cram, The Substance of Gothic (Boston, 1917), p. 146. Cram persistently used the phrase "élan vital" in his writings long after Bergson went out of popular favor.
14. Cram, My Life, p. 10.
15. As with the Pre-Raphaelite movement, the literature for the Aesthetic Movement is extensive. A few of the more important works include: Remy de Gourmont, Decadence and Other Essays on the Culture of Ideas, tr. William Aspenwall Bradley (New York, 1921); Gustave L. Van Roosbroeck, The Legend of the Decadents (New York, 1966); and Holbrook Jackson, The Eighteen Nineties (New York, 1922). Jackson's study, though dated--it was originally published in England in 1913 and in the United States in 1922--is both detailed and highly readable.
16. Cram, My Life, pp. 7-8.
17. Ibid., pp. 8, 63.
18. Jackson, The Eighteen Nineties, p. 57.
19. Richard Hovey (1894-1900) was born in Normal, Illinois, and like Louise Guiney, had a Civil War general for a father. He attended Dartmouth College and became the college's laureate and

author of its popular song, "Men of Dartmouth."
After briefly studying for the ministry (Episcopalian), he took a trip to New England in 1887
and met Carman and Tom Meteyard (another future
member of Cram's artistic circle). Hovey's best-
known poetic works were probably his Vagabondia
Songs (Songs from Vagabondia, More Songs From
Vagabondia, and Last Songs from Vagabondia),
written in collaboration with Carman and illustrated by Meteyard. Hovey also won distinction
for his translation of the works of the Belgian
dramatist Maurice Maeterlinck. The best study
of this poet is Allan Houston Macdonald, Richard
Hovey, Man & Craftsman (Durham, North Carolina,
1957).

20. Cram, My Life, pp. 13-16. Louise Imogen Guiney
(1861-1920) was born in Roxbury, Massachusetts,
the daughter of an Irish-born father who became a
brigadier general in the American Civil War. A
devout Roman Catholic, she was appointed post-
mistress of Auburndale, Massachusetts by President Cleveland, but was boycotted by prejudiced
Protestant townspeople. Her nearby Boston
friends (including Cram) undertook a national
campaign to get people throughout the country to
buy their stamps from her and were successful in
their quest. Guiney left the United States in
1901, however, and lived in England until her
death. A prolific poet, admired by Edmund Gosse,
Robert Louis Stevenson, Richard Watson Gilder,
and others, her best known works are collected in
The Roadside Harp and Happy Ending. For the best
biography of her to date, see E.M. Tenison,
Louise Imogen Guiney: Her Life and Works, 1861-
1920 (London, 1923).

21. Ibid., p. 15.

22. Ibid., pp. 18-19.

23. As one writer has claimed of Hovey's Songs from
Vagabondia: "The volume's vivacity and originality took the country by storm, and collegians
went about chanting Hovey's poems as more than
twenty-five years before Oxonians had chanted
Swinburne's first series of Poems and Ballads."
Henry Leffert, "Richard Hovey," Dumas Malone
(ed.), The Dictionary of American Biography, V
New York, 1932), p. 273. The poet Mallarmé also
lauded Hovey's Songs. Macdonald, Richard Hovey,
p. 170.

24. In describing the contents of Knight Errant's

first issue, Guiney noted: "And the doughty
Cram swings his sword at the world generally."
Letter of Louise Imogen Guiney to Herbert E.
Clarke, June 20, 1892, Grace Guiney (ed.),
Letters of Louise Imogen Guiney, I (New York,
1926), p. 38.

25. "Cross Currents," The Architectural Record, II
(October-December, 1892), 216-220. Nonetheless,
the Record considered the universities better
suited to relating the past to the present. Not
everyone, however, so cavalierly dismissed the
Knight Errant and its creators. Walter Crane,
the English artist who was then visiting Boston
and who was to contribute some work to the
journal, depicted Cram and his friends as "a
cultured group of young men...who had been inspired by the recent English revival of printing
and book decoration and the higher forms of art
generally." He described their magazine as "a
nicely printed quarterly...with a tasteful cover
design by Mr. [Bertram] Goodhue." Walter Crane,
An Artist's Reminiscences (New York, 1907), p.
371.

26. Alfred Kazin, On Native Grounds (New York, 1942),
p. 20.

27. Ralph Adams Cram, Black Spirits and White (Chica-
go, 1895). The stories were entitled: "No. 252
Rue M. Le Prince," "In Kropfsberg Keep," "The
White Villa," "Sister Maddalena," "Notre Dame des
Eaux," and "The Dead Valley."

28. Letter of Ralph Adams Cram to [Robert Underwood]
Johnson, February 6, 1895, The Century Collection, New York Public Library.

29. Cram, My Life, p. 94.

30. Ralph Adams Cram, The Boat of Love: A Masque for
Music, in Poet Lore, XLVI, (Summer, 1940), 165-
177.

31. Ibid., 166.

32. Holbrook Jackson described this poem (The Hound of
Heaven) as "a work which well might serve as a
symbol of the spiritual unrest of the whole nineteenth century." Jackson, The Eighteen Nineties,
p. 172.

33. Huysmans (1848-1907), christened Charles-Marie-
Georges, was born in Paris of a French mother and
Dutch father. Despite his stultifying work as a
clerk in the Ministry of Interior for more than
thirty years, he successfully became a littéra-
teur. À rebours (Against the Grain), published

in 1884, established his reputation as the most important Decadent novelist in France. Seven years later he published Là-bas (Down There), a novel of Satanism and witchcraft, but shortly thereafter went on a monastic retreat and returned to the Catholic Church.

34. Among Cram and his friends, Richard Hovey's works represented the finest and most extensive use of medieval themes in longer poems and dramas written in blank verse. The most notable of these included: The Birth of Galahad, Launcelot and Guenevere, The Marriage of Guenevere, The Quest of Merlin, Taliesin: A Masque, and his uncompleted The Holy Grail.

35. Ralph Adams Cram, Excalibur: An Arthurian Drama (Boston, 1909), unpaginated advertisement.

36. Cram, My Life, p. 94.

37. Ibid., p. 84: The full title of this work is: The Decadent: Being the Gospel of Inaction: Wherein Are Set Forth in Romance Form Certain Reflections Touching the Curious Characteristics of These Ultimate Years, and the Divers Causes Thereof. The jesting subtitle contrasts oddly with the general sobriety of the work itself, of which one hundred and twenty-five copies were privately printed by Copeland and Day, both friends of his.

38. One of these friends is named "Wentworth" and is a man who, like Cram, professes to be both a socialist and a monarchist. Interestingly, "Wentworth" is also the name of Cram's first partner in architecture.

39. Ibid., pp. 3-20, passim.

40. Ibid., pp. 10, 27-36, passim.

41. Ibid., pp. 36-41, passim.

42. Larzer Ziff, The American 1890's: Life and Times of a Lost Generation (New York, 1966), p. 348.

43. Cram, My Life, p. 20.

44. Cram, Ministry, p. 51.

45. Cram, My Life, pp. 19-20. In his recollection of his younger years, Van Wyck Brooks cited this Anglo-Catholic, royalist Order with certain favor as a reaction against the Puritan tradition in New England. Van Wyck Brooks, Scenes and Portraits: Memories of Childhood and Youth (New York, 1954), p. 107.

46. Ralph Adams Cram and John Rodwaye, unpublished encyclical entitled "Order of the White Rose" (St. George's Day, 1899), pp. 1-4, Louise Imogen

Guiney Papers, Holy Cross College. See also
Cram's letter to Miss Guiney (?, 1899) in the
same collection.

47. Letters of Louise Imogen Guiney to Mrs. Herbert
     E. Clarke, June 24, 1896 and to Herbert E. Clarke,
     November 8, 1896, Guiney (ed.), Letters to Louise
     Imogen Guiney, I, pp. 116,147.

48. Letter of Louise Imogen Guiney to the Reverend
     W.H. Van Allen, May 8, 1899, ibid., pp 256-257.

49. Letter of Louise Imogen Guiney to Herbert E.
     Clarke, June 23, 1899, Grace Guiney (ed.),
     Letters of Louise Imogen Guiney, II (New York,
     1926), p. 4.

CHAPTER III

THE MAKING OF A GOTHICIST

Increasingly the Middle Ages fell into disrepute in the centuries following its demise, so much that Henry Fielding could revile: "O! more than Gothic ignorance." Nor did Gothic architecture escape the general contempt felt for its historical matrix. For the tasteful Augustan in eighteenth-century England--and it is England with which we are chiefly concerned--Renaissance and classical building ruled triumphant. Despite or, more probably, because of this situation, a few men of means and imagination rebelled. 1750 marks a critical point in Gothic Revival history, for it was in that year that Sir Robert Walpole's son Horace began to convert his Baroque villa at Twickenham into the Gothic mansion that is Strawberry Hill. What began as the whim of one man became in less than a century virtually a national style.[1]

As noted previously, Romanticism, particularly as it manifested itself in poetry, fiction, and the penchant for the archaeological, gave an enormous impetus to Gothicism. So, too, did patriotic fervor. Noting that medievalism had never fully vanished from England, one historian of the period has justly concluded that the post-Napoleonic generation, in search of a national style to complement its growing self-awareness, eagerly seized upon Gothic.[2] The most decisive factor in launching the English Gothic Revival, however, may not have been the cultural or nationalistic one, but rather, that of social control--cheap social control, more precisely. England counted herself fortunate that she had escaped the Jacobinism and social upheavals of the French Revolution, but after Waterloo came Peterloo and a growing fear that her escape had been only of temporary duration. Prefiguring and inverting Marx's theorem, the established order decided that the cure for lower-class unrest was to be religion. There was a problem, however. For the preceding half century very few churches had been built, despite a burgeoning population. The Church Building Act of 1818 attempted to remedy matters, and in the next fifteen

years some six million pounds were expended to construct some two hundred and fourteen churches, of which
one hundred and seventy-four were more-or-less Gothic
in style. Why Gothic rather than the still dominant
Classical? Brick was cheaper than stone.[3] The desire
for social control may have initiated the Gothic Revival, but religious considerations were to sustain
and to give it distinctive character. Without the
Catholic Emancipation Act of 1829, the Oxford Movement,
the Ecclesiological Society, and the compelling sales-
manship of Augustus Pugin, the Revival might well have
been short-lived.

The energetic, almost frenetic church building
activity which followed the Act of 1818 brought up the
question of honest construction, the hallmark of medieval Gothic architecture. As Peter Collins has observed
apropos of this church building: "Cheapness had been
achieved by using cast iron for columns and tracery,
and by making the walls of plastered brick. Thus the
more extensively archaeological studies developed, the
more violently was the objection raised that these
churches were not true Gothic at all, but pitiful
shams."[4] Unfettered from serious restrictions by the
Emancipation Act, Catholics had begun to give more
thought to their churches. Due to the special needs of
liturgy, these churches differed from Protestant ones,
thus forcing architects to consider more seriously honest interior as well as exterior construction. The
practical effect of this, however, was much less significant than might have been anticipated: English
Catholics, by and large, eschewed their Gothic heritage
in favor of the Italianate.

More greatly concerned with the proper relationship between liturgy and church architecture was the
Ecclesiological Society. Founded in 1839 and originally called the Cambridge Camden Society, this offshoot
of the Oxford Movement attempted to push the Established Church in the direction of Anglo-Catholicism. More
concerned that religious edifices by "correct" than
beautiful, the Ecclesiologists decreed that Anglicans
must build in the Gothic style, and the Decorated Gothic, at that.[5] Indeed, by so insistently and persistently debating the relative merits of truth and beauty,
they created a dilemma which no Gothicist, contemporary
or later, could entirely avoid.

No one single person deserves more credit for attempting to formulate and systematize guiding principles for the Gothic Revival in England than did Augustus Welby Pugin (1812-1852).[6] The son of a French é-

migré who had fled during the Revolution and who, as a draftsman, was an authority on Gothic, Pugin, reared as a Protestant, converted to Catholicism in 1834. His life saddened by deep personal tragedy (his first two wives died at an early age), he threw himself wholeheartedly into the cause of convincing his coreligionists that they had no alternative but to adopt the Gothic style. Only a few wealthy Catholics heeded his plea, but his major works--Contrasts (1836), True Principles of Christian Architecture (1841), and Apology for the Revival of Christian Architecture in England (1843)--were not easily dismissed by Protestant Gothicists, despite their objections to his religious bias and polemics.

Besides being an apologist, Pugin was a practitioner of Gothic architecture, though few of his works ever lived up to their high drawing-board promise. He did, however, assist young Sir Charles Barry in rebuilding the Houses of Parliament after the latter bested ninety-six other competing architects in 1836 with his Gothic designs.[7] Whatever one may think of the aesthetic results, Barry's victory gave notice that Gothic, in regard to public buildings, was no longer to be considered outré.

Pugin went insane in the last few years of his life and died in 1852 at the age of forty. By that time another brilliant advocate for the Gothic had come forth: John Ruskin. The differences in view between Pugin and Ruskin, however, were pronounced. The former was a devout Catholic; the latter so markedly anti-Catholic, at least in his writings, that Sir Kenneth Clark concluded that his diatribes amounted to a classical case of defense mechanism.[8] Pugin, the architect, was primarily concerned with a building's construction; Ruskin, the art critic, with its ornamentation. Pugin's greatest influence was on church architecture; Ruskin's on civil.[9] The indigenous medieval Gothic was most suitable as a style for nineteenth-century England, according to Pugin; Ruskin basically agreed, but so popular did his descriptions of Venetian Gothic prove, that he became largely responsible for the introduction of foreign elements. One could continue with such comparisons, but the real point is that Ruskin, despite his disillusionment with the Revival (he abhorred the mass destruction of old buildings in the name of a "sane" or "logical" restoration), successfully carried on the popularizing activities of Pugin both at home and abroad.

By the 1850's or certainly by the death of Prince Albert in 1861, Gothic architecture had been elevated virtually if not fully to the rank of a national style. A handful of rather bizarre mansions had been the chief result of the late eighteenth-century's dalliance with Gothic; after Waterloo and through the early years of Victoria, Gothic's popularity expanded, though not much beyond the province of church building. After the Crystal Palace and Great Exhibition, however, a proud and powerful England passionately embraced this style with fewer and fewer reservations. No longer could the movement be described as the picturesque preserve of a few aristocrats or as the archaeological quest of religionists to find the true style. Midway through the century the Revival had become the especial concern of the middle class. Sir Gilbert Scott (1810-1877), a self-made man, symbolized this triumph and concern. Neither an unabashed medievalist[10] nor a Catholic, Scott adopted Gothic largely because it seemed consonant with the nation's historical past. In his forty years as a practicing architect, he and his assistants were reputedly responsible for more than a thousand buildings.[11] As Clark has so nicely understated: "Gilbert Scott must have changed the appearance of England considerably."[12] But Scott was not alone. The names of Butterfield, Bodley, Burges, and Barlow, of Street and Shaw, and of Waterhouse and Webb, illuminate the roster of High Victorian Gothic architects. And if one can look beyond their abuse of polychromy, their confusing eclecticism, and their occasional inability to withstand overusing pinnacles and parapets, cusps and crockets, one can applaud their energy and audacity in trying to find a modern use for a medieval style. This last phase of Victorian Gothic might have represented Philistinism; but it was able to withstand challenges and to endure almost as a credo until the turn of the century.[13]

The Gothic Revival was by no means limited to England, though certainly it flowered most luxuriantly there. Nineteenth-century France enjoyed a corresponding if diminished resuscitation of medieval architecture, thanks, in no small measure, to the efforts of one man: Eugène Viollet-le-Duc (1814-1879). Like his counterpart across the Channel, Pugin, Viollet-le-Duc served as the leading publicist for his nation's nineteenth-century Gothic Revival. His writings on medieval architecture ran to no fewer than sixteen volumes. Similarly, both men were singularly more successful in enunciating the principles of Gothic than applying them

to their own buildings. There the comparisons stop,
however. Pugin was a religious zealot; Viollet-le-Duc
a strong anti-clericalist. Whereas for the Englishman
the ultimate rationale for the use of Gothic rested
with its religious affinities, for the Frenchman,
Gothic was pandemically applicable due to its principles of structural integrity. The latter's was the
argument for Gothic Rationalism, and, as such, did
much to bridge the gap between builders of the nineteenth and twentieth centuries.[14] Pugin, moreover,
for all the bitter criticism he engendered, did exert
a pronounced influence on the English Gothic Revival.
Viollet-le-Duc, in contrast, fought a lonely, uphill
battle against the École des Beaux-Arts, arbiter of
French taste during the last half of the century.
Choosing largely to ignore the nation's medieval heritage, the École decreed that appropriate Renaissance
and Baroque works should serve as models for the glory
of the Second Empire.[15]

The French may have had a rich medieval heritage
but, relatively speaking, decided to ignore it; Americans, on the other hand, possessed no such heritage
but acted as though they did. Indeed, in the century
between the 1830's and the 1930's, American architecture accommodated no fewer than three interrelated but
essentially separate phases of Gothic revivalism. The
primary reason that this exotic transplant took root
does not seem difficult to fathom. Its efforts to
achieve cultural nationalism notwithstanding, the nation throughout the nineteenth century continued basically to take its artistic cues from Great Britain.
Each of the three phases of this country's Gothic Revival corresponded to an English phase. Several leading American Gothicists, moreover--Upjohn, Vaughan and
Bodley--were born and received their training in England.   Viewed in this light, the American Gothic Revival appears to be much more a protracted case of
"conspicuous emulation" than of any sincere quest to
recapture a fanciful medieval spirit. This seems so--
until one comes to Ralph Adams Cram.

The Jacksonian Era swept away the proportioned
and symmetrical classicism of the Early National Period, in politics as well as art, replacing it with a
decidedly less restrained and asymmetrical romanticism.
Democracy in politics and eclecticism in the arts became the values of the generation which lived during
the thirty years prior to the Civil War. Along with
the Grecian, Egyptian, and Italian, the Gothic style
became a widespread fad which found expression in pub-

lic buildings, homes, and churches. The nation's most
popular architect and architectural critic, Alexander
Jackson Davis and Andrew Jackson Downing, respectively, though appreciative of and catering to the variegated stylistic tastes, were Gothicists by preference.
So also were the age's two finest church builders,
Richard Upjohn and James Renwick.[16] The former's
Trinity Chruch and the Church of the Ascension, and
the latter's Grace Church and St. Patrick's Cathedral,
gave New Yorkers in particular and Americans in general the distinct feeling that Gothicism need not be the
special preserve of England.

It would be a serious mistake, of course, to assume that this early Gothic Revival represented any
sort of golden age for architecture. It assuredly did
not, though it scarcely constituted an age of unrelieved failure, as some critics, Cram included, would
have us believe. Though Downing, who well understood
the principles of medieval Gothic design and construction, would warn his fellow architects to express
their materials clearly,[17] many, if not most, resorted
to plastered brick rather than stone. Also, like
their counterparts in England, the early American
Gothicists usually fell prey to too much archaeology
and too little creative innovation. By the 1850's,
with the movement already in its waning years, the so-
called Carpenter's Gothic brought the style to the
verge of ridicule.

Despite continued problems, the outlook for American architecture during the years following the Civil
War was by no means one of unrelieved gloom, though
Cram considered the entire fifty-year period, 1830-
1880, "worse than at any time or in any place recorded
in history...."[18] For one thing, the American Institute of Architects, established in 1857, was beginning
to take a more active part in standards of taste. In
addition, the nation's first schools of architecture
were established at M.I.T. (1865) and at Columbia University (1881), and were working towards similar goals.
Further assistance came from an international quarter.
Ever since Napoleon III had endowed the École des
Beaux-Arts with new prestige, Paris held out the promise of suitable training for aspiring young American
architects.[19] Richard Morris Hunt (1828-1895), the
first American student to take advantage of this situation, brought back from the École a passion for the
chateaux of the Loire and the atelier method, whereby
a master architect employs and concomitantly instructs
his younger assistants. Aside from a number of public

buildings (such as New York's Lenox Library and Metropolitan Museum of Art, and Washington's National Observatory), Hunt catered to the vulgar ostentation of the newly rich. Yet if his Biltmore, the French Renaissance chateau designed for William Vanderbilt at Asheville, North Carolina, and the Breakers, created for Cornelius Vanderbilt at Newport, indicate that artistic tastes had not proceeded, pari passu, with the nation's growing wealth, Hunt could not be faulted for poor execution. He was, as one critic has observed, "no rebel questioning the validity of the historic styles but a scholarly eclectic who refined other men's barbaric treatment of them...."[20]

It was not only Hunt who attempted to elevate public taste. The Centennial Exposition of 1876 in Philadelphia, by exhibiting the latest European trends in art, helped to produce both "a new artistic conscience" and "a growing refinement of taste to serve."[21] Add to this the continued and growing influence of the École des Beaux-Arts, and the stage was ready for a change of scenery, if not an altogether new production. Two figures now emerged from the wings to offer memorable performances of architectural virtuosity: Charles Follen McKim and Henry Hobson Richardson.

Born in a mining town in Chester County, Pennsylvania, McKim (1847-1909) studied engineering at Harvard but then elected architecture as a vocation.[22] After an apprenticeship with Russell Sturgis and additional study at the École, he aided Richardson with the latter's Brattle Square Church in Boston before establishing his own firm. Specializing first in the neo-classical and then in the Renaissance style, McKim and his two partners, William Mead and Stanford White, produced much of New York's finest late nineteenth- and early twentieth-century public and private building. Even a partial list of their edifices reads like a tour guide to the city's architecture of that period: the University Club, the Century Club, the Villard Mansion, the J. Pierpont Morgan Library, Low Library (Columbia University), Madison Square Garden, Pennsylvania Station, Washington Square Arch. In addition, the firm designed the Boston Public Library and the Rhode Island State Capitol, modeled respectively along majestic Renaissance and Classical lines. When one also considers their impressive array of residences built for the rich and famous--William and Harry Payne Whitney, James Gordon Bennett, John Jacob Astor, Mrs. Mark Hopkins, Charles Dana Gibson, Levi

Morton, and George Eastman--it is easy to understand the high stature that accrued to McKim and associates.

Impressive as their works were, however, the original and revolutionary genius of Richardson (1838-1886) stands out preeminently in the last quarter of the nineteenth century.[23] Born near New Orleans into a family of considerable wealth, he became the second American neophyte architect to receive training at the École. Unlike Hunt or McKim, however, he had derived his greatest inspiration neither from the French chateaux nor from the Italian classicism or Renaissance, but from the Romanesque religious art of southern France and northern Spain. The Brattle Square Church, commissioned in 1870, marked his initial foray into the Romanesque and his first major work. In 1872 he began what was to become one of his most splendid works, Trinity Church in Boston. A gourmand, though one whose health problems should have forced him to eat and drink abstemiously, he labored frenetically, once telling a friend that he could "never take the time to die."[24] Over the next decade and a half designs for a large number of remarkably fine churches, college buildings, private homes, railroad stations, and monuments, as well as the Albany City Hall, flowed from his fertile imagination. Although the Allegheny County Court House and Jail in Pittsburgh and the Marshall Field Wholesale Store in Chicago, two of his most stunning achievements, were unfinished at the time of his sudden death, his reputation by then had been well secured. As far as Cram was concerned, Richardson, whom he idolized, would be remembered, "not as the discoverer of a new style, but as the man who made architecture a living art once more."[25]

In point of fact, Cram considered Richardson and McKim to be the age's architectural giants. As a young man in the 1880's, he watched the construction of McKim's Boston Public Library directly in front of Trinity Church and deemed that when finished it would "probably be the finest architectural monument in the United States."[26] Some fifty years later he was to observe: "No greater contrast could be imagined than that between Trinity Church and the new Library across the way. On the one hand, an almost brutal, certainly primitive, boldness, arrogance, power; on the other, a serene classicism, reserved, scholarly, delicately conceived in all its parts, beautiful in that sense in which things have always been beautiful in periods of high human culture." Complementary rather than competing, Richardson's projects and genius were "bold,

56

dominating, adventurous," while McKim's were of "grace," "refinement," and "sensibility."[27] With a striking analogy, Cram concluded: "Nothing led up to Richardson and McKim though much followed on. They came like sudden portents, an architectural Mussolini sweeping away at a breath the farrago of an outworn superstition, an architectural Matthew Arnold with his new gospel of 'sweetness and light.'"[28]

The Gilded Age's High Victorian Gothic Revival, in contrast to the works of Richardson and McKim, received no paeans of praise either from Cram or, for that matter, from a number of other architectural critics, though it currently enjoys considerably more critical esteem. It was a popular style, to be sure; but the quality of its achievements, according to its critics, failed to live up to that of its corresponding phase in England. In fact, one might well argue that it actually represented a retrogression from the Early Victorian Revival in the United States. The earlier Revival, though suffering from too great a dependence on archaeological models and the use of questionable materials, achieved a certain respectability, largely as a result of adhering to accepted Gothic principles. The Revival of the 1860's and 1870's, however, all too often created structures which, as one critic has put it, "had lost all systematic proportion, all certainty of symbolism, all real sense of form."[29] In contradistinction to the Early Revival, the High Revival tended to adorn its creations with a plethora of Gothic devices—pointed arches, clustered columns, turrets, parapets, fretted window-frames—quite irrespective of the crazy-quilt, kaleidoscopic results which would emerge. Ultimately the High Victorian Revival, characterized by illogical additions and by the misuse of polychromy and Italianate models, the result of too much reading or misreading of Ruskin (who, for Cram, had become "quite the most unreliable critic and exponent of architecture that ever lived"),[30] ran aground.

Besides its endemic weaknesses, this phase of the Revival suffered at the hands of external sources as well. The Centennial Exposition, through its wide variety of architectural examples, had given an added centrifugal impetus to architects desiring to break away from then-dominant trends, of which the Gothic was one. Secondly, while there were a few Gothicists of genuine merit, such as Ware and Van Brunt (although the latter eschewed the style in mid-career), even their works paled before the non-Gothic examples of

Richardson and McKim, Mead and White.
If the hypothesis that nineteenth-century American architecture closely followed English trends is correct, there would have been a Late Victorian Gothic Revival in any case. Given the questionable yield of the High Victorian harvest, however, there was no indication whatsoever that the Late Revival would prove artistically successful. That it did, to a very great extent reflects the achievements of Ralph Adams Cram. Before more closely examining his work, however, it is first necessary to complete the analysis of his genesis as a Gothicist.

Cram returned from his second trip to Europe approximately one thousand dollars in debt. Entering an open competition for additions to be made to Charles Bulfinch's Massachusetts State House, he won the second prize of thirteen hundred dollars,[31] paid off his debts, and decided to form his own office. Needing a partner who could handle the business and practical details (as opposed to the actual designing), he joined forces with Charles Francis Wentworth, and the two opened office--"Cram and Wentworth, Architects"--at One Park Square, Boston, in or around 1889.[32]

All things--his early reading of Ruskin, his two trips to Europe (particularly Venice), his conversion to High Anglicanism--pointed to an intellectual and emotional acceptance of Gothic on Cram's part. But there were other reinforcing and no less important factors as well. Possessing a first-rate mind and no little degree of self-assurance, he probably had no intention of toiling in the shadows of another man's work, and by 1890, the shadows of both Richardson and McKim were long. There was also a very practical consideration. In the United States, as in England, the High Victorian period, in contrast to the Early Victorian one, witnessed a decided shift in emphasis in the use of Gothic, away from ecclesiastical architecture and more towards public and domestic. If Cram and Wentworth were to establish a genuine reputation for themselves, it may have seemed the course of wisdom to enter church building, the less crowded area of specialization. Yet the practical basis for Cram's decision should not be overemphasized. Had a certain opportunism predominated in him, he logically could have turned sharply at some point in his career to the ascendant modes of modernist expression in terms both of style and type of building. As it was, in his fifty years as an architect, he never abandoned his preference for Gothic churches.

From the inception of his career, Cram never con-
tented himself with simply building churches or other
structures. Instead, he persistently attempted to
educate the public as to what constituted good and bad
architecture. While not reaching the extent of Viollet-le-Duc's, his writings on architectural subjects
are voluminous. Even before settling upon architecture as a profession, he gave considerable thought to
the history and nature of art, and once engaged in his
practice, he began to lecture widely and to commit to
print his ideas, particularly as they related to ecclesiastical art. The heart of these reflections became embodied in Church Building, which was first published in 1899 and which no person interested in Cram
can afford to neglect. Not only does this book offer
a clear indication of what he was trying to achieve in
his early work, but because his views on art and ar-
chitecture--for better or worse--were to remain remarkably consistent, it also provides a guide and
yardstick for the study of his later work. There
exists an additional reason for concerning ourselves
with his aesthetic vision. If the Church Building of
1899 had been the work of a still relatively obscure
architect, by 1914, the year of its second edition,
it had become the work of a highly respected master
builder, and, as such, could be challenged but no
longer ignored by any ecclesiastical specialist, Gothic or otherwise. At this point, it is useful to examine some of his more important and characteristic
points of view.

A central problem for the study of the Gothic Revival (or, for that matter, of any architectural revival) rests with considering to what extent the movement was archaeological and to what extent it was innovative. By definition, the Revival was bound to
secrete certain overtones of archaeology. Architecture might not be quite the "seamless web" that is
history, but in its revivalistic phases it ineluctably
strives to capture the continuity between past and
present. Overdone, the revival becomes pure archaism
bereft of the saving graces of transmutation and
growth. While it may be true that the ultimate test
lies in the trained eye and mind of the beholder, it
is crucial to know how the architect himself viewed
the problem vis-à-vis his work: result can never be
fully separated from intent.

For Cram, architects were to avoid archaeology
at all costs. While still an apprentice at Rotch and
Tilden, he chided: "many architects go so far in

59

their love for the [Gothic] style that they not only
copy the deficiencies as well as the beauties, but
they make modern necessities conform to Gothic forms.
It does not seem as though such servile copying as
this is true art."[33] In other words, for the Revival
to be legitimate, Gothic forms would have to conform
to modern needs and not vice versa. Cram, of course,
did not mean to denigrate the past per se. Indeed,
he reasoned that only through a careful study of the
past could one build for the present and future. It
seems worthwhile to quote him at some length on this
matter, since this viewpoint served as the touchstone
not only for his theory of art, but for his general
critique of society as well:

> ... when we build here in America, we are
> building for now....It is art, not archae-
> ology, that drives us. From the past, not
> in the past. We must return for the fire
> of life to other centuries, since a night
> intervened between our fathers' time and
> ours wherin the light was not. We must re-
> turn, but we may not remain. It is the
> present that demands us,--the immutable
> Church existing in times of the utmost
> mutability. We must express the Church
> that is one through all ages; but also we
> must express the endless changes of human
> life, the variation of environment. This
> is church architecture; the manifestation
> through new modes of the ecclesiastical
> past; unchangeableness through variety;
> the eternal through the never-fixed.[34]

The nineteenth-century Gothic Revival had largely
failed, in his opinion, simply because it had been
guilty of too great an attachment to the past and too
little regard for the present. Though Pugin readily
confessed to a concern for "antiquity, not novelty,"[35]
Cram believed that the Englishman had escaped archae-
ologism and, by emphasizing the essential principles
of medieval architecture, had positioned the Revival
on solid ground. His successors, however--Scott,
Street, and Pearson--were "masters of archaeology"
and, as such, caused the movement to retrogress. Fortunately, some Late Victorian Gothicists, such as
Bodley, Garner, Sedding, and Vaughan, "with their sen-
sitive appreciation of architecture as a living
thing," had returned to Pugin's theories, had revivified the movement, and, in Vaughan's case, had brought
these principles to the United States.[36]

There was more than their appreciation of medieval principles which linked Pugin and Cram, though it is improbable that the latter was fully aware of this. Those who knew Pugin claimed that he had arrived at his religion by way of aesthetic appreciation; he never denied it.[37] Once converted, however, he wholeheartedly enlisted beauty in the cause of religion. Cram's experience appears similar. His passion for beauty long antedated his zeal for religion, but once having discovered his High Anglicanism, he merged the two, though he never subordinated one to the other. "Until we realize," he wrote, "that beauty of whatever kind in any church is put there to the glory of God and not to the admiration of the passers-by, we may study and labor in vain." Yet he cautioned: "Art has been, is, and will be forever the greatest agency for spiritual impression that the Church may claim.... Art and religion cannot be dissociated without mutual loss, for in its highest estate the former is but the perfect expression of the latter."[38] Like Keats, he had construed truth and beauty as a balanced equation.

During the 1890's Cram enunciated various subsuming principles for church building which indicated his overall sympathy with certain general turns the Gothic Revival had already taken. For Anglicans--and at this stage of his life Cram had a narrow religious concern--only the Gothic was an appropriate style. This was exactly what the Ecclesiological Society had decreed. Even Richardsonian Romanesque, integral and organic as it was, was unsuitable for Anglican church building since it bore "no relationship to national, racial or historical Christianity in the United States."[39] As a corollary to this proposition, Cram also insisted that the architect, if he were to achieve a successful church, must be sympathetic to its faith. This tendency to fuse art and morality characterized the thinking of virtually all the leading Gothic polemicists of the nineteenth century-- Pugin, the Ecclesiological Society, Ruskin, and Cram. Only Viollet-le-Duc seems to have escaped this pitfall, and it was precisely his amoral Rationalism which upset other value-conscious Goths. Cram inveighed: "Church building is not simply an ordinary proposition in architectural design, but rather a problem governed by higher principles and more enduring laws than obtain in any other form of the great art of building."[40] More will be said later concerning Cram's belief in the necessity for Anglicans to build in Gothic and the function of art as an instrument of morality.

In terms of other strictures respecting ecclesiastical architecture, physical location was to be paramount in determining church design. There were distinct and separate methods for designing acceptable country churches, village churches, city churches, and cathedrals. The materials used, the massing, the proportions--all were dependent on not only what one was trying to achieve, but where. Brick, for example, would be suitable for country churches, but not for great cathedrals; village churches need not necessarily have high walls, but city churches, in order to prevent being dwarfed by large buildings, did. Also, city churches and cathedrals needed more refined materials and greater ornamentation than did houses of worship in less populated areas. There were certain basic principles, however, which applied to Gothic churches, regardless of location. "A church is organic," he asserted, "and every line, every mass, every detail, must be carefully considered and perfectly adapted to its ends, forming an essential part of a great and living whole."41 In other words, honesty--in terms of design, construction, and decoration--was essential for success.

In the area of design, Cram made one of his more original contributions to the Gothic Revival by stressing the English Perpendicular style. There were three styles or stages of development in medieval English Gothic architecture: the early or Norman Gothic, the Decorated or Edwardian Gothic, and the Perpendicular Gothic of the fourteenth and fifteenth centuries. The Ecclesiologists had decreed that only the Decorated was acceptable as a style for the nineteenth-century Revival.42 Cram, however, insisted that the true course for nineteenth-century revivalists to pursue was that of the Perpendicular, which, though born at the end of the fourteenth century, had never fully developed but had been preternaturally destroyed by Henry VIII's rift with Rome and the subsequent apostasy of England to Protestantism.43 Specifically, this is what he had meant when he said that we must build from, but not in the past. Given the direction it had been taking, the Perpendicular, he conjectured, would in all probability have constituted the true flowering of medieval English Gothic, the perfect art form for the true, sacramental, Anglo-Catholic religion. Symbolized by the work of Bishop William of Wykeham, builder of the great Winchester Cathedral and the "greatest Gothic of all," the Perpendicular had provided a logical, beautiful, and modern architecture for the churches of its age. There seemed no reason, therefore, why that style could not do the same for the modern age. "Were we to continue as now," Cram cautioned, "building essays in archaeology, to-day in French Flamboyant, to-morrow in Early English, here in Decorated, there in François premier, we should still be following out the old principle of artificiality. One style, and one only, is for us; and that is the English Perpendicular."[44] If other modern Gothicists also preferred the Perpendicular-- and some did--none, to my knowledge, articulated as did Cram the possibilities of developing this continuum between past and present.

Honesty in construction and decoration were no less vital than truthfulness in design. According to Cram, the artist should never attempt to conceal the true nature of the material he uses. When confronted with such "sham" construction as steel columns covered by applied stone or girders doing the work of arches and vaults, he became irate. There was no substitute, so he argued, for masonry. Stone and, on certain occasions, brick were legitimate materials for church building; plaster and lath were not. He knew, of course, that stone could be quite costly, and hence the temptation to employ cheaper materials. Yet stone, though it might involve a greater initial expense, was both "permanent" and "respectful." Build only a little but well, he advised, not a good deal and poorly.[45] To a surprisingly large extent, he actually practiced what he preached. Where funds were plentiful, as for the Cathedral of St. John the Divine, the Princeton Chapel or the East Liberty, Pennsylvania Presbyterian Church, he spared no expense while plying his craft; when they were at a premium, he built less lavishly, though his work never appeared cheap or tawdry.

Preferring a simple massing for a church's exterior, Cram believed that it was the church's interior which rightfully should express a richness of fabric and ornamentation. Anglo-Catholic churches, the overwhelming interest of his early career, centered around the chancel and sanctuary. One could properly build a simple nave, he argued, but the altar, the most sacred part of the church, must stand out as the quintessence of beauty. Whether it be the altar-stone or reredos, the greatest care must be taken to insure that beauty would be commensurate with the sanctity of these church parts.

One of Cram's most significant and controversial contributions to the Gothic Revival was his insistence that--especially when it concerned ornamentation--the machine could never rival the individual craftsman for excellence of work. This ideal was shared by William Morris and by the entire generation of Anglo-American arts-and-crafts revivalists: good artists alone produced good work, and the design and execution of a work were inseparable. Sculpting, wood carving, stained glass, metal design, glazes, needlework, illumination, tapestry--these were allied but by no means subordinate arts, and vis-à-vis architecture, stood as complementary labors. Virtually all of Cram's churches--both early and late--are marked by the rich and almost always successful use of these arts. In church after church, one finds, for example, the exquisite sculpture of Lee Lawrie or Sterling Calder, the wood carving of John Kirchmayer, and the stained glasses of Charles Connick and Nicola d'Ascenzo.[46]

Cram's animus against the machine was paralleled by his opposition to other innovations. The tendency in churches to remove columns and all obstacles to vision, and to build low side walls, steep roofs supported by heavy trusses, and polygonal chancels, all met with his disapproval. So, too, did the use of lath, plaster and steel in the construction of vaults.[47] Underscoring the importance of tradition, he wrote: "The Church is essentially immutable, and essentially her architectural expression must be the same. The old ideals persist and control us in our labors. Following them, we can hardly go wrong, the danger lies only in breaking recklessly away."[48] In his reluctance to espouse innovations in church architecture, whether in the nature of design, materials, or the use of the machine, Cram has appeared almost as a troglodyte to some later critics. As Roger B. Stein, contrasting the effect Ruskin had on Cram and Frank Lloyd Wright, has noted: "Wright was able to shape the old elements of art, nature, and morality into a new architectural synthesis, to create in a sense the Madonna of the future, while Cram could only rearrange the old elements mechanically and produce merely anachronistic Cimabues or Duccios."[49] By persistently articulating his opposition to modernism in the arts and architecture, moreover, Cram gave his critics an abundance of fuel for their fires. Yet he never looked at himself as an artistic innovator, but as the upholder and modifier of a sacred tradition. Organic change, not revolution, became his credo as

64

assuredly did his conviction that modernism equalled
revolution. And if it is true--as well it may be--
that by influencing an entire generation to build in
Gothic, Cram delayed the acceptance of modernism in
ecclesiastical architecture, far from rejecting the
charge, he would have been pleased.

One can argue, nevertheless, that at least a
small part of the modernist critique against Cram de-
rives from the anomaly created by building churches in
the midst of an increasingly secular society. It may
have been his belief that churches still played a vital role, rather than his actual methods of design and
construction, which have made him seem so hopelessly
outmoded. Certainly his general approach to ecclesiastical architecture was not totally removed from the
secular architecture of the modernists. The dicta
that one should build honestly and beautifully and
that the edifice, both in its totality and in its relationship to its milieu, should form an integral,
organic whole, apply equally to both. Moreover, he
never objected to the use of new structural materials
like steel and concrete when, as with commercial
buildings, it seemed appropriate. Indeed, it was precisely the utilization of these aids which, in his
opinion, had catapulted the nation's architecture to a
position of world leadership by the 1920's.[50] Also,
if by functionalism is meant that "form follows function," then Cram's churches were decidedly functional,
with all parts serving a purpose, in this case, the
worship and glorification of God. Or to state the
problem in somewhat different terms: a "functional"
modern office building prides itself on the absence of
useless parts and ornamentation; in a High Anglican or
Roman Catholic church, the various parts and ornamentation are indispensable components of function. As
with archaism, what constitutes modernism is to some
degree a subjective matter.

Over the years Cram's conception of what comprised good Gothic architecture remained basically un-
changed. While he was to retract his pronounced emphasis on the English Perpendicular and his narrow
concern for Anglo-Catholicism,[51] his later writings
basically reflected an elaboration of early principles. Still clearly noticeable would be the influence
of the earlier nineteenth-century Gothicists: the
Ecclesiologists' demand that the Gothic best served
Anglican churches, Viollet-le-Duc's advocacy of Gothicism's structural honesty, and Pugin's insistence
that beauty was an avenue to religion. Yet Cram's importance in American architectural history extends

far beyond his role as an advocate for medieval building. Unlike that of a Pugin or a Viollet-le-Duc, his
work fully lived up to his theories of art, providing,
as one historian has noted, "a comfortable standard
of beauty that even the simplest could appreciate."[52]
Reactionary or not, Cram was to become the high priest
of the Late Gothic Revival and one of the nation's
leading and most popular architects.

NOTES

1. The literature of the Gothic Revival in England, not surprisingly, has become abundant. The best contemporary account is to be found in Charles L. Eastlake, A History of the Gothic Revival (London, 1872). Oddly, more than half a century elapsed before another significant treatment of the movement appeared in the form of Sir Kenneth Clark's provocative classic, The Gothic Revival (London, 1928). Other works which I found most helpful for understanding the Revival include Robert Furneaux Jordan, Victorian Architecture (Middlesex, 1966); Basil F. L. Clarke, Church Builders of the Nineteenth Century (London, 1938); Henry-Russell Hitchcock, Architecture, Nineteenth and Twentieth Centuries (Baltimore, 1958); and John Summerson, Heavenly Mansions (London, 1949). Not a history of the movement as such, but filled with acute pertinent perceptions is Peter Collins, Changing Ideals in Modern Architecture, 1750-1950 (London, 1965).

2. Jordan, Victorian Architecture, pp. 60, 76.

3. Sir Kenneth Clark, The Gothic Revival, 3rd ed., rev. (New York, 1962), pp. 94-96.

4. Collins, Changing Ideals in Modern Architecture, pp. 106-107.

5. Clark, The Gothic Revival, p. 171.

6. For details of Pugin's life and work, see Benjamin Ferrey, Pugin: Recollections (London, 1861); Michael Lomax-Trappes, Pugin, a Medieval Victorian (London, 1932); Denis Gwyn, Lord Shrewsbury, Pugin and the Catholic Revival (London, 1946); and Phoebe Stanton, Pugin (New York, 1971).

7. Ironically, Barry was a classicist by preference.

8. Clark, The Gothic Revival, p. 197.

9. Clarke, Church Builders of the Nineteenth Century, p. 145.

10. Though Scott did at one point declare that "every aspiration of my heart had become mediaeval" (quoted in Clarke, Church Builders, p. 163), it does not seem to me that his commitment to medievalism even nearly approached that of others, such as Pugin, Ruskin or Morris.

11. Jordan, Victorian Architecture, p. 97.

12. Clark, The Gothic Revival, p. 175.

13. A number of critics, moreover, have noted the overall influence exerted by nineteenth-century Gothicism, particularly in its later manifestations, on the functional and organic styles of the twentieth century. See, for example, Jordan, Victorian Architecture, pp. 258-260.

14. For a helpful analysis of Viollet-le-Duc's Rationalism, see Summerson, Heavenly Mansions and Collins, Changing Ideals, pp. 198-217.

15. Despite this situation, Viollet-le-Duc was successful in his unceasing attempts to restore--for better or worse--a number of France's medieval works. Among his more significant restorations must be included the Cathedrals of Notre Dame, Chartres, and Laon, as well as the famed walls of Carcassonne.

16. The most complete treatments of the Early Gothic Revival in American ecclesiastical architecture are to be found in Phoebe B. Stanton, The Gothic Revival & American Church Architecture: An Episode in Taste, 1840-1856 (Baltimore, 1968), and William H. Pierson, Jr., American Buildings and Their Architects: Technology and the Picturesque, the Corporate and the Early Gothic Styles (Garden City, N.Y., 1978).

17. As Downing wrote: "When we employ stone as a building material, let it be clearly expressed. When we employ wood, there should be no less frankness in avowing the material." Quoted in Wayne Andrews. Architecture, Ambition and Americans (New York, 1947), p. 107.

18. Ralph Adams Cram, The Gothic Quest (New York, 1907), p. 148.

19. Fiske Kimball, American Architecture (New York, 1928), p. 125. Many of the major architects of the second half of the nineteenth century--Hunt, Richardson, McKim, Carrère, Hastings--studied at the École, which Cram thought at that time "was the one school in the world with a logical, consistent, and inspiring system of education." Ralph Adams Cram, My Life in Architecture (Boston, 1936), p. 37. Cram, however, developed stronger reservations about the school at a later time.

20. Oliver W. Larkin, Art and Life in America, rev. ed. (New York, 1960), p. 247. For a biting description of the artistic tastes of the nouveaux riches, see Russell Lynes, The Art-Makers of Nineteenth Century America (New York, 1970), pp. 408-417, 447-481. For a quite different point of

view, see Wayne Andrews, Architecture, Ambition
and Americans. While not overlooking some of the
negative effects produced by the new wealth of
the Gilded Age, Andrews argues that this wealth
made possible some major innovations in architecture. And as Lewis Mumford has pointed out,
those innovations, achieved by technology in the
areas of heating, lighting, ventilation and construction, considerably brightened the "brown decades" of the late nineteenth century. Lewis
Mumford, The Brown Decades (New York, 1931), pp.
107-181, passim.

21. Talbot Faulkner Hamlin, The American Spirit in
Architecture (New Haven, 1926), pp. 165-166.

22. For studies of McKim and his work, see Alfred
Hoyt Granger, Charles Follen McKim (Boston, 1913),
Charles Moore, The Life and Times of Charles
Follen McKim (Boston, 1929), and Leland M. Roth,
The Architecture of McKim, Mead & White (New
York, 1973). Also see William H. Jordy, American
Buildings and their Architects: Progressive and
Academic Ideals at the Turn of the Twentieth Cen-
tury (Garden City, N.Y., 1972), pp. 314-375.

23. The best study to date of Richardson and his work
is Henry-Russell Hitchcock, The Architecture of
H. H. Richardson and His Times, 2nd ed., rev.
(Hamden, Connecticut, 1961).

24. Andrews, Architecture, p. 168.

25. Ralph Adams Cram, "Style in American Architecture," The Architectural Record, XXXIV (September,
1913), 236.

26. Ralph Adams Cram, Letter to Mr. White, (n.d.),
Department of Rare Books & MSS, Boston Public
Library.

27. Cram, My Life, pp. 35,33.

28. Ralph Adams Cram, American Church Building of Today, (New York, 1929), p. v.

29. Alan Gowans, Architecture in New Jersey (Princeton, New Jersey, 1964), p. 97.

30. Ralph Adams Cram, "The Influence of the French
School on American Architecture," The American
Architect and Building News, LXVI, (November 25,
1899), 66. Ruskin, for Cram, had become a "bigot"
and "absurd" as a result of "his frantic advocacy
of certain forms or architecture." Though not explicitly spelled out, he was doubtlessly referring, at least in part, to Ruskin's conversion
from English Gothic, as championed in The Seven
Lamps of Architecture, to Italian Gothic, which

69

he lauded in his later <u>Stones of Venice</u>. Then, too, there was Ruskin's diatribes against Catholicism.

31. Certain unnamed lobbyists approached Cram, telling him that for a "consideration" they would have the judgement reviewed so that his design would win first prize. Cram refused the offer. Cram, <u>My Life</u>, pp. 67-68.

32. The exact year when this partnership commenced presents a moot point. The stationery of Hoyle, Doran and Berry, successors of Cram, lists 1889. Yet Cram in his autobiography (p. 70) offers 1890 as the date. The problem is compounded, moreover, by the existence of certain material found in the Cram Papers. Two cards sent to the architect on the occasion of his fiftieth birthday (December 16, 1913) conveyed congratulations not only for this special occasion but for the twenty-fifth anniversary of his career in architecture as well.

33. Ralph Adams Cram,"Journal, 1881-1885" (n.p.), unpublished MS., Department of Rare Books & MSS., Boston Public Library.

34. Ralph Adams Cram, <u>Church Building</u>, 3rd ed., rev. (Boston, 1924), p. 13.

35. Stanton, <u>Pugin</u>, p. 11.

36. Cram, <u>Church Building</u>, pp. 263-264.

37. Clark, <u>The Gothic Revival</u>, p. 126.

38. Cram, <u>Church Building</u>, pp. 85, 9, 270.

39. Arthur Tappan North, <u>Ralph Adams Cram</u> (New York 1931), p. 7.

40. Cram, <u>Church Building</u>, p. 261.

41. Ibid., p. 125.

42. Yet as Sir Kenneth Clark has observed: "But whether or not 'Decorated' is really the best style of Gothic architecture, it was certainly the worst style for the Gothic Revival." Clark, <u>The Gothic Revival</u>, p. 171. In his preface to the second edition of <u>The Seven Lamps of Architecture</u>, Ruskin, who scorned the Perpendicular, advised nineteenth-century Gothicists to pursue the thirteenth-century or Norman style.

43. Cram refers in bitter terms throughout his writings to the premature death of English Perpendicular. For the most complete exposition of this view, see his <u>Ruined Abbeys of Great Britain</u> (New York, 1905).

44. Cram, <u>Church Building</u>, pp. 266-268.

45. Ibid., pp. 22, 43.

46. When Church Building was first published, Cram
    claimed (p. 230) that the allied arts at that
    time nearly surpassed architecture proper.
47. Ibid., pp. 57, 61.
48. Ibid., p. 205.
49. Stein, John Ruskin, p. 208.
50. Virginia Pope, "Architecture of America Molds
    Beauty Anew," The New York Times Magazine (De-
    cember 19, 1926), 3.
51. Cram, Church Building, p. 276.
52. Nelson Manfred Blake, A Short History of American
    Life (New York, 1952), p. 675.

CHAPTER IV

THE HIGH PRIEST OF THE GOTHIC REVIVAL

On the last Sunday of the year 1879, Colonel
Oliver Peabody, a scion of one of Boston's oldest fam-
ilies and a founder of the brokerage firm, Kidder,
Peabody and Co., and his wife Mary Lothrop Peabody,
the daughter of the Unitarian minister for whom
Richardson built his Brattle Square Church, left their
home to attend religious services at Kings Chapel in
Dorchester. A blizzard halted their progress, forcing
them to stop at the simple wooden chapel of All
Saints' in Ashmont. This day being the Feast of the
Holy Innocents, the rector of All Saints' fittingly
preached a sermon on the loss of children. He was
totally unaware that the Peabodys had lost their sole
daughter but a few months earlier. Within a short period of time, Oliver and Mary Peabody, moved by what
they had heard, were confirmed as Episcopalians and
joined the parish of All Saints'. They did more than
"join," moreover. Over the next twenty years they
were to contribute more than half a million dollars
for the erection of a new church. Samll wonder, indeed, that one architectural historian could refer to
these events as "the miracle of Ashmont."[1] The events
surrounding Ashmont may or may not have been miracu-
lous, but for Cram, they were certainly opportune.
Minor successes came quickly to Cram and Wentworth. Their first commission--remodeling a tenement
dwelling in nearby Brighton--brought six hundred dollars and was followed by ones to build another tenement house and a few private domiciles. Cram wished
to build churches, however, and towards this end his
earliest ambitions were thwarted. For more than a
year after opening his office he had unsuccessfully
sought commissions for at least five churches.[2] Finally, in late 1891 his frustration came to an end as
he received the award for All Saints'--his first
church commission.
It is unusual for an architect in the earliest
years of his career to achieve a notable triumph.
More often than not, success comes only after repeated

efforts at experimentation. All Saints' provides an exception to this general rule. In a sense, of course, Cram was not a "beginning" architect. Several years of apprenticeship, two trips to Europe, and at least a full decade of serious thought had enabled him to approach the Ashmont project with a clear idea of what exactly he would try to achieve. Then, too, there was the example of the English Late Victorian Gothicists, particularly Henry Vaughan, whose recent Chapel at St. Paul's School in Concord, New Hampshire and St. Mary's Church in Dorchester felicitously captured the spirit of English Perpendicular. So convincing were the latter's works that Cram after nearly fifty years could refer to Vaughan as his "local mentor."[3]

Late medieval English Gothic provided the inspiration for All Saints', but not its raison d'être. While it was to be suitably Anglican and Anglo-Saxon in its derivation, the church, warned Cram, "could not be simply a study in archaeological experiment; it must be essentially a church of this century, built, not in England, but in New England." He elaborated:

> This, it seems to me, must be the governing principle of modern church architecture. To study the work of our forefathers until we understand it and feel its power, comprehend its motive, and then with this as a foundation go on developing it little by little until it gradually ceases to have the close resemblance to its model that at first is inevitable. We have been without instinctive art for two centuries, and we cannot now, simply by an act of will, re-create what has so long been non-existent. We can only begin where we left off in the sixteenth century, and work steadily and seriously toward something more consistent with our temper and the times in which we live.[4]

As Douglass Shand Tucci has pointed out, Cram, in attempting to revivify rather than merely copy English Gothic, was following in the wake of Vaughan, who, in turn, had learned this precept from George Bodley, his English mentor and celebrated Late Victorian Gothicist.[5]

One of the most critical areas in which Cram attempted to develop the work of his Gothic forbears was that of composition and massing. Following

Ruskin's advice, most of the High Victorian Gothicists had concentrated on detail and ornamentation to the neglect of structure. At Ashmont Cram radically deviated from this tendency and eventually convinced many of the Late Victorian Gothicists in the United States to do likewise.[6] "A good church," he reasoned, "from an artistic standpoint, is composed of sanctuary, choir and nave of the utmost simplicity of design, gravity of massing, refinement of proportion, classicism of composition; and beyond this, of bounding walls, following varied lines, giving space, distance, variety, mystery."[7] To a pronounced degree All Saints' successfully incorporates these principles. Eschewing both transepts and central tower, Cram used a western tower to prolong the nave to one hundred and seventy feet. Correspondingly, he blended his masses and voids so as to strike a balance between light and shadow, thereby achieving his intent of drawing attention to the altar. Though this scarcely seems extraordinary today, it represented at the time, at least for one critic, a prototype for future Gothic design.[8]

In attempting to mediate between past achievement and present needs, Cram showed an ability to compromise. Pews or fixed seats had become de rigueur in modern churches, particularly American ones, in order to afford a more direct view of the altar and pulpit. Cram did not believe that this was a valid consideration, arguing that a church, after all, "is not a theatre, but a temple of public worship...."[9] To permit fixed seating while avoiding the undesirable effects of an auditorium, he devised an ingenious scheme. Placing seats in the nave proper, he countered what might then have been unfortunate consequences by building large stone piers to separate the nave from the narrow aisles or ambulatories which, in turn, received low, small windows. The outcome proved aesthetically triumphant, and, incidentally, did not harm the acoustics.[10]

While not falling under the rubric of literal innovation, Cram's decision to build a west rather than central tower defied contemporary usage. Then in vogue, the cruciform design with its central tower seemed to him totally unsuitable for smaller churches (with naves under two hundred feet) like All Saints'. To maintain a sense of perspective, he designed a powerful west tower. With little cut stone detail, the tower might easily have appeared altogether too somber had he not designed a west portal built completely of cut stone and with niches, figures, and foliated tracery to counterbalance the tower's stolidity. Controversial as it was, this tower became the model for countless future ones.[11]

Cram lavished proportionately as much care on the materials used at All Saints' as he did on its design. From the outset he dismissed the use of brick largely because American architects had employed it so "hideously." Smooth sandstone or limestone was acceptable, but its cost, particularly that involving its refinement, was too dear. Detesting rough or "quarry-faced" stone, he discovered smooth "seam-faced" granite, which had the desirable qualities of being cheap and abundant (at least in the East), and which had a "wealth of tone and color that is matchless." For the church's cut stone, he selected a gray Nova Scotia sandstone for the exterior and a Lake Superior red stone for the interior.[12]

Cram bestowed on the interior of the church all the wealth of detail and ornamentation which he had studiously excluded from its exterior. To secure this richness, he employed some of the finest talent of the day. Once completed, the chancel, the focal point, in his opinion, of a Gothic church's beauty, represented the careful efforts of such outstanding craftsmen as John Evans, J. Kirchmayer, and individuals representing the firm of Irving and Casson. And if the chancel ultimately proved too small for the church's need, most viewers would forgive Cram his error, praising, instead, the remarkable twenty-five-foot-high reredos of white Caen stone, the elaborate chiselled-brass candlesticks and cross set in jasper, the unassuming but stately triangular lectern of darkly stained oak. Moreover, no admirer of stained glass windows should have been disappointed by those of All Saints'. Designed in later years by Charles Connick, who was to work closely with Cram on numerous projects, they constitute an exemplary recrudescence of that medieval art.

One of the most distinguished efforts at All Saints' proved to be the altar-piece. Originally Cram had planned to invite Burne-Jones to do this work, but the famed artist died. After a delay of several years, he selected George Hallowell, a personal friend whom he claimed John Singer Sargent had adjudged to be "the painter with the greatest power and promise in America."[13] Combining what the architect called "the colour of Giorgione, with hints of the drawing of Dürer," this Boston artist created an altar-piece which won widespread national and international praise.[14] Dying prematurely, Hallowell never fully realized his early potential. His death was a painful loss for Cram, for professional as well as personal reasons. Though it seems fair to say that he considerably exaggerated Hallowell's talents, Cram never again was to find a painter whose work would genuinely satisfy him. Indeed, if there is one perceptible and consistent weakness in all his ecclesiastical buildings after All Saints', it is the mediocrity of the painting, especially when contrasted with the excellence of the other allied arts.

Though largely finished in its exterior by 1893, All Saints' was sporadically to occupy Cram for the next twenty years and lesser known architects for an ensuing score of years after that. Cram scarcely cited the church in his autobiography; critics, preferring to dwell on his larger, more prestigious buildings, followed suit. Only recently has its true excellence as one of the nation's finest suburban churches been emphasized. In one of his more modest moments, Cram attributed the real beginning of the late Gothic Revival in America to Vaughan's St. Paul's Chapel.[15] It was a case of misguided modesty. The true origins of the Revival are to be found in "The Miracle of Ashmont."[16]

It was not only the All Saints' commission which marked 1891 as a portentous year in Cram's career. Early small successes had permitted Cram and Wentworth to expand their modest office in 1891 and to acquire a promising young draftsman named Bertram Grosvenor Goodhue. Indeed, it may well have been the latter's superb perspectives for All Saints' which ultimately convinced the building committee to award the contract to the firm.[17] Probably no one foresaw that by the time Goodhue was to leave the firm in 1913, he and Cram were to have established one of the most celebrated partnerships then exisitng in American architecture. Few would then have disagreed with Louise Imogen Guiney's earlier prejudiced but apt observation that "Cram and his partner, my dear Bertram Goodhue, are bound to put character into everything they touch."[18]

Nearly six years Cram's junior, Goodhue was born in Pomfret, Connecticut on April 28, 1869. Under the influence of a mother who painted and sketched, he had decided by the age of nine to become an architect. Like his future partner, Goodhue early fell under the spell of the Pre-Raphaelites, particularly the painter Burne-Jones. Though he attended college (Russell's

College in New Haven), he had received no formal instruction in architecture before coming to New York, where he worked for several years as a draftsman under Renwick on the completion of St. Patrick's Cathedral. When at the youthful age of twenty-one he won the award for a projected cathedral in Dallas (which he never did build), he began to search for a young firm with which he could associate himself. For reasons not clear, he chose Cram and Wentworth and was accepted as a draftsman at a salary of twenty dollars a week.[19] Because of his fine work, but also because, as Cram candidly admitted, it was financially easier to pay him part of the firm's profits rather than a regular salary, Cram and Wentworth took in Goodhue as a full partner in 1895.[20]

Cram and Goodhue were closely associated for nearly a quarter of a century, and the result of their collaboration was awesome in terms both of quantity and quality. Specializing in ecclesiastical architecture, they made Gothic their favored mode of expression, with Cram leaning toward the English Perpendicular and Goodhue more receptive to the various continental varieties. They did, however, design their churches in other styles as well: Spanish Renaissance, Byzantine, Colonial and Romanesque.[21] Moreover, they by no means confined themselves exclusively to the building of churches. Schools and colleges, public and commercial buildings, and a few private residences were all part of their efforts. Sometimes Cram played the more important role in the conception and design of the edifice; sometimes Goodhue. Sometimes they shared the responsibility more or less equally.

"From the very beginning," wrote a distinguished architectural historian, the work of Cram and Goodhue "was superlative." He added (with more than a little magniloquence): "The bad Gothic of the sixties and seventies had been eclipsed by the worse Romanesque of the eighties and nineties. Anglican and Evangelical alike awaited a new gospel of beauty, and so when these two knights, their lances in rest, with the cry of 'Dieu le veult' ["God wills it] on their lips, charged the cohorts of ugliness and sham, a paean of thanksgiving for deliverance ascended from every pulpit." Their work, he concluded, had demonstrated "the perfect union of the austerity of Cram and the exuberance of Goodhue."[22]

It was precisely the complementary nature of Cram's and Goodhue's respective talents that struck other architects. Charles Maginnis, himself an established Gothic architect and friend to both men, contrasted Cram's "austere" quality of mind and "logical enterprise of pencil" with Goodhue's "flamboyance." To Maginnis, Cram recalled Charles McKim, while Goodhue reminded him of McKim's long-time partner, the colorful Stanford White.[23] Goodhue, as Thomas Tallmadge observed, "was an architect's architect, the god of designers, the darling of the draughting-room...."[24] Cram, on the other hand, was, at least to Oliver Larkin, the man of intellect, the man "who could justify the flying buttress in the age of Bryan." He was the architect more concerned with values than, as was the case with Goodhue, beauty for its own sake.[25] Cram, too, was keenly aware of the differing but mutually sustaining talents possessed by Goodhue and himself. Acknowledging his partner's extraordinary ability with regard to ornament and details for churches,[26] he readily confessed his own impatience with and lack of sufficient imagination for these items. Instead, his primary concern rested with the "organism of a building, with the allied considerations of form, proportion, composition...."[27]

During the 1890's the firm began to establish a reputation for itself, but chiefly on a regional (New England) basis. Work progressed on four churches commissioned during the firm's earliest years of existence—All Saints' in Ashmont, Christ Church in Hyde Park, the Swedenborgian church in Newtonville, and St. Paul's in Brockton—and new commissions were obtained in the form of other churches, libraries, school buildings and private residences. By the decade's end, however, the firm, now known as "Cram, Goodhue and Ferguson" (the latter having replaced the deceased Wentworth),[28] was still searching for the architect's dream: a commission whose execution would bring a widespread reputation.

Late in 1897 the dream appeared to have a chance of being transformed into reality when the Japanese government announced that it planned to rebuild its houses of parliament. The Reverend Arthur May Knapp, a Unitarian minister living in Japan and father of one of Cram's friends, suggested to Cram that he draw up a set of proposed sketches and he would then obtain for him a personal audience with government officials. Cram, who esteemed Japanese art as among the world's finest, immediately consented. Deploring the "dull and very Teutonic banalities" which were being introduced into the Flowery Kingdom, he and Goodhue based

79

their sketches, completed in but a few weeks, on the indigenous art of the Ashikaga and Fujiwara periods. Then in January, 1898, design in hand, Cram boarded the S. S. Peru and arrived the following month at Yokohama. True to his word, the Reverend Knapp had provided sufficient contacts with Japanese officials. The prime minister, the Marquis Ito, was appreciative of a foreigner's understanding of and liking for Japan's traditions. He approved of the designs and three months later was prepared to include in his forthcoming budget a substantial amount of money to be awarded Cram and Goodhue for a complete set of preliminary designs. In what ecstatic state of mind Cram left Japan, one can only imagine. When his ship reached Vancouver, however, he was horrified to learn that the Ito ministry had fallen, and with it, the project for the houses of parliament. The trip, of course, had not been a total loss. He had enjoyed encountering a different culture and civilization, which he subsequently described in his splendid Impressions of Japanese Architecture (1905), and had met a variety of interesting persons, including the expatriate Americans, Lafcadio Hearn and Ernest Fenollosa. But the disappointment remained. Cram returned empty-handed, and the new Japanese government soon opted for a Renaissance style for their government buildings.[29]

Cram's professional disappointment was offset two years later by an event bringing great personal happiness. On September 20, 1900, at New Bedford, Massachusetts, the thirty-six-year-old architect gave up his life as a bachelor to marry Elizabeth Carrington Read, a native Virginian, daughter of a former Confederate officer, and schoolteacher of considerable charm. After a honeymoon trip to Italy, the couple returned to the United States, settled in the Boston suburb of Brookline, and two years later had their first child, a daughter whom they named Mary Carrington.

Shortly after the birth of his first child, Cram received another opportunity to secure a major commission, in this instance, the most important domestic one of his career to date. The government had invited Cram, Goodhue and Ferguson, along with approximately a dozen other firms, to compete for the rebuilding of the United States Military Academy at West Point, an ambitious project which was to cost an estimated six and one-half million dollars.[30] Though deeply flattered, Cram, even in retrospect, could never understand why "we had been included amongst firms of more notable status and accomplishment...."[31]

80

Their initial incredulity overcome, Cram and Goodhue faced the problem of selecting an appropriate style
for their sketches.[32] The older buildings at West
Point had been done in a sort of mid-century, pseudo-
military Gothic, but the most recent addition to the
campus, Cullum Hall, had been designed by McKim, Mead
and White, using their well-known Classic features.
Cram guessed--and correctly--that most of the competitors, influenced by this recent move and the École des
Beaux-Arts, would be following the precedent of McKim
and his partners.[33] For Cram and Goodhue, however,
their choice of style, Gothic, seemed almost foreor-
dained. On this occasion, it was to be a secular Goth-
ic--the English Perpendicular being considered too "delicate"--one which hopefully would avoid being merely
"archaeological." The partners were delighted, in
fact, to be able to turn to a non-religious but still
medieval style of Gothic, particularly since they feared they were becoming stagnant as a result of too much
concentration on ecclesiastical architecture.[34]
    The results of the competition were announced in
1903. Despite the fact that the architects who served
as the jury (George B. Post, Cass Gilbert and Walter
Cook), selected by the competitors themselves, were
basically classicists, the award went to Cram, Goodhue
and Ferguson.[35] The jury believed that "the character
of the design is such that it cannot only be constructed with economy, but that it will harmonize with the
character of the landscape, and that it can be readily
developed into a satisfactory and complete plan."[36]
Montgomery Schuyler, the doyen of that generation's
architectural critics, praised the design: "With all
its bold picturesqueness and with its aspect of
even wilful freedom and originality, one is apt to
overlook what a success it is of careful and deferen-
tial conformity, one might almost say of compromise.
For it does effectively mediate between the existing
buildings." He approved, moreover, that "all this work
is of a piece, that it is the appropriate architectural
expression of the United States Military Academy, with
its tradition of a hundred years, and that it gives the
sense of an indigenous growth and not of an exotic
transplantation."[37] Euphoric over their victory, Cram
and Goodhue began work on the project which was to con-
sume several years, produce some excellent buildings,
bring national renown to the firm, and, at the same
time, leave a feeling of unallayed bitterness between
the architects and the government.
    At first the project went smoothly. Under terms

of the award, the firm had to maintain a New York office, but this possible problem was obviated by Goodhue's desire to relocate there under any circumstances. With Goodhue gone, Cram, who had moved his family back to Beacon Hill,[38] took full responsibility for the firm's Boston commitments and, indeed, moved to larger offices. Though separated geographically, Cram and Goodhue were able to sustain a remarkable rapport and spirit of cooperation as far as the project was concerned. In essence, they agreed to a division of labor under which each would bear primary responsibility for certain aspects of the work, with the rest to be undertaken conjointly. Over the next several years, Goodhue produced the West Point Chapel and two of its Cadet Barracks; Cram designed the Post Headquarters, Riding Hall and Power Plant; they jointly completed the other edifices. The modern viewer on a tour of the Academy can only marvel at the complementary quality of the buildings achieved by these two diverse architectural virtuosi.[39]

Until the time of the West Point commission, Gothic had generally fallen into disuse as an accepted style for collegiate building. Far from welcoming its reappearance, numerous critics feared that it represented retrogression for the nation's architecture. Yet as Schuyler observed, if "faithfully applied to modern conditions," Gothic, by capturing the spirit but not the literal forms of medieval building, could indicate a forward movement.[40] This was precisely Cram's intention. Mindful of the Academy's earlier Gothic buildings, as well as Cullum Hall, he and Goodhue designed their additions to achieve a sense of organic growth. The site for each new building was carefully chosen to blend with both the other buildings and the school's picturesque landscape. The new Chapel, for example, from its hilltop position dominated the campus, but in no way detracted from other component parts. Simple but powerful massing—one of Cram's strong points—characterized each building, whose native stone served to accentuate the fittingly rugged austerity of the Academy. The partners deliberately chose to keep their ornamentation to a minimum, except for the Post Headquarters and Chapel, where richer elaboration seemed suitable. Always searching out the finest craftsmen, Cram was able to persuade Lee Lawrie to undertake the stone sculpting for these latter two with remarkably fine attendant results.[41] So successful in particular did the Chapel prove that one critic could praise it as "a very perfect soldier's

church."[42] Dazzled by what he saw, the once dubious
Schuyler proclaimed that the example of West Point
marked the successful reemergence of Gothic as a legitimate style for secular design.[43]

If the artistic part of the project was a virtually unqualified success, the practical aspects told a
markedly different story. Though the relations between
the firm and West Point officials remained amicable,
difficulties developed with the United States government. Troublesome bookkeeping complications seemed resolved when the government agreed to certain "supplementary contracts." However, the change of administration from Roosevelt to Taft brought in a new Secretary
of War, J.M. Dickinson, who adamantly refused to pay
the last bill submitted by the firm, a bill which
amounted to no less than $35,000.[44] Dickinson claimed
that these supplementary contracts were void since his
predecessor did not have the right to have agreed to
them in the first place. Moreover, he was now threatening that unless Cram and Goodhue withdrew their latest claim, the government would sue to recover all
moneys paid under the contracts. The two architects
refused to withdraw the claim, but even the powerful
and astute Elihu Root, largely responsible for the initiation of the project, could not get the government to
reimburse them. Meanwhile, Washington announced that
no further sums would be given Cram and Goodhue, thus
ensuring that they would not complete their work at
West Point, and began calling other architects for discussions. The matter remained stalemated until 1925,
the year after Goodhue's death, when a zealous Comp-
troller General brought suit against Cram to recover
nearly $22,000 which had been paid under terms of
these same supplementary contracts. A United States
District Court in Boston subsequently decided against
the government. Then, oddly enough, the government
asked Cram to do one more building at West Point, and,
more oddly, Cram accepted. Epilogue: that last claim
filed by Cram and Goodhue was never honored.[45]

While work on the West Point buildings was still
in progress, Cram and Goodhue combined their efforts
for what the former called "the last, and I think the
best, of the projects on which we worked together in
complete unity": St. Thomas' Church (Episcopal) in New
York.[46] Standing at Fifty-Third Street and Fifth Avenue, the old St. Thomas', designed by Richard Upjohn
and completed in 1873, had been destroyed by fire in
1905. As Goodhue was particularly preoccupied at this
time with West Point and other work, Cram and Frank

Cleveland, one of his young draftsmen who would later become a partner, drew up sketches, largely in English Gothic, that won the commission to rebuild the razed church. Soon afterwards Cram revised his design to include more elements of the French Gothic. Goodhue objected to these changes and submitted his own sketches, but the church's building committee preferred Cram's revisions.

That Cram was moving away from his earlier pervasive commitment to the English Perpendicular is underscored by his free translation of the French Flamboyant style for St. Thomas'. Limited in his conceptions by the paucity of available space, he declined to use either flying buttresses or transepts, but, instead, chose to rely solely on columns for the building's principal support.[47] There was a medieval French precedent for this in Bourges Cathedral, which was constructed without transepts. Similarly, the clerestory windows were patterned on the proportions of those of the Troyes Cathedral, while the Cathedral of Le Mans, with its arcade of two stories, provided the inspiration for the chancel and gallery.[48]

Inspiration is not necessarily the equivalent of archaeology and there is much of original vitality to be found in St. Thomas'. Realizing that the church eventually might be literally overshadowed by neighboring commercial buildings, Cram rejected height for mass. The especially thick walls which he consequently prescribed, more characteristic of French than English Gothic, added a realistic three-dimensional effect to the edifice. By carefully balancing his masses with voids, moreover, he was able to elicit a sense of repose, at least from the grateful Montgomery Schuyler.[49] A traditionalist by choice, Cram clearly demonstrated with St. Thomas' that he was quite willing to defy tradition when it served no useful purpose: the church faces east and its altar west in contradistinction to medieval practice. Contravening another cherished tradition (Ruskin's), instead of designing four equal pinnacles to adorn the tower, he emphasized one at the expense of the other three.

Cram's adroit massing, of course, was not the only factor responsible for the overall beauty of St. Thomas'. The materials used--Kentucky limestone for the exterior, South Carrollton sandstone for the interior--provided a certain compelling grandeur and warmth, respectively. Far more important was the magnificent interior decoration, the basic responsibility for which rested with Goodhue, whose talent for de-

84

tails seemed limitless. The octagonal oak pulpit, the elaborate oak-carved chancel, the bronze grill of the altar rail, the lectern of inlaid wood--all reflected the uncompromisingly high standard of craftsmanship which Goodhue and his partner incessantly sought and usually found. It has been the reredos, however, which has deservedly drawn most attention. Soaring some eighty feet above the altar, the reredos was completed within a ten-month span during World War One and reflected the joint, harmonious efforts of both Goodhue and Lee Lawrie.[50] Few quarreled when the American Institute of Architects later awarded its Gold Medal to Goodhue for this work. Even before this altar screen was begun, Schuyler hailed the new church as "one of the chief architectural ornaments of New York." It promised, moreover, "to be the masterpiece of either or both of the architects," and that, concluded the critic, "is saying a great deal."[51]

After St. Thomas', perhaps indeed their architectural chef-d'oeuvre, Cram and Goodhue drew apart, each pursuing lines dictated by his respective genius. Cram, representing by self-admission "the reactionary tendency," returned to what Maginnis called his "massive English sobriety,"[52] as evidenced by his Fourth Presbyterian Church in Chicago, smaller New England churches, and collegiate buildings at Princeton. Goodhue, on the other hand, became decidedly more adventurous and began to experiment in the Spanish Renaissance and Byzantine styles in his Maryland Cathedral and several buildings for the San Diego Exposition. By 1913 their fruitful association of more than two decades was terminated by mutual consent. For Cram, who at least in print always lavishly praised Goodhue, his partner had "few peers in his own day and generation" and had provided "the most stimulating and illuminating experience of a long and varied life."[53] Goodhue, for his part, offered a witty but accurate estimate of Cram: "There are two kinds of genius. The fictitious kind starves in the garret; while the other does not starve himself into being one. Mr. Cram is a well-fed genius."[54] Beneath the witticism, however, there seethed great discontent. Thanks to recent evidence, it is now known that Goodhue was convinced--rightly or wrongly--that his partner received too much of the credit for their mutual work. He fumed in a telegram to Cram: "You know my demand that work be credited personally, and that under present limelight... to call everything firm's was only another way of having it credited to yourself. Insist you make perfectly clear in the future... that firm's designs are each of marked individuality, enumerating if you choose your buildings only, though preferably mine as well.... Practically every clause of present partnership agreement has been violated. Am preparing draft of a new one..."[55] Except for the discerning few, their subsequent dissolution of partnership came as a distinct shock and, as one critic noted, as "a rupture regretted by the entire profession."[56] Speaking of the Gothic creations of Cram and Goodhue, another critic termed them "by far the most notable in this movement." He added: "To see any one of them is to be immediately aware of the paucity of noble architecture over the country generally, and to be stirred with the undreamed of possibilities before us as a rich nation beginning to be capable of expressing itself in the noblest forms for the highest enjoyments of the spiritual life."[57]

After their split Goodhue gradually abandoned the Gothic and ultimately developed a singular style best exemplified in his Nebraska State Capitol, which Cram termed "his masterpiece" and "perhaps the greatest example of vital, modern architecture in the United States."[58] Almost literally, Goodhue lost his life in a tragic battle with Nebraska's politicians, as he attempted to save his building from their philistine attacks. At least one critic thinks that, had he lived, Goodhue "would have become one of the foremost exponents of the modern movement in architecture."[59] A radical departure from other state capitols, Goodhue's work, according to another critic, very nearly inaugurated a new and major battle in the sporadic but intense fight to achieve something tantamount to a national style in architecture.[60]

While Goodhue had begun large-scale experimentation after the completion of St. Thomas', Cram, too, showed that he was capable of provocatively innovative conceptualization. In 1909 he accepted the position of chief architect for the Rice Institute at Houston. There was one major problem, however: although it possessed three hundred acres and a building fund of ten million dollars, Rice had, as yet, not a single building. Cram, forced to start entirely from scratch, immediately excluded from consideration the Mission, Colonial, Georgian, and Gothic styles as being unsuitable. He noted: "We wanted something that was beautiful, if we could make it so, Southern in its spirit, and with some quality of continuity with the historic and cultural past. Manifestly the only thing to do was to invent something approaching a new style (though not too new)...."[61] Reflecting, in part, the influence of

his travels throughout the Mediterranean, from France
to Turkey and from Italy to Syria, the style (most
pronouncedly embodied in the Administration Building)
contained "elements from a dozen sources knit together
as well as possible in a unity that was, substantially,
Gothic and Christian, but with the use of no Gothic
forms...."[62] More than the style perhaps, it was the
colors used which gave Rice its most distinctive character: rose-colored brick, red granite, rose-and-
white marble; various colored marbles from Vermont,
Tennessee, Greece, Italy, and Switzerland; glazed,
iridescent tiles and green bronze.[63] Cram was convinced that he had achieved a wholesome type of modernism at the new university. Whether he did or not
is problematical, though Henry-Russell Hitchcock,
scarcely one of his greatest admirers, thought that
this "Byzantoid" style was considerably more successful than most of his efforts in Gothic.[64]

While undoubtedly interesting, the architecture
at Rice Institute represents a deviation for Cram, who
continued to do the major portion of his work in Gothic. Once the West Point commission had been secured,
moreover, various colleges and universities began increasingly to solicit his talents. When in 1906
Princeton asked Cram for assistance in obtaining "stylistic unity and consistency of plan," he was only too
happy to oblige. He insisted, however, on the use of
Gothic, "the perfected style of our ancestors developed as the architectural expression of scholarship, at
Oxford and Cambridge, Winchester, Eton and the other
great schools and colleges of England as they were before the victory of the Renaissance...."[65] Cram need
not have worried. Dean Andrew West of the Graduate
School earlier had urged the selection of a style akin
to that used at Oxford or Cambridge, and the university's trustees had readily agreed.[66] So, too, had the
university's president, Woodrow Wilson, who, addressing an alumni group in 1902, argued: "By the very
simple device of building our new buildings in the
Tudor Gothic style we seem to have added to Princeton
the age of Oxford and Cambridge; we have added a
thousand years to the history of Princeton by merely
putting those lines in our buildings which point every
man's imagination to the historic traditions of learning in the English-speaking race. We have declared
and acknowledged our derivation and lineage...."[67]
Wilson, West, the trustees, and Cram were of one mind:
Collegiate Gothic was the most fitting symbol of the
Anglo-Saxon tradition of higher education. In 1907

Cram's unofficial role became formalized as he was appointed Supervisory Architect at Princeton, a position which he was to hold and relish for the next twenty-two years.

Wilson and West may have concurred in their choice of Gothic as the style for the university's burgeoning campus, but there was one aspect of this expansion over which they quarreled bitterly. Wilson, who had fought to democratize the school by abolishing its quasi-aristocratic eating clubs, insisted that the new Graduate College be built on-campus, hoping thereby to effect a greater intermingling of graduate with undergraduate students. West, who earlier had supported Wilson even to the point of declining the presidency of the Massachusetts Institute of Technology, now balked, insisting that the proper site for the Graduate College was off-campus, thus effectively segregating graduates from undergraduates. Such a separation, he hoped, would enable the graduate students to attend to their more "serious" work. At one point, Wilson even refused the bequest of a half-million dollars which had been donated by one of West's friends because it carried with it the stipulation that the Dean of the Graduate School, that is to say, West, should decide the location. Ultimately, however, Wilson was forced to yield in the face of another bequest, this one of several million dollars of which West was declared to be the executor.[68]

Given his official position and the fact that he was directly responsible for the design of the Graduate College, Cram could not avoid becoming involved in the heated Wilson-West controversy, though from all available evidence it would seem that he managed the situation with tact and adroitness. It certainly helped that Wilson and Cram greatly respected one another. Wilson, whose personal selection of Cram as Supervisory Architect had prevailed, impressed Cram with his interest in and understanding of architectural details. Indeed, the architect was to recall how Princeton's president would get down on the floor with him to work over sketches for the various buildings. "I have never had a better client," he claimed, "and few as good."[69] Yet by 1909 Dean West had convinced him that the Graduate College should be located away from the undergraduate campus.[70] Cram did admit in early 1911 that he and Wilson had "differed radically," but at the same time he called Wilson "the greatest man in America today," correctly predicting that he would win the 1912 presidential election![71]

Whatever the politics of the controversy, it is manifest that Cram, in his tenure as Supervisory Architect, did much to transform Princeton physically. The Gothic style at Princeton did not originate with Cram. During the Gilded Age, President James McCosh, breaking with the university's traditional Georgian style, overseered the erection of several buildings designed in the Venetian Gothic popularized by Ruskin. Credit for the initiation of Collegiate Gothic at Princeton, however, belongs to William A. Potter, whose Pyne Library was completed in 1901. At the same time, the firm of Cope and Stewardson, which had so successfully utilized Collegiate Gothic at Bryn Mawr during the 1890's, advanced this new trend with their Blair and Little Halls.[72] But it was Cram who was responsible for a long-range plan which would give the school an unmistakable Gothic consistency. After completing Campbell Hall in 1909, he began the prodigious task of building the Graduate College. Opened four years later, it drew almost unanimous praise.[73] Proctor Hall, the Refectory, even the rather odd, hexagonal Cleveland Tower--all blended to give the graduate campus the aura of medieval academe. Admittedly, Cram may have adhered too rigidly to a major axis in his planning, thus diminishing Princeton's pleasing informality. Yet for the most part his grand design was intelligent and artistically successful. There were even elements, such as emphasizing the nature and function of his materials, in his work which modernists could in good conscience laud.[74]

After the war, Cram, in addition to supervising the work of others (notably the Philadelphia firm of Day and Klauder), offered a final contribution of his own to the campus: the Chapel. Scarcely the small, simple English chapel that he had long praised--it is the third largest collegiate chapel in the world--this awesome creation, dedicated in 1928, more nearly resembled a cathedral in its size, and power, and cost of two and one-half million dollars. Not without reason, detractors have referred to it as "the God Box."[75] Cram might even have appreciated the witticism. After all, by his request one of the twenty-four Elders carved under the Chapel's south portal bore his features.[76] Who, finally, was most responsible for the widespread popularity which Collegiate Gothic was to achieve during the first three decades or so of the twentieth century? The question remains a moot one. It may have been Cope and Stewardson; it may have been James Gamble Rogers with his superb work at Yale and

Duke University. It certainly may have been Cram.
By 1911, Cram's reputation as a leading architect
(and the leading Gothic architect in the United
States) had been securely established. West Point,
St. Thomas', Rice Institute, Princeton, numerous
churches throughout the country--all had contributed
to making him one of the nation's most sought-after
designers. Accordingly, in 1911 he was asked to
undertake the most ambitious project he had yet en-
countered. He knew that it would be a most difficult,
though highly desirable assignment. It is doubtful if
he foresaw that it would stand uncompleted at the time
of his death. To this day, New York's Cathedral of
St. John the Divine remains an architectural conundrum.
    In 1889 the Episcopal Diocese of New York an-
nounced an open competition for the design of a
Cathedral. The competition for this major edifice
proved as varied as it was intense. Some sixty designs in all were submitted, embodying virtually every
shade of the Gothic as well as the Romanesque, the
Richardsonian influence then being at its height.
There were even compositions based on the Renaissance
style, including a most interesting one by Carrère and
Hastings. Cram, who had returned from his initial
two trips to Europe and was currently doing odd jobs,
was so eager for the prize that he somehow managed to
enter two designs: one rather servilely following
Richardson's Romanesque, the other, an unsophisticated
Gothic model. (The submission of two designs indicates more than an eagerness to win; Cram clearly had
not as yet become a confirmed Gothicist.) According
to Cram, of all the sketches entered--his own included
--only two escaped what he called "antiquarianism."
Halsey Wood's design defied categorization. Unique in
the extreme, it was a harbinger of modern architecture, or at least of that modernism of which Cram
approved. The other design, a blend of the Romanesque
and Byzantine conceived by the partners Grant La
Farge and George L. Heins, was chosen, although Cram
believed Wood's was the better.[77]
    The cornerstone for St. John the Divine was laid
in 1892, but the project soon went awry. Try as they
certainly did, La Farge, the son of a noted artist,[78]
and Heins, his partner and brother-in-law, were not
able to overcome certain major obstacles. Foremost of
these problems were the treacherous foundation conditions which made every architectural addition
hazardous. Moreover, La Farge's plan to place a huge
dome over the church's crossing, topped by a large

pyramid-like tower, seemed next to impossible.[79]   As
the years passed, the work slowed down but criticism
accelerated. At least as early as 1899, Cram, for
one, had publicly called the designs for the cathedral
ridiculous.[80]
    Heins' worries over St. John's ended in 1907 when
he died. For his partner, however, his death presented not only a terrible personal loss, but a final insurmountable crisis as well. The contract which Heins
and La Farge had signed stipulated that should one of
the partners die, the contract might be voided. It
now remained to be seen whether or not the church's
trustees would reengage the surviving partner's services. La Farge ably defended his work,[81] but objections continued to mount. An anonymous article in
American Architect attacked La Farge for having turned
a possibly decent Byzantine church into a dreadful
Gothic one. Citing, in addition, the poor lighting
and heating in the cathedral, the critic demanded a
reconsideration of the proposed nave (a very major reconsideration) "before it is too late, to save money
and avoid a still more hybrid effect."[82] A year after
Heins' death, Cram stirred the juice in which La Farge
was already so uncomfortably stewing. First, in an
editorial he wrote for his own magazine, Christian
Art,[83] he took a gratuitous potshot at the original
competition for the commission, describing it as
"humiliating to the architectural profession in its
revelation of the fundamental weakness of American
architects in the matter of church building...." As
for the ill-fated partners, Cram approvingly cited
their original youth, enthusiasm and strength and
regretted that Heins had died before his work could
perhaps be vindicated. Nowhere in his editorial did
Cram flatly state that the designs should be altered.
But having described them as being "in every particular without historical or archaeological precedent,"
Cram left little doubt as to his inclinations.[84]
    In 1911 the trustees made their decision: La
Farge was to be replaced in favor of Cram. While most
"gratifying," his appointment was also exceedingly
"embarrassing," for it presented the delicate problem
of an architect replacing one of his vocational
brethren against the latter's wishes. After consulting other architects, Cram went to La Farge himself
and proposed that the two continue the venture jointly. Both the diocesan bishop and trustees refused,
however, adhering firmly to their decision that Cram,
Goodhue and Ferguson should alone be responsible for

future work. Cram reasoned that the church officials had concluded that Gothic would be the proper style for a great cathedral rather than Romanesque, which had by now lost the great popularity it had commanded when the project began.[85] His reasoning is by no means unconvincing since Gothic had once more become the most desirable style in ecclesiastical architecture.

At least one person, however, does not believe Cram manifested much probity in the matter. John La Farge, S.J., a Jesuit priest and brother of Grant La Farge, has conjectured that Cram perhaps may have attempted clandestinely to secure the commission for himself. Describing the Gothicist as "a born lecturer, a skillful writer and a persuasive personality," Father La Farge queried: "Just how far Mr. Cram used personal influence is, of course, a matter of dispute. It is said...that he received a severe professional censure for his interference." Grant La Farge never spoke of the matter, but, according to his sympathetic brother, the denouement was both economically and professionally damaging.[86] Father La Farge admitted, nonetheless, that his brother possessed a bad temper and often had been absent from his duties. More pertinent, he also confessed that he had never attempted to substantiate the charges leveled against Cram.[87] Consequently, one can only conclude that La Farge's case against Cram, interesting though it may sound, remains moot.

Whatever the full circumstances surrounding the affair, Cram immediately began working to transform the cathedral, which John La Farge estimated had already cost two million dollars,[88] from a Romanesque-Byzantine-cum-Gothic structure to one of a more orthodox composition of French and English Gothic. By the fall of 1913 a full, though tentative, set of plans for the completion of the cathedral was made public.

Receiving the difficult assignment to complete the Cathedral of St. John the Divine merely solidified Ralph Adams Cram's position as "the outstanding protagonist for the Gothic revival" in the United States.[89] His actual innovations in building had been relatively few, though as Ruskin had wisely pointed out, originality of expression does not depend on invention. What most distinguished his Gothic creations was the startling beauty--sometimes quiet, sometimes overpowering--they effected. At times adhering to medieval architectural theory and practice, at times modifying them, he strove to bridge the gap of centuries

and to make Gothic a living force in the modern world.
If, for some, he seemed guilty of the archaeology he
so roundly condemned, for others, he had succeeded in
his quest. As Montgomery Schuyler asserted: "That
they [Cram and Goodhue] have done the best Gothic
churches thus far erected in America hardly seems an
extravagant claim...."90

Yet Cram never considered architecture--Gothic or
otherwise--to be an end in and of itself. Architecture, like any other art form, was inextricably linked
to larger ideals and values. And just as there was
"good" and "bad" art, so, correspondingly, there were
"good" and "bad" ideals and values. It only remained
to discover, to differentiate, and to act upon them
accordingly. In that quarter century between the time
he and Charles Wentworth opened their office at One
Park Square and the outbreak of World War One, Cram
labored incessantly to educate others to his distinct
point of view. As Charles Maginnis accurately observed: "Cram has always been more than the architect. He has been a vital and developing force in the
intellectual life of the nation."91

NOTES

1. Douglass Shand Tucci, The Gothic Churches of Dor-
    chester: Readings in Modern Boston History (Bos-
    ton, 1972), pp. 23, 25.
2. Douglass Shand Tucci, All Saints' Church: An In-
    troduction to the Architecture of Ralph Adams Cram
    (Boston, 1973), pp. 61-62.
3. Ralph Adams Cram, My Life in Architecture (Boston,
    1936), p. 39.
4. Ralph Adams Cram, "All Saints' Church," The
    Churchman, LXXIX (April 15, 1899), 559, 563.
5. Douglass Shand Tucci, Church Building in Boston,
    1720-1970 (Concord, Mass., 1974), pp. 65, 93.
6. Agnes Addison, Romanticism and the Gothic Revival
    (New York, 1938), p. 139. In this respect he was
    much influenced by the ideals of the École des
    Beaux-Arts.
7. Ralph Adams Cram, Church Building, 3rd. ed., rev.
    (Boston, 1924), p. 116.
8. Tucci, All Saints' Church, pp. 80-82.
9. Cram, "All Saints' Church," 560.
10. Ibid; see also, Tucci, All Saints' Church, pp. 87-
    91.
11. Tucci, All Saints' Church, pp. 76-80.
12. Cram, "All Saints' Church," 562. He thought that
    English architects, in contrast, used brick more
    skillfully.
13. Cram, My Life, p. 17.
14. Ibid., p. 195; Tucci, All Saints' Church, p. 133.
15. Cram, My Life, p. 36. St. Paul's Chapel was built
    in 1888.
16. Tucci concurs in this judgment, as does Marcus
    Whiffen in his American Architecture Since 1780
    (Cambridge, Massachusetts, 1969), p. 173. Cram's
    assessment of Vaughan's importance in this matter
    found very little contemporary support, according
    to Tucci. Church Building, pp. 91-92. Throughout
    this fine study Tucci makes an impressive case for
    Cram's innovativeness. Even the hostile Henry-
    Russell Hitchcock offered some faint praise, cal-
    ling All Saints' "the least anachronistic" of
    Cram's works. Architecture, Nineteenth and Twen-
    tieth Centuries, (Baltimore, 1958), p. 400.
17. Another influencing factor doubtlessly was the low
    estimate of cost offered by the firm. The figure
    they gave for chancel and nave, for example, was
    slightly under forty thousand dollars. Tucci, All

94

Saints' Church, p. 62.

18. Letter of Louise Imogen Guiney to W.H. Van Allen, June 13, 1898, Grace Guiney (ed.), Letters of Louise Imogen Guiney, I (New York, 1926), p. 227.

19. Charles Harris Whitaker (ed.), Bertram Grosvenor Goodhue--Architect and Master of Many Arts (New York, 1925), p. 28.

20. Cram, My Life, p. 76.

21. Particularly fine examples of their non-Gothic achievements must include Cram's Colonial-style Second Parish Church of Boston and Goodhue's La Santissima Trinidad built in Havana in the style of the Spanish Renaissance.

22. Thomas E. Tallmadge, The Story of Architecture in America, 2nd ed., rev. (New York, 1936), pp. 259-261.

23. Charles Maginnis, The Work of Cram and Ferguson (New York, 1929), p. 4. Maginnis, who meant his analogy to be complimentary, probably did not know that William Mead (of McKim, Mead and White) had once said that his purpose in the firm was "to keep Charles McKim and Stanford White from killing each other." Cram, My Life, p. 83.

24. Tallmadge, Architecture, p. 259. While much has been rightly made of Goodhue's talents as a draftsman, there has been a tendency to overlook Cram's ability in this same area. Robert Tappan, who worked for Cram in the 1920's, denied Russell Sturgis' contention that Goodhue had done all of the firm's drafting and found his mentor to be an excellent draftsman. Letter from Robert Tappan to The American Architect, CXXXIX, (January, 1931), 66. For further praise of Cram's drafting abilities, see George H. Allen, "Cram--The Yankee Medievalist," The Architectural Forum, LV (July, 1931), 80.

25. Oliver W. Larkin, Art and Life in America, 2nd ed., rev. (New York, 1960), p. 339.

26. Goodhue was awarded the American Institute of Architects' Gold Medal for his reredos in St. Thomas' Church (New York).

27. Whitaker, Goodhue, p. 30.

28. Wentworth, who died of tuberculosis, was replaced by Frank Ferguson, who, in turn, remained a partner until his death in 1926. Like his predecessor, Ferguson took care of only the business concerns of the firm.

29. Ralph Adams Cram, Impressions of Japanese Architecture and the Allied Arts, 2nd ed.,rev. (Boston, 1930), pp. 19-21, 38; Cram, My Life, pp. 98-100.

30. Among the more prominent individual architects or
firms that also entered the competition were included: Daniel Burnham, Heins & La Farge, Carrère
& Hastings, and McKim, Mead and White (who dropped
out soon after the competition opened). Secretary
of War Elihu Root was responsible for having procured the building funds from Congress. Thomas
J. Fleming, West Point: The Men and Times of the
United States Military Academy (New York, 1969),
pp. 281-282.
31. Cram, My Life, p. 102.
32. West Point's decision to build in a single integrated style reflected the successful implementation of the principle of unity at the Chicago
World's Fair of 1893. Hitherto, it had been deemed impractical. Stephen E. Ambrose, Duty, Honor,
Country: A History of West Point (Baltimore,
1966), p. 241.
33. Besides Cram, Goodhue and Ferguson, only three
firms or individual architects submitted Gothic
sketches: Cope and Stewardson, Heins and La
Farge, and C. C. Haight.
34. Cram, My Life, pp. 102-105.
35. Montgomery Schuyler hinted that, as classicists,
the judges were not really fit to pass verdict on
a Gothic design. He felt, moreover, that bowing
to the predilections of the officials at West
Point, they had accepted a Gothic design against
their will. Schuyler also peevishly wondered
aloud why every leading architect in the country
had not been invited to submit a design. Montgomery Schuyler, "The Architecture of West Point,"
The Architectural Record, XIV (December, 1903),
477-478. For a splendid collection of Schuyler's
essays and articles, see William H. Jordy and
Ralph Coe (ed.), American Architecture and Other
Writings by Montgomery Schuyler, 2 Vols. (Cambridge, Mass., 1961).
36. Charles Moore, Daniel H. Burnham: Architect Planner of Cities, I (Boston, 1921), p. 196.
37. Schuyler, "The Architecture of West Point," 490,
492.
38. From 1887 until his death in 1942 (and with the
exception of the two years spent in Brookline
after his marriage), Cram resided on Beacon Hill,
which, according to him, "means more than geographical nomenclature; like Boston, of which it
was for so long a time the very heart and soul, it
is a state of mind." Cram, My Life, p. 219.

39. Lewis Mumford, notwithstanding his deep-seated admiration for Louis Sullivan and functionalism, admired Cram for his Gothic achievement at West Point, which he considered "of great esthetic interest." Sticks and Stones (New York, 1924), p. 194.
40. Montgomery Schuyler, "The Work of Cram, Goodhue & Ferguson," The Architectural Record, XXIX (January, 1911), 87. Skeptical at first about the use of Gothic for West Point, Schuyler, sometime between 1903 and 1911, became convinced of its wisdom.
41. Lawrie also was to provide stone sculptures for Cram's public library in Pawtucket, Rhode Island, and for the central portal of New York's St. John the Divine.
42. James McFarlan Baker, American Churches, II (New York, 1915), p. 7.
43. Schuyler, "The Work of Cram, Goodhue & Ferguson," 109.
44. Letter of Ralph Adams Cram to Louise Imogen Guiney, September 30, 1919, Louise Imogen Guiney Papers, Holy Cross College.
45. Cram, My Life, pp. 110-113.
46. Ibid., p. 79.
47. His refusal to use any steel in the columns, however, proved unfortunate. Several years after the church was completed, the north wall began to bulge dangerously, and it became necessary to position steel beams across all the columns and above the ceiling. St. Thomas Church (New York, 1965), p. 5.
48. Ibid., p. 4.
49. Montgomery Schuyler, "The New St. Thomas's Church, New York," Scribner's Magazine, LIV (December, 1913), 794.
50. St. Thomas Church, pp. 43-44.
51. Schuyler, "The New St. Thomas's Church, New York," 794, and "The Work of Cram, Goodhue & Ferguson," 71-72.
52. Whitaker, Goodhue, pp. 32; Maginnis, Cram and Ferguson, p. 4.
53. Whitaker, Goodhue, pp. 32, 30.
54. George H. Allen, "Cram--The Yankee Mediaevalist," 80. On another occasion when Cram told a reporter that he was interested "in nearly everything but banking and finance," Goodhue reputedly chuckled. The Boston Evening Record, August 3, 1897.
55. Tucci, All Saints' Church, p. 52.

97

56. Tallmadge, Architecture, ·p. 261. Maginnis, however, rightly saw the rupture as a blessing for Goodhue. Obscured by Cram's reputation both as a writer and as "the symbol of the Gothic idea" in the public's mind, the full extent of his talents became apparent only after their professional separation. Charles D. Maginnis, "Ralph Adams Cram," The Octagon, 15 (February, 1943), 13.

57. Von Ogden Vogt, Art & Religion (New Haven, 1921), pp. 191-192. The most sustained analysis of the work of Cram and Goodhue remains that written more than sixty years ago by Montgomery Schuyler ("The Work of Cram & Ferguson," The Architectural Record, XXIX (January, 1911), 1-112). Quite favorable though by no means uncritical, Schuyler's assessment is that Cram and Goodhue had produced the finest Gothic churches in the country. Moreover, he praised their "scholarship" for not having prevented "originality," one way of saying that their works were not archaeological (p. 45). For a less sympathetic view of Cram's "scholarship," see Henry-Russell Hitchcock, Architecture, pp. 393, 400-401. While admitting that Cram was "then the most esteemed Gothic practitioner," Hitchcock considers his Gothic creations to be "lifeless and crude" in comparison to their English counterparts from which they largely had derived.

58. Cram, My Life, pp. 114, 79.

59. Suzanne La Follette, Art in America (New York, 1929), p. 290.

60. Tallmadge, Architecture, p. 263.

61. Cram, My Life, pp. 124-125.

62. Ibid., p. 126.

63. Ibid., p. 127.

64. Hitchcock, Architecture, p. 401

65. Ralph Adams Cram, "Princeton Architecture," The American Architect, XCVI (July 21, 1909), 23, 30.

66. John Burchard and Albert Bush-Brown, The Architecture of America: A Social and Cultural History (Boston, 1961), p. 291.

67. Donald Drew Egbert, "The Architecture and the Setting," in Charles G. Osgood et al., The Modern Princeton (Princeton, N.J., 1947), p. 94.

68. For good accounts of this interesting battle, see Alexander L. George and Juliette L. George, Woodrow Wilson and Colonel House: A Personality Study (New York, 1956), pp. 36-47; Arthur S. Link, Wilson: The Road to the White House (Princeton, N.J.

1947), pp. 59-91; Ray Stannard Baker, Woodrow
Wilson: Life and Letters, II (Garden City, N.Y.,
1927), pp. 275-360: Andrew Fleming West, The
Graduate College of Princeton (Princeton, N.J.,
1913); Arthur S. Link (ed.), The Papers of Woodrow Wilson, XVII-XX (Princeton, N.J., 1974, 1975),
passim; Henry Wilkinson Bragdon, Woodrow Wilson:
The Academic Years (Cambridge, Mass., 1967), pp.
353-383.
69. Letter of Ralph Adams Cram to Ray Stannard Baker,
[n.d.], Baker, Wilson, p. 176; Bragdon, Wilson,
p. 357.
70. Bragdon, Wilson, p. 363.
71. Letter of Samuel Huston Thompson, Jr. to Woodrow
Wilson, January 25, 1911, Link, Papers, XXII
(Princeton, N.J., 1976), p. 375.
72. Cram was extremely impressed with Walter Cope's
work, so much that had Cope not died before the
commission was awarded, Cram was convinced he
would have won the West Point competition. Cram,
My Life, p. 119.
73. Egbert, "The Architecture and the Setting," p. 87.
74. Ibid., pp. 108, 94-95. Egbert, for example, sees
(p. 95) the Cubist influence at work, particularly in the "blockiness of form" found in the Chapel. It is very doubtful whether Cram would have
appreciated the comparison, however, since he
heartily loathed this style.
75. Russell Lynes, The Tastemakers (New York, 1954),
p. 36. Egbert, for one, believes (p. 120) that
the Chapel does represent a fitting religious
symbol for the school. For a more extended analysis of the Chapel, see Richard Stillwell The
Chapel of Princeton University (Princeton, N.J.,
1972).
76. Cram apparently delighted in such professional
jokes. He and Goodhue placed a dollar sign on
the Brides' Portal of St. Thomas' which was only
discovered in 1921. Also, the archivolts of the
Synod House of St. John the Divine featured the
figures of Cram, Goodhue, and Ferguson. Unknown
to Cram, some craftsmen managed to depict him as
a gargoyle on the Refectory at Princeton and on
the cornice of the Chapel of St. George's School
in Newport, Rhode Island which Cram designed for
his friend John Nicholas Brown. The Boston Herald, February 13, 1931.
77. Wood, "potentially one of the greatest architects
of modern times," died soon after the competi-

tion, according to Cram, as a result of a broken heart. Cram, _My Life_, pp. 167-170. La Farge and Heins were classmates at M.I.T. and later commenced their partnership in New York in 1886. La Farge had worked briefly in H.H. Richardson's office.

78. La Farge's father, John La Farge, was, along with Louis Tiffany, especially celebrated for his stained glass windows. Cram, however, preferred the windows of other artists, notably Charles Connick. La Farge, incidentally, did do the chancel for St. Thomas' Church.

79. James M. Fitch, "St. John the Divine," _Architectural Forum_ (December, 1954), p. 115.

80. Ralph Adams Cram, "The Influence of the French School on American Architecture," _The American Architect and Building News_, LXVI (November 25, 1899), 66.

81. Grant La Farge, "St. John the Divine," _Scribner's Magazine_, XLI (April, 1907), 385-401.

82. [Candidus], "The Cathedral of St. John the Divine: A Criticism," _American Architect_, XCI (May 18, 1907), 203-204.

83. Cram founded and edited _Christian Art_, a journal devoted to news and criticism of Christian art in Europe and the United States. The journal lasted only two years (1907-1908).

84. Ralph Adams Cram, Editorial in _Christian Art_, II (March, 1908), 305-306.

85. Cram, _My Life_, pp. 171-172. Since the choir and crossing had already been completed, the switch to Gothic has been called "one of the most bizarre and arbitrary decisions." William H. Pierson, Jr., _American Building and Their Architects: Technology and the Picturesque, the Corporate and the Early Gothic Styles_ (Garden City, N.Y., 1978), p. 264.

86. How "damaging" the loss of the commission was is problematical. La Farge subsequently went into partnership with other architects (including his son Christopher) and remained relatively active until his death. Oliver La Farge, the author and anthropologist, was one of his three sons.

87. John La Farge, S.J., _The Manner Is Ordinary_ (New York, 1954), pp. 389-390.

88. Ibid., p. 390.

89. Vogt, _Art & Religion_, p. 196.

90. Schuyler, "The Work of Cram, Goodhue & Ferguson," 45.

91. Maginnis, _Cram and Ferguson_, p. 3.

All Saints' Church - Ashmont, Massachusetts
Photo by Paul J. Weber
Courtesy Hoyle, Doran and Berry

Ralph Adams Cram aboard the S.S. Peru en route to Japan (1898)
Courtesy Ralph Adams Cram II

Ralph Adams Cram in Japan

West Point - Cadet Chapel
Photo by Pfc. Levicoff
Courtesy United States Military Academy

West Point - Headquarters Building
Photo by Murphy
Courtesy United States Military Academy

St. Thomas' Church - New York City
Courtesy Hoyle, Doran and Berry

Rice Institute - Administration Building
Photo by Tebbs & Knell
Courtesy Hoyle, Doran and Berry

Princeton University - Graduate College
Courtesy Hoyle, Doran and Berry

Princeton University - Proctor Hall
Photo by Paul J. Weber
Courtesy Hoyle, Doran and Berry

Princeton University - Chapel
Courtesy Hoyle, Doran and Berry

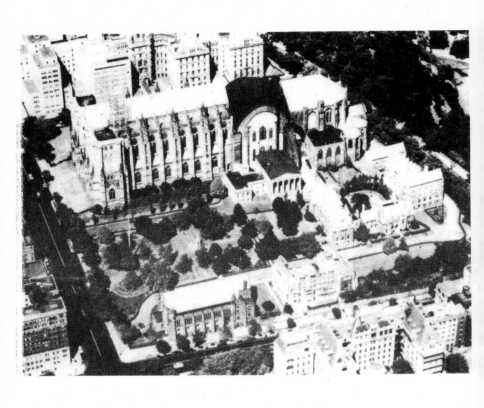

Cathedral of St. John the Divine - Aerial View
Courtesy Cathedral of St. John the Divine

Cathedral of St. John the Divine - ~~Entrance~~ West Façade
Courtesy Cathedral of St. John the Divine

Library and Garden at Whitehall, Estate of Ralph Adams Cram
in Sudbury, Massachusetts
Photo by Paul J. Weber
Courtesy Hoyle, Doran and Berry

St. Elizabeth's Chapel at Whitehall
Courtesy Hoyle, Doran and Berry

CHAPTER V

THE ARCHITECT AS MEDIEVALIST

Some time after the turn of the century Cram wrote to his friend Louise Guiney, then in self-imposed exile in England, that while he was "a good and patriotic American," he was forced to "think of my own land only with a shudder, as a vile prison that cages the dear people I love."[1] Unlike the poet, he never became an expatriate--at least not in the literal sense of the term. Frequent, sometimes yearly trips abroad he did take, especially after 1900, but he seems not to have considered seriously the possibility of actually abandoning his homeland. In 1916, for example, he received an opportunity to purchase a reasonably priced house in his beloved England, but found suitable excuses to reject it.[2] On a realistic level, familial responsibilities may have militated too strongly against such uprooting; cynically speaking, perhaps he was just too much of Goodhue's "well-fed genius." Expatriation, however, can imply a state of mind as well as the literal act of renouncing one's country of birth. Those representing the former, the spiritually expatriated, are usually more numerous though less conspicuous than those exemplifying the latter. While their alienation does not result in physical exile, it does force them to remain as quasi-strangers in their own land. Such seems to have been the case, at least to a degree, with Cram.

In the second half of the nineteenth century a painful sense of this spiritual expatriation began seriously to afflict a growing number of American artists and intellectuals. In his preface to The Marble Faun (1860), Nathaniel Hawthorne had strikingly sounded the note of the artist's alienation when he wrote: "No author, without a trial, can conceive of the difficulty of writing a Romance about a country where there is no shadow, no antiquity, no mystery, no picturesque and gloomy wrong, nor anything but a commonplace prosperity.... Romance and poetry, like ivy, lichens, and wall-flowers, need Ruin to make them grow."[3] Meant primarily for writers, Hawthorne's perception might well have applied a generation later to the malaise experienced by the young architect from Hampton Falls. Actually, Cram's alienation needs to be qualified. As an artist, he did find in the Gothic those elements of mystery and shadow which Hawthorne so cherished, and very successfully incorporated them into his work. Yet architecture, as he never tired of repeating, was not an end in itself, but only a mode of expression of its larger society or civilization, and for him, contemporary society seemed diseased. Increasingly alienated, between the 1890's and the outbreak of World War I he began to develop a philosophy and program of neo-medievalism, not as a placebo, but as a panacea.

Knowing of his involvement with the innovations of the Aesthetic Movement (and his admiration for William James), one might readily suppose that Cram was generally amenable to experimentation and change. Quite the contrary. Like Edmund Burke, he kept an open mind only as a prelude to closing it. More precisely, he accepted change as does the true reactionary, not as something good per se, but as a means of reverting back to earlier values, traditions, and truths--in short, to some imagined Golden Age. As he observed: "After all, there is no longer the possibility of novelty in ideas, except where these are indefensible by any argument based on history and precedent: the fundamental laws--spiritual, ethical, philosophical--were long ago either revealed or determined, and the only excuse for their reiteration today is that so many of them have been forgotten and overlaid by the detritus of loose thinking, it must fall to some to rescue them from their temporary (but curiously periodic) oblivion."[4] There could, then, be no justifiable breaking from established fundamental truths, but only an organic working out of them. In this sense, change implied sound growth, not deviation. Desirable changes--artistic, religious, political, economic, social--only brought the traveler back to the one correct course. Or, as Cram reasoned: "It is impossible for any man, or woman either, to invent a new policy of government, a new religion, or a new art."[5] Having discovered various "truths" for himself, he had only to spell them out for the benefit of non-believers.

The artist, the artist of moral conscience at least, was, to Cram's way of thinking, by no means free to express himself totally as he saw fit. "The man who offends in his art, particularly in his architecture," he cautioned, "is an enemy of society. He is no better than the owner and publisher of a yellow journal; he is no better than Matisse--and worse than that I cannot say. I repeat, he is the enemy of the people. He is bringing to bear an influence for evil on society, instead of an influence for good."[6] Whether it be the poet who "glorifies the hideous shape of atheism" or the musician who "exalts the morbid and the horrible," the irresponsible artist, however technically competent, should be condemned.[7] The triad of truth, beauty, and goodness simply was not to be construed subjectively. Art, especially architecture, which takes the other arts and "binds them in one, harmonizing, controlling, directing them, and lifting them up in a great structural Te Deum,"[8] is, in a very real sense, religious, and the artist, to use Cram's phrase, must concern himself with "the ministry of art," which involves nothing less than the redemption of human character. In the years before the Great War, Cram, through his books, articles, and numerous lectures, became as much "minister" as practitioner of art.

In general, he felt little but contempt for modern art (see Chapter VIII). His violent dislike of Matisse was partly symbolic, for his epithets of scorn might have applied to virtually all the modernists. Cram understood that art was not a sort of Kantian noumenon or thing-in-itself. It was, ultimately, an expression of that society which had nurtured it. As for his contemporary age: "The perfect chaos of society, the mingling of myriad races and traditions, the anarchy of industry, the muddleheadedness of theology, the breakdown of the nineteenth-century educational system, the general aimlessness and uncertainty of things react inevitably on art..."[9] Modern art, as part of the infrastructure of modern society, had deviated from the fundamental laws so vital to a wholesome civilization. To redefine those laws it was first necessary to trace them back to their greatest flowering: the Gothicism of the Middle Ages.

Gothic, for all its variations, represents a distinct, organic style. But as Cram averred in a lecture delivered in 1904, "Gothic...is less a method of construction than it is a mental attitude, the visualizing of a spiritual impulse."[10] By stressing Gothic as "spiritual impulse," Cram was setting himself against the rationalism of Viollet-le-Duc and the English realists, that is to say, their conception of Gothic as a method of construction. However, he was

117

not arguing, like the German Nazarenes, that all art
or architecture derived from religion. As far as he
was concerned, domestic art and architecture reflected, and should reflect, existing social conditions.
Their sensuous manifestations in ancient Athens and
later in Venice, for example, sanely derived from the
natural beauty of the surroundings. While a certain
amount of diversity was warranted in general architectural expression--and naturally Cram was most concerned with architecture--this was not the case for
ecclesiastical architecture. He wrote: "We are not
at liberty to pick and choose among the tentative
styles of a crescent Christianity...we must return to
the one style our forefathers at last created for the
full expression of their blood and faith."[11] We must,
in other words, return to the Gothic. Actually, he
believed that the West had produced three major styles
of architecture--the Greek, Byzantine, and Gothic--and
he also looked favorably upon the Lombard, Romanesque,
and Norman styles. Nevertheless, only the Gothic provided "the sanest and most promising basis"[12] for contemporary Christian art: "There is no single subject
for design that calls out so much imagination, that
demands such a use of architectural power, that makes
possible such enduring and honorable monuments as a
Christian church."[13]

At this point it becomes necessary to take a
closer look at what Cram meant when he spoke of
"Christianity." Of the multitude of sects which com-
prise this great religion of the West, he was basically concerned only with two: the Anglican Church and
the Roman Catholic Church. A devout Episcopalian, he
constantly spoke in cordial terms of "our sister," the
Roman Catholic Church.[14] Indeed, having scourged the
Reformation in virtually all of his writings and having acknowledged the existence of a single, true
faith, he poses a mild enigma in never having converted to Catholicism.[15] In any event, he spent much time
and effort working for the restoration of Christian
unity (see Chapter VIII), via the reconciliation of
these two churches, which, he boasted, "can claim more
fully the honour of being absolutely out of touch with
what we are pleased to call 'Modern Civilization.'"[16]

In Cram's view, both the Anglican and Roman Catholic Church could properly use only the Gothic architecture which was developed in Europe between the mid-
twelfth and mid-sixteenth centuries. That which antedated this period "was barbarism, and barbarism followed after, but those four centuries saw Christianity

118

bring into being its own perfect and final mode of expression."[17] It logically followed, for him at least, that only one in sympathy with these two faiths could construct their buildings. While strongly sympathizing with Catholicism as a faith, however, he positively abhorred its art forms which dominated in the late nineteenth and early twentieth centuries. Writing in a Catholic magazine in 1894, he did not hesitate to excoriate the Church, claiming that "by her art as a whole," it "verily appears what Puritan bigotry declared her to be." In the same article he suggested--and one can only wonder if this was applicable to himself--that would-be converts might no longer hesitate if only the Church cultivated her "natural" art and beauty.[18] Instead, it seemed "helpless, chained hand and foot by utter artistic depravity, ignorance, and self-satisfaction."[19]

As Cram pleaded for the Catholic Church to pursue beauty (which in part involved building in the Gothic style), various Protestant denominations in the United States ironically were beginning in the first two decades of the twentieth century to adopt the Gothic mode for their churches. At first he attempted to discourage these Congregationalists, Presbyterians, Methodists, and Baptists from using the style which he had largely earmarked for Anglicans and Roman Catholics. He believed that the architecture of a given church should reflect its particular tenets and manner of worship. Accordingly, the rich splendor of a Gothic edifice scarcely seemed congruent with the relative simplicity of a Presbyterian service. The art of these various sects could be genuinely moving if only it honestly reflected the denomination's true spirit. Increasingly, however, Cram came to view the Gothic style as a kind of missionary force for the achievement of Christian unity. Some of his finest Gothic churches were built precisely for these diverse Protestant groups.[20]

As high priest and hierophant of the Gothic Revival in the years before World War I, Cram strove to make that form of architectural expression popular with Americans. Despite his general success, he never assumed that it was about to become the national style. Such an occurrence seemed altogether impossible in light of the country's diversity: "It is evident that art cannot coordinate society; society must coordinate art, and, as it shows at present not the faintest tendency toward its own coordination, the day of a 'national style' is evidently a long way off."[21]

Both suitable and legitimate, Gothic represented the
style for Episcopalian and Roman Catholic churches and
a style for colleges and universities. The most that
one could ask for other buildings was that they reflect styles consonant with their spirit and purposes
and heed canons of taste. To say that he did not anticipate the elevation of Gothic to the level of national style, however, is not to say that volition was
lacking. In order that wish might become act it was
necessary for "a returning to other days--not for the
retrieving of pleasant but forgotten forms, but for
the recovery of those impulses in life which made
these forms inevitable."[22] More important than the
style itself, in other words, were its nutrients. Because of a theory of history he had developed, he had
good reason to believe that "a returning to other
days" was imminent.

The theory of historical progress did not necessarily begin with the Enlightenment, but assuredly
that movement was most instrumental in transforming
modern man's viewpoint from a hope to a conviction.
After a painfully slow ascent over the centuries, man
had climbed, in the metaphor of the Marquis de Condor-
cet, to the threshold, the tenth and final stage, of
human perfection. This legacy of the Enlightenment
was worked out in greater detail and in various forms
by its nineteenth-century heirs. Auguste Comte, for
example, predicated progress and perfection on man's
reaching the "positive" stage of development, after
having passed through the earlier "theological" and
"metaphysical" stages. For Karl Marx, perfection
would come inevitably with the triumph of the proletariat over the bourgeoisie and a subsequent classless
society. For many, perhaps the most important con-
firmation of meliorism came from Charles Darwin's
theory of evolution, which seemed to verify once and
for all the optimistic prognosis advanced by the
philosophes. While a growing lack of confidence could
be perceived by the end of the century, the belief in
progress generally held away until the cataclysm of
1914.

Strictly speaking, Christianity does not accept
a progressive view of history. Tainted by original
sin and the fall from grace, mankind does not--indeed,
cannot--"progress" in any real secular sense. The
true Christian ultimately must disavow the worldly,
historical City of Man in favor of the spiritual, a-
historical City of God if he is to obtain redemption.
Carried to its logical conclusion, this view posits

history as a more-or-less nugatory force. Some Christians, however, refuse to accept the implications of this reasoning and, instead, define history as the unfolding of Divine Will. This second group is further divided into those who contend that God's design for man is inscrutable and those who, with more than a little hubris, vouchsafe to explain the blueprints of Providence to the unenlightened. Cram belongs to this latter group. Though his concept of history was undeniably Christian in the final analysis, it was Christian with some strange twists.

History, for Cram, was neither the inevitable linear progression suggested by the philosophes and their legatees nor the generally static view implied in Christianity. It was cyclical. The roots of his thinking on this subject are extremely obscure. A very well-read and erudite man, he was aware, in all probability, of the ancient Greeks' concept of history as a circular movement, but nowhere in his writings does he refer to this. He did admire Walter Pater, who frequently concerned himself with the Greek philosophers, particularly Heraclitus and his "perpetual flux." In <u>Marius the Epicurean</u>, for example, Pater used such phrases as "continual change," "inexhaustible energy," and "rhythmical logic."[23] Yet any possible connection between the Oxford don's ideas and Cram's theory of history is much too vague to be drawn. Besides, Cram's only direct references to Pater are of the most general nature. It is unlikely, furthermore, that the architect had read Giambattista Vico (1668-1744), the philosopher and legal scholar whose cyclical view of history and general works have remained in eclipse until quite recently. He much admired the contemporary work of Oswald Spengler (1880-1936), whose morphological concept of history became internationally celebrated, but to impute direct influence in this instance is impossible since he developed his theory before Spengler's saw the dark of the printer's ink. For want of solid evidence it becomes necessary to conclude that Cram developed his theory of history in an independent fashion--a conclusion which by no means seems totally far-fetched.

As early as 1908, Cram began describing his historical theory as "rhythmical" or "vibratory."[24] History, according to this theory, revealed itself through a series of cycles, each of which encompassed roughly five hundred years. Within each cycle there were two waves, one ascending, the other descending, or, put another way, one representing historically

121

dominant forces, trends, and values, the other representing recessive ones. There is much here which suggests the Hegelian interplay of thesis and antithesis, especially since the parabolically ascending and descending waves do intersect at points which Cram called "nodes." But no synthesis--as in Hegelianism--results from the ensuing clash. Rather, the waves begin to reverse positions: dominant becomes recessive and vice versa. The newly dominant wave, however, will in turn yield to a recessive one in the following five-hundred-year cycle. While he found these cycles at work in the centuries before Christ, only the subsequent period of time engaged Cram's interest. He discerned that in these years anno Domini nodes had never failed to appear with striking regularity: 450-550, 950-1050, 1450-1550. Invariably, these one-hundred-year periods witnessed the decay of dominant waves and the flowering of the hitherto recessive ones. In every case the transition was marked by an epochal event. The Roman Empire, for example, gave way to the Dark Ages, the Carolingian Renaissance yielded to Europe's tenth-and early eleventh-century decline, and the Middle Ages receded before the push of the Renaissance. By this reasoning, that ascendant undulation which reached its nodal point sometime around the mid-nineteenth century, though still strong, should have already begun to ebb in the face of the rising recessive one. And indeed Cram saw the process at work as evidenced by the Gothic Revival. Though centrifugal forces characteristic of nodal periods were stronger than centripetal ones, their struggle indicated that another historical cycle rapidly was drawing to its close. By the middle of the twentieth century, he reckoned, a new dominant wave should be clearly ascendant.

Argued with conviction and in a compelling style, Cram's theory of history, for all its interest, suffers from all sorts of internal and external deficiencies. First of all, his schema is totally arbitrary, its dates and events selected to fit preconceived notions. There are not, for example, many persons--scholars or otherwise--who consider the Renaissance to be a virtually unmitigated disaster. Secondly, one finds a patent partisanship with regard to his dominant waves. One can safely infer that Cram lamented the ebbing of the Roman Empire, Carolingian Renaissance, and Middle Ages. Yet he could scarcely wait for the diminution of the dominant wave of his own contemporary cycle. Further, the theory, as presented, purports to be more than a theory: it assumes its own proof. It possesses, moreover, all the rigidity of scientific determinism, which, when put forth by others (and with better qualifications), he found highly repugnant.[25] Blatantly inconsistent, Cram mistook his own subjectivity for historical inevitability. And one could go on with criticisms. Rather than completely dismiss his views on history, however, one would do better to pick and choose judiciously. Invalid premises will ultimately result in an invalid argument, but along the way one may find interesting, useful, and even accurate propositions. For all his mistaken notions and faulty methodology, Cram did glean some valuable insights from the past.

Just as he deplored architecture which was merely archeological or antiquarian in content, so likewise was Cram unwilling to justify studying the past qua past and without possible application to contemporary society. Despite his artistic sensibilities, he was determined in good utilitarian fashion to seek in the past what was useful for the present, more specifically, the present of the West. Admiring the ancient Greeks and, to a somewhat lesser degree, the Romans, he nonetheless rejected their civilizations as appropriate models because they were pagan ones. The Byzantine civilization, in contrast, was not pagan, but its history belonged more properly to the East. Only one civilization seemed to provide a suitable paradigm for the West: the Middle Ages.

To embrace medievalism as a paradigm for nineteenth century Western culture was to strike at the heart of that age's received ideas and living experience. In an age conspicuous for its triumphs in science and technology, its secularism, its inclination (however grudged) toward democracy, the medieval quest seemed both retrogressive and hopelessly quixotic. For Comteans and others, modernity had been achieved proportionally as the beliefs and traditions of the Middle Ages were swept into the historical dustbin. As Louis H. Sullivan, the great pioneer in modern architecture, perceived the problem at the turn of the century: "Thus in his ever-flowing moment of initiative, the man is clearly at the parting of two ways--The one leading him away from his fellow men, and the other toward them. Upon the choice of the way has ever depended and now as surely depends the course of those two great factors in the social history of man, which we shall call Feudalism and Democracy."[26] While modernists, virtually by definition, were im-

placable foes of medievalism, there were others who
looked to the Middle Ages precisely because it held
out the hope of mitigating the worst evils of modernism. Differing over what constituted the quintessen-
tial truths and usefulness of medievalism, these
critics concurred in their vision of the Middle Ages
as a cynosure for their own age. As Alice Chandler
has observed: "Medievalism was influential because
it fitted in with the dominant pattern of the age.
It provided the most relevant answer that the past
could offer to the problems of a new society."[27]
Increasingly, the most important of these critics--
John Ruskin, Charles Eliot Norton, William Morris,
and, of course, Ralph Adams Cram--came to perceive
their art and art commentary as complementary and
sometimes even ancillary to larger social criticism.

Famous as a critic of both art and architecture,
Ruskin in mid-life launched a scathing attack upon
the evils of laissez-faire industrial capitalism in
a collected series of essays, Unto This Last (1862).
Sympathetic to the assorted grievances of the workers,
to whom he addressed a spate of hortatory letters,
Ruskin became convinced that Western society must
remodel itself along the economic and social lines
that had formed the matrix of the Middle Ages.
Though later in life he would call himself a socialist
and even a communist, he was, at heart, a Tory democrat, much like Disraeli. Society, as he perceived
it, was straining toward anarchy, and a revived spirit
of feudalism, with its sense of hierarchy, repose, and
benevolent paternalism, appeared the best, perhaps the
only, means of averting disaster. Ruskin was aware of
the discrepancy between the medieval ideal and reality, but as he observed: "The things that actually
happened were of small consequence --the thoughts that
were developed are of infinite consequence."[28] In
short, for Ruskin, as for Georges Sorel and his conception of the general strike, the myth was to become
the efficacious agent.

Medieval ideals also permeated the social criticism of Charles Eliot Norton, Harvard Professor of
Fine Arts, distinguished man of letters, and close
friend of Ruskin. A genteel scion of prominent New
England forbears who was doomed to live in an age
which had come to respect gentility less and less,
Norton lectured his students and readers of his books
and articles on the wonders of Dante and medieval art
and, with equal fervor, on the lewdness and debauch-

eries of the Renaissance. Evincing the same narrow
Protestant bigotry as Ruskin, he refused to credit the
Catholic Church with inspiring the art of the Middle
Ages. Unlike Ruskin, however, he also refused to give
good grades to feudalism. Cathedrals, the most ambitious examples of medieval art, were "the work neither of ecclesiastics nor of feudal barons. They represent, in a measure, the decline of feudalism, and
the prevalence of the democratic element in society."[29] For Norton, much like Cram, there existed a
reciprocal relationship between art and the people en
masse. Art could transform mediocrity into excellence, malady into health, but only when an essential
truth was fully grasped: "In their highest achievements the arts are not so much the instruments and expression of the solitary individual artist, as the
means which the nation adopts, creates, inspires for
the expression of its faith, its loftiness of spirit.
They are the embodiment of its ideals; the permanent
form of its poetic moods. When the nation is great
enough to require great art there will be artists
ready for its need."[30]

Yet the scholar found little evidence of such
benign development in his own society. An elitist at
heart, he preached fervently to the proverbial unwashed who, for all his efforts, remained, as far as
he was concerned, unwashed. Norton's America was not
ready for great art. Forever extolling the virtues
of a democratic medieval communalism, moreover, the
Harvard professor was sometimes optimistic but usually
skeptical with regard to the aspirations and abilities
of his democratic countrymen. Nor did he share his
friend Ruskin's contempt for the prevailing system of
economics: laissez-faire capitalism, for all its
faults, was acceptable to Norton and his brethren who
comprised the Genteel Tradition. Ultimately, Norton,
unlike Ruskin, could never fully shed his inheritance
of nineteenth-century liberalism. There was, however,
a contemporary of Ruskin and Norton who could read
democracy into the Middle Ages and then use that
reading as a point of departure to reach a fusion of
socialism and democracy as a panacea for the ills of
society.

Poet, novelist, social critic, craftsman, William
Morris, "as much as anyone of his time," it has been
noted, "was a latterday version of the Renaissance man
--a compliment he would not have valued, given his
hatred of the Renaissance with its emphasis on individual genius."[31] In his detestation of that era im-

mediately following the Middle Ages, Morris likely
would have agreed with Victor Hugo's assessment that
the Renaissance was a sunset which history had mistaken for a dawn. For Morris, it was the medieval example which held out hope for the anomie and deracina-
tion produced by modern industrialism. In turning to
the Middle Ages, this creative genius drew inspiration
from Ruskin and from Karl Marx, who declared the fourteenth century to be a golden one for the workingman
who had then--and for the last time--owned his means
of production and found self-respect and fulfillment in
his daily work. Recognizing that the material conditions of workers in the late nineteenth century had
become better rather than worse, Marx's predictions to
the contrary, Morris at first concerned himself primarily with the drudgery and joylessness of work experienced by the proletariat rather than with the
problem of wages. In essays, pamphlets, lectures, and
in his two utopian novels, A Dream of John Ball (1888)
and News from Nowhere (1891), he sermonized on the
polarity between the independent worker of the Middle
Ages and his modern counterpart, the slave to the
machine. Unlike others who shared his views, moreover, Morris literally practiced what he preached,
making herculean efforts to revive the arts and crafts
as they had more or less existed in the Middle Ages.
Ironically, since his goods--whether finely bound and
printed books from the Kelmscott Press or richly designed wallpaper and bric-à-brac--were so expensive
that only the well-to-do could afford them, only a few
craftsmen actually were able to escape dehumanization
wrought by the machine.

For all his efforts, both literary and active,
Morris ultimately abandoned medievalism as an impossible ideal. Scoffing at those who failed to see the
medieval ideal as futile for the modern world, he
lashed out: "Then there are others who, looking back
on the past, and perceiving that the worker of the
Middle Ages lived in more comfort and self-respect than
ours do, even though they were subjected to the class
rule of men who were looked on as another order of
beings than they, think that if those conditions of
life could be reproduced under our better political
conditions the question would be solved for a time at
least. Their schemes may be summed up in attempts,
more or less preposterously futile, to graft a class
of independent peasants on our system of wages and
capital."[32] Morris had turned, to use E. P. Thompson's description, from "romantic" to "revolutionary."

Marx had triumphed over Ruskin, dialectical materialism over A Dream of John Ball, and the class struggle
over the vision of a peaceful and productive medieval
communitarianism.
The difference in the assessment of the Middle
Ages by Ruskin, Norton, and Morris ultimately proved
large. While all three esteemed the Middle Age's art
and architecture and either denigrated or played down
the influence of the Church, Ruskin also valued that
period's social order, Norton its spirit of democracy,
and Morris its psychological and social benefits for
workers. In other words, these critics drew selec-
tively from the variegated ideas and institutions of
that earlier historical epoch. Not so Ralph Adams
Cram, who developed an integrated view which could and
would serve, he hoped, as a model for regenerating
modern civilization.
The single most important element of medieval
civilization was, for Cram, as for Pugin, the religious one. Aside from its strictly theological importance, this great age of faith--never reached before, never equalled since--had produced in the West
"a Christian commonwealth, not a pagan aggregation of
egotistical units, knotted and writhing in a Laocoön
struggle for life."[33] Respectful as he was of the period's brilliant scholastics[34] and eminent churchmen,
he most admired the monastic orders for the invaluable
role they performed in the achievement of this commonwealth. It was not only a matter of their preservation of learning both during and after the Dark Ages,
their solicitude for the physically and spiritually
ill, and their simple religious piety. Quite as important were the vows of poverty, chastity, and obedience which they took and which Cram construed broadly and symbolically. Modern man, he insisted, could
learn much from these three strictures, whose implications applied fully as much to secular as religious
life. Poverty, for example, connoted despising wealth
for its own sake and elevating communal well-being
above that of the individual. Chastity encouraged
service over selfishness, as well as freedom from
lusts. Finally, obedience served as a necessary ce-
menting element for society, one which had dangerously
eroded in modern times. This obedience was not to be
confused with authoritarianism. On the contrary,
monasticism "was the only democracy the world has ever
known which was at the same time a pure democracy and
a success."[35] Carried away with the virtues of monasticism, an exuberant Cram once confessed to Louise

127

Guiney: "My solemn conviction is that the great demand of the present century is for a monastic order
which will take in married men with their wives and
children!" He dolefully admitted, however, that he
did not think it would prove feasible.[36]

Another characteristic of the Middle Ages which
so impressed Cram was the balance struck between liberty and order, between the individual and society:
"Liberty was a mania amongst the Medievals, and it was
they who laid all the foundations of such liberty as
men have possessed ever since, but they knew, as we
do not, that liberty means obedience, precise and
highly articulated society, communal action as opposed
to individualism. Knowing this they produced the
greatest unity, achieved by and expressed through liberty and individuality, history has thus far recorded
....It was the exact antithesis of anarchy."[37] For
Cram, there existed a vast difference between the concept of individualism at work in the Middle Ages and
that operative in the modern world. Paradoxically,
it was not despite but because of hierarchical order
that the individualism of the former was superior:
"It was all a question of ability, of capacity, and,
whatever their faults, monasticism and feudalism were
the great agencies for enabling any man, whatever his
previous status, to achieve whatever position in life
his abilities warranted him in demanding."[38]

Nowhere was the acceptance of individual ability
better exemplified than in the craft guilds of the
Middle Ages, "the golden age of the workingman."[39]
With specific regard for the arts, Cram deplored contemporary union discouragement of the apprentice system practiced in medieval times. Not only was union
parochialism preventing able craftsmen from advancing,
but those seeking to employ such craftsmen were being
forced to go to Europe for this talent. According to
the indignant architect, it was precisely the lack of
skilled artisans, in tandem with the loss of religious
zeal and disregard for law, order, and obedience,
which accounted for the nation's failure to produce a
single great edifice on the level of the Pyramids, the
Taj Mahal, Greek and Buddhist temples, and Chartres.
"By itself," he confessed, "architecture is nothing;
allied with the structural crafts and the artist
crafts, it is everything,--the greatest art in the
world; for it is a plexus of all the arts; it assem-
bles them in a great synthesis that is vaster than any
art by itself alone, that gathers them together in the
perfect service of God and man."[40]

In the final analysis, the nation's lack of skilled craftsmen could be attributed to the pernicious economic system which had replaced the more equitable order of the Middle Ages. "In place of a communism that developed true personality," Cram lamented, we have "an individualism that destroyed personality." Disregarding "the splendid liberty of medieval society," we have constructed "an economic system that, through mechanics, capitalism, the wage system, and division of labour, has become a very sordid kind of slavery." What could be done? He suggested that we vigorously search for dedicated artisans, those few still imbued with pride of workmanship. Pursuant to this end, he advised the cumulation and circulation of a "White List" of both skilled and promising workers. These recommendations were merely palliatives, however. Ultimately, we must return to a guild system modeled after that of the Middle Ages, one, not incidentally, which would provide for a division of profits in lieu of the wage system.[41] At this point it becomes important to note the vital difference between Cram and William Morris with respect to the workingman. Both strongly accepted the necessity of fulfilling the worker's creative instincts but differed strongly as to the means for securing this. Basically anti-capitalist but also fundamentally anti-union, Cram could accept nothing less than slightly modified practices of the medieval guilds. Morris, on the other hand, called for a socialism based on the realities of contemporary life. Though linked by a common loathing for industrialism, the two represented the antithetical responses of conservatism and socialism as conduits for fundamental change.

The Middle Ages was, in sum, "the nearest approach to the Christian Commonwealth man has thus far achieved."[42] Built on the foundations of true Christianity, its society was an organic one in which religious and secular elements grew and flourished symbiotically. Politically hierarchical yet decentralized, economically productive but cognizant of human needs and instincts, socially homogeneous without stifling individual aspirations, it manifested a balance of the dynamic and static, the innovative and traditional. It was only such a vital society that could have produced the splendors of the stained glass window and Gothic spires. But "the great thousand years" of medievalism reached its apogee, began the downward course of its trajectory, and sometime in the mid-fifteenth century reached its nodal point, where it met the rising curve of soon-to-be dominant forces. Those new forces, once in ascendancy, were, in Cram's opinion, to prove utterly disastrous for the West.

The medievalist from Hampton Falls by no means rejected the Renaissance in toto. On the contrary, he viewed that age almost as a Manichaean struggle between the forces of light and darkness. The earlier Renaissance, the flowering of Dante, Giotto, and their spiritual heirs, Pico della Mirandola and Botticelli, was a continuation of the finest impulses which had coursed through the Middle Ages. By the middle of the fifteenth century, however, the darker elements of the Renaissance had arrived, "hatching the cockatrice of neo-paganism from the eggs of Christian civilization."[43] Symbolized by the martyrdom of Savonarola, the secular impulse became dominant over the spiritual, the individualistic over the communal, and the authoritarian over the democratic. In place of the worship of God, the Renaissance now built an altar to the false gods of intellect, selfishness, and force. Art, as a result, began to suffer. Cram was certainly not arguing that the Renaissance had no artistic genius. Reflecting the social matrix from which it had evolved, however, it was an inescapably decadent art which "the painters and sculptors and poets wrought out of the inheritance of mediaevalism to clothe its pagan nakedness," and which "bears the mark of the beast."[44] While he readily admitted that "we have forgiven Alexander VI and Leo X, Torquemada and Machiavelli, for the sake of Leonardo, Botticelli, [and] Donatello," he posed an important question by asking: "Are we the heirs of the Pagan Renaissance, or of the Great Thousand Years of Christianity?"[45] For his part, the answer was never in doubt.

As with the Renaissance, he differentiated between a "true" and "false" Reformation. "The true reformation," he wrote, "lies in the revolt of the soul of Europe against the degraded morals of a paganized Church; the false reformation in the assault on the Church as well as on its paganism."[46] In other words, he came down on the side of Erasmus the reformer rather than Luther the revolutionary. Cram did not deny that the Church badly needed reform. He scarcely could in light of its growing worldliness which had culminated in the "insolent triumph"[47] of St. Peter's. But Luther, going beyond necessary purgations, effectively had shattered Christian unity, the keystone of Western civilization. Calvin fared no better at Cram's hands. Despising that theologian's insistence on the doctrine of predestination, he simply dismissed him as being "un-Christian."[48] Moreover, Luther, by having "killed all art but music in Germany," had set the stage for the mass destruction of Catholic art.[49] Yet this was but the beginning, for the entire Reformation, "by its substitution of a manufactured religion for that of God's revelation, dried up the springs of spiritual energy which are the source of the art-impulse."[50] For the first time in history, lamented Cram, religion had seemingly turned against art. He had evidently forgotten or conveniently overlooked the egregious "Bonfire of Vanities" perpetrated by his beloved Savonarola.

If Cram experienced a genuine dislike of Luther and Calvin, his detestation of England's Henry VIII, "the incarnation of all the moral evil of the Renaissance," was virtually boundless. Henry, although he remained basically Catholic in theological matters and vigorously opposed Luther, closed the English monasteries and confiscated their wealth. Cram admitted that there had been religious corruption and perhaps the acquisition of too much power. Yet rather than instigating corrective reforms, Henry, driven by pleonexia and greed, utterly destroyed "the most highly organized form of Christian society then existing," as well as its priceless art treasures.[51] Luther, Calvin, Henry VIII, as well as Zwingli and the Anabaptists--all had contributed to the Reformation, that stupendous event which had caused "the greatest breakdown on record."[52]

The false principles and malefactions of the Renaissance and Reformation initiated a new spiritual and social decline for the West. Following the disasters of the sixteenth century, Western civilization became imbued with the "savage hatred" of the seventeenth century, the "chaos and violence" and "empty formalism" of the eighteenth century, and the "mental self-satisfaction" and "materialism" of the nineteenth century.[53] A few hundred years after the Renaissance and Reformation, the Industrial Revolution completed the destruction of medievalism. Like these two earlier shattering events, it had stemmed from an honorable impulse, in this case the material amelioration of the human condition. Yet it, too, had gone awry, shaking "the very foundations of religious society" and establishing "economic conditions in which art could no longer endure."[54] Worse still, it had shackled the West with that capitalism whose seeds had been planted in the nefarious soil of Renaissance and Reformation malfeasance.

Without the slightest question, Cram's sense of history was filled with a myriad of distortions and errors of fact and interpretation. All of this is not to say that it was totally devoid of worth; he could, in fact, occasionally point to historical facts which various scholars have missed. For example, he was quite correct in noting that the notorious <u>droit du seigneur</u> was the feudal exception rather than the rule. He was not necessarily wrong, moreover, to argue the merits of medieval laws based on customs and traditions in contradistinction to the plethora of laws ground out by modern legislative institutions,[55] and arguments such as those for Christian unity and the guild system similarly are questions of values more than of historical authenticity. His most telling weakness as an amateur historian is not so much that he was guilty of factual errors but that his vision was too roseate. For him, the Middle Ages represented a spiritual, cultural, and institutional utopia without major blemish. Some of the worst abuses recognized as part of the medieval totality he either blithely ignored or managed to attribute to other historical eras, particularly those of the Renaissance and Reformation. It was quite true, for example, that the Inquisition reached its zenith in the sixteenth century; he failed to note, however, that this glorious institution had its birth with the thirteenth-century Albigensian Crusade. Also, can one really state with any degree of assurance that the ruthlessness and authoritarianism of the Renaissance despots was worse than that of the Middle Ages? King John's not-so-loyal barons would not have said so; neither in all probability would the countless numbers of peasants and serfs who stood at the base of the feudal pyramid. Nor was Cram being terribly historical when he flatly declared that Protestants were the heirs of the Medici and Borgias.[56] One critic, though friendly to the architect, scoffed irreverently at Cram's medievalism: "If the learned doctor could have his way he would have us living in walled towns, vassals of some baron or bishop, and we would be dragging the stones to the rising cathedral, yoked to wooden carts, chanting the <u>Dies Irae</u>." In more sober tones, he added: "We would have to bind ourselves, as Mr. Cram has done, to the bigotry, persecution, famine, pestilence, and abysmal ignorance of all outside the hierarchy."[57]

Cram's historical interpretation of the lengthy

132

period following the Renaissance and the Reformation also leaves a good deal to be desired. Again, the chief problem is less one of factual accuracy than of judgment and balance. Aside from a few kind words for the Stuarts and the abortive architectural revival during their years, as well as the expected plaudits for aristocratic lineage and hierarchy, he found virtually nothing at all to praise.[58] Few rays of sunlight, he would have us believe, brightened the almost unrelieved gloom of this three-century-old morass.

Bleak as the picture he had painted of Western civilization was, Cram could see positive forces--the ascending curve, as it were--at work. From approximately the middle of the nineteenth century, counter forces had been struggling to undermine the baneful effects of, as he termed them, the three R's: the Renaissance, Reformation, and (Industrial and French) Revolution. The Pre-Raphaelites, the Decadents, Wagnerian music, Christian socialism, a monastic revival, the Gothic Revival--all had given promise that the heretofore dominant forces were beginning to recede and that the five-hundred-year historical cycle was drawing to its inglorious close. Moreover, his trip to Japan in 1898 seemed to indicate that the medieval spirit and principles he so greatly admired were not the sole legacy and domain of the West.

Cram genuinely appreciated the art and architecture of Japan (as well as that of China and Korea) largely because it had stemmed from the same wholesome impulses that had characterized the Gothic style of the West. Like the Gothic, it had symbolized "the triumph of a great religious ideal, the manifestation of a fully achieved self-knowledge, the rising of a people out of barbarism, the development of the splendid virtues of heroism, sacrifice, chivalry, and worship."[59] Whereas the great traditions of Western art --the Classical, Byzantine, and Gothic--lasted as major forces for no more than a few centuries, Japan's art endured for more than a millennium, from the mid-seventh to the mid-nineteenth century. Cram did perceive a decline in her art shortly after it had peaked during the early Tokugawa period of the seventeenth century. It was the arrival of Commodore Perry and his "black ships" in the 1850's, however, which spelled doom for indigenous culture, substituting the worst of Western art for the best of Eastern. The architecture which had resulted, according to an appalled Cram, "would dishonour a trans-Mississippi city or a

133

German suburb."[60] At the end of the nineteenth century most of her vital art had been destroyed by the foolishly adopted policy of westernization. Distressed, he lamented: "In three centuries we have sold our birthright for a mess of pottage. Japan bartered hers in less than forty years." [61] (Unfortunately, Cram never indicated if his cyclical view of history applied to Japan as well as the West.)

Yet in Japan, as elsewhere, art was but a graphic manifestation of deeper social and spiritual dynamics. What had produced her splendid works had not been primarily her creative geniuses (though obviously they were necessary), but her values, traditions, and institutions. Like the West during the Middle Ages, Japan had been fundamentally a religious society. Shinto, her native religion, had provided an ethical tradition and had made possible through its emphasis on duty and obedience the flowering of chivalry imparted by the samurai code of Bushido.[62] Buddhism, imported from India via China, had offered further contributions. As a dedicated Christian, Cram could not resist the impulse to proselytize any more than could the actual missionaries who had been invading the Orient since the sixteenth century. Still, he cautioned that Japan must be approached as a "pagan but lofty civilization" and held out his religion, "not as to a barbarian tribe of African fetish worshipers, but as the Apostles offered it to the Athenians, respecting what they had come to destroy."[63] He was sure that certain traditions and values derived from Shinto and Buddhism should and would remain secure, even with the eventual triumph of Christianity.

As devout a Christian as he was, Cram was an equally devout Anglo-Saxonist who considered the racial differences between East and West to be insurmountable. The West, nonetheless, had much to learn from Japan, where the "artistic impulse" was the last to die.[64] Despite a certain decline (in her craftsmanship, for example), the vestiges of greatness—her sense of religion, her communalism as opposed to the individualism which had been raging in the West since the Renaissance, her artistic achievements—were constant reminders that the "Gothic spirit" knew no geographical boundaries. Having only recently declined, she might quickly reverse direction, return to her former ways, and provide a fitting model for Western regeneration. It was not at all surprising that Cram favored Japan in her early twentieth-century war with Russia.[65]

While Japan provided Cram with one source of hope that modernism might soon give way to a recrudescence of medievalism, an eminent American man of letters provided another. Though the Aesthetic Movement was dead and one could hear clearly the death rattles of the arts and crafts movement, in the years immediately preceding World War One the architect was able to find a person whom he considered a kindred spirit. Whether or not Henry Adams thought of the relationship in reciprocal terms is another matter.

In attempting to impart a quasi-scientific basis to history--the idea of historical cycles is not scientific per se--Cram displayed certain striking similarities to the famous American historian. In his Education, A Letter to American Teachers of History, and The Rule of Phase Applied to History, Adams had turned, however ambivalently, to science for an analysis and interpretation of contemporary maladjustments. With a brilliant if faulty coup de main, he advanced a rigidly deterministic explanation for civilization's imminent collapse.[66] "The American professor," he counseled, "should begin his annual course by announcing to his class that their year's work be devoted to showing in American history 'a universal tendency to the dissipation of energy' and degradation of thought, which would soon end in making America improper for the habitation of man as he is now constituted...."[67] Fully as alienated from the modern world as was Adams, Cram, at least at this time, did not posit as dismal a prognosis for mankind's future. Whereas the historian cited the Second Law of Thermodynamics as proof that civilization must inexorably end sometime around the middle of the twentieth century, the architect advanced his cyclical theory of history to predict the coming ascendancy of positive forces.

Although Cram developed his peculiar historical theory quite independently of Adams,[68] the overall influence of the latter's writings is undeniable. When Cram wrote in his autobiography that "life began to widen out and take on a certain consistency and unity through multiplicity," and, at another point, noted "the decline of the parabolic trajectory that began some five hundred years ago,"[69] he was resorting to distinctly Adamsesque language. More striking, he frankly admitted that, like Admas', his life had been "a search for that education the schools could not give."[70] It is to their medievalism rather than their scientific history, however, that one turns for a more apt comparison between the two.

In all his writings Henry Adams only once chose to create a work of joy. That work, of course, is Mont-Saint-Michel and Chartres, one of his finest. Wearied by the personal tragedy of his wife's suicide and living in a world he professed not to understand, he sought temporary refuge in the resplendent past of the High Middle Ages. "All artists," he sighed, "love the sanctuary of the Christian Church and all tourists love the rest."[71] But it was more than just the Christian Church which so deeply moved him. "Modern science, like modern art, tends, in practice, to drop the dogma of organic unity," he wrote, although "all experience, human and divine, assured man in the thirteenth century that the lines of the universe converged."[72] Christianity, as opposed to paganism, community rather than anarchy, the centripetal instead of the centrifugal--these seemed Adams' personal choices, though made impossible by unyielding laws of a value-free science and a civilization which was rapidly dissipating its vital energies.

Adams had Mont-Saint-Michel and Chartres privately printed in 1904 for distribution to a chosen few. Cram only discovered this work when his friend Barrett Wendell loaned him his personal copy. One can only begin to imagine his satisfaction upon reading the book, particularly since its point of view was so remarkably similar to what he had been preaching for many years. Determined to secure his own copy, Cram was gratified a few years later when he found himself in Paris at the same time as Adams' nieces, who were his friends and purportedly the persons for whom the book had been written. One of these ladies introduced him to Adams, who also was in Paris. Though he never offered any account of their meeting, Cram left the city with an autographed copy of the work.[73]

The architect was now determined that Chartres should come out in a public edition, a condition to which its author had steadfastly refused to accede. "In this, and for once," Cram remarked, "his judgment is at fault."[74] Lunching with Adams in Washington one day in 1912, in his position as a director of the American Institute of Architects he invited him to become an honorary member of the organization. When Adams assented, Cram rather insidiously requested that he permit Chartres to be published under the Institute's auspices. Startled, Adams at first demurred, protesting that no one really wished to read it. Pressed further by Cram and the two other luncheon guests (one of whom was his niece), the harassed historian finally yielded, saying: "Oh, very well, be it on your own head; I give you the book. You may do what you like with it, but don't bother me about any details."[75] Shortly thereafter he complained that he had been placed in the position of almost religiously pleading the cause of medieval Christianity, "with my Chartres for Evangel, and Ralph Adams Cram for St. John the Baptist." He moaned despairingly: "They will beatify me after all."[76] And yet Adams did acknowledge his appreciation to Cram slightly more than a month after his waspish comment. "I shall feel myself even more flattered," he wrote, "if you give additional stamp of authority to my work."[77]

The following year Houghton Mifflin brought out the first public edition of Adams' remarkable work. Adams remained unimpressed, disdaining, through probably not seriously, Cram's "flaming preface."[78] In the fashion of the true curmudgeon that he was, he peevishly worte a friend that "the Society of Architects has stolen my volume about Mont-Saint-Michel ...."[79] A month later he denounced its publication to this same friend in even more scathing tones: "Don't say I let 'em publish Chartres. I kicked so as to be a credit to my years. But what could I do? One can't make a fool of oneself to that point. Let the architects do that."[80]

Whatever his real feelings were--and one cannot take his self-effacing, self-deprecating words at their face value--Adams autographed and sent the first publicly printed copy of his masterpiece to the delighted Cram. As the latter humbly noted in his last years: "If the world owes me anything for what I have done (a question open to debate), it certainly does so for my having been able to act as agent in making available to the public this great and singularly distinguished work."[81] Analyzing the writings on Gothic architecture of both Adams and Cram, one critic found them to be "less scientific, more imaginative" than others, "but full of suggestion and well worth reading."[82] Much more flattering was the observation of another writer who credited the two men with the very continuance of the Gothic tradition in twentieth-century America.[83] Cram could not and would not have asked for a finer compliment.

Despite his incessant diatribes against the West in the quarter century before the outbreak of World War One, Cram could not accurately be classified as a latter-day Jeremiah. Unlike the Biblical prophet, the architect was convinced of an impending change for the

better. Change--change in general--invariably took
one of two forms: the one striving to push the ascending curve of subordinate historical forces upward,
the other seeking to prevent the decline of presently
dominant ones. "At this moment," he noted, "the descending and ascending curves cross, the tangential
reactions are very much mixed, and no wonder helpless
humanity is confused." He added: "Half the so-called
reforms of today, and those most loudly acclaimed and
avidly accepted, are really no more than the desperate efforts of a dying force to prolong for an hour
its pitiful existence, to postpone for a day its inevitable plunge into the sea of oblivion."[84] To effect the desired positive changes, it was necessary to
let a moribund society die a nautral death or even to
hasten its demise. This doubtlessly would cause some
jarring dislocations, but the new society which would
supplant the old one would more than compensate. As
Herbert Spencer might explain, it was sometimes necessary to be cruel in order to be kind.

The widespread transvaluations which Cram wished
for and predicted amounted to a virtual revolution--
more precisely, a revolution of reaction. He explained: "Whether we know it or not, --and some of us act
by instinct rather than conviction,--we are fighting
the battles of a new civilization, which, like all
true civilizations, is also the old."[85] Fully confident of civilization's future, he annoucned: "...we
are at the end of an epoch of materialism, rationalism, and intellectualism, and at the beginning of a
wonderful new epoch, when once more we achieve a just
estimate of comparative values; when material achievement becomes the slave again, and no longer the slave-
driver; when spiritual intuition drives mere intellect
back into its proper and very circumscribed sphere;
and when religion, at the same time dogmatic, sacramental, and mystic, becomes, in the ancient and sound-
ing phrase, 'One, Holy, Catholic, and Apostolic,' and
assumes again its rightful place as the supreme element in life and thought...."[86] The making of a medievalist had been complete. Yet Cram insisted that
restoration served only as a prelude to reconstruction. Addressing the Contemporary Club of Philadelphia in July, 1913, he noted that the West was re-
tracing its steps to the Christian Middle Ages, "not
that there we may remain, but that we may achieve an
adequate point of departure; what follows must take
care of itself."[87] Less than a year later a violent
incident in far-off Sarajevo was to set in motion
events which would considerably diminish his optimism.

NOTES

1. Letter of Ralph Adams Cram to Louise Imogen Guiney, n.d., Louise Imogen Guiney Papers, Holy Cross College.
2. Letter of Ralph Adams Cram to Louise Imogen Guiney, May 12, 1916, ibid. The house in question was selling for $2000.
3. Nathaniel Hawthorne, Preface to The Marble Faun, The Centenary Edition of the Works of Nathaniel Hawthorne, IV, ed. William Charvat et al. (Columbus, Ohio, 1968), p. 3.
4. Ralph Adams Cram, The Ministry of Art (Boston, 1914), pp. vii-viii.
5. Ralph Adams Cram, "The Relation of Architecture to the People," Supplement to Art and Progress, I (July, 1910), 21.
6. Ibid., 20. Cram frequently expressed his pronounced distaste for Matisse.
7. Cram, Ministry, pp. 114-115.
8. Ralph Adams Cram, "Architecture As an Expression of Religion," The American Architect, XCVII (December 28, 1910), 219.
9. Ralph Adams Cram, Church Building, 3rd ed., rev. (Boston, 1924), pp. 255-256.
10. Cram, Ministry, p. 57.
11. Ibid., p. 240. By "forefathers," Cram meant the northern races of Europe--the Franks, Teutons, Burgundians, Normans, Saxons, and Danes. The southern and eastern influence had provided only "alien blood." Cram, "Architecture As an Expression of Religion," 218.
12. Ralph Adams Cram, Editorial in Christian Art, I (April, 1907), 19.
13. Ralph Adams Cram, "The Influence of the French School on American Architecture," The Architect and Building News, LXVI (November 25, 1899), 66.
14. Cram, "Architecture As an Expression of Religion," 216.
15. Cram's son believes that had his father been living in more recent times the ecumenical spirit of the Catholic Church would have induced him to convert. Interview with Ralph Wentworth Cram, August 9, 1972. At the time of his death the Brooklyn Tablet also wondered why he had never converted: "God alone understands why he did not embrace the faith which inspired the humble

builders of his beloved old world cathedrals."
James F. Johnson, "Ralph Adams Cram: Idealist,
Scholar, Architect," Christian Property Adminis-
tration, 8 (January-February, 1944), 9-10.

16. Ralph Adams Cram, The Gothic Quest (New York,
1907), p. 184.

17. Ralph Adams Cram, Editorial in Christian Art, II
(January, 1908), 209.

18. Cram, Gothic Quest, pp. 237, 251-252.

19. Cram, Church Building, p. 269. At least as late
as 1907 he was still complaining about the
Church's lack of artistic taste. Editorial in
Christian Art, I (August, 1907), 235.

20. James F. White, "Theology and Architecture in
America: A Study of Three Leaders," A Miscellany
of American Christianity: Essays in Honor of H.
Shelton Smith, ed. Stuart C. Henry, (Durham, N.C.,
1963), pp. 379-380. Some of these fine Protestant churches which were built in Gothic include
the Euclid Avenue Presbyterian Church (Cleveland),
the First Presbyterian Church (Oakland), the
First Congregational Church (Montclair, New Jersey), and the Swedenborgian Church of Bryn Athyn,
Pennsylvania.

21. Cram, Church Building, p. 257.

22. Cram, Ministry, p. 46.

23. Walter Pater, Marius the Epicurean (London, 1968
[copyright, 1885]), p. 75.

24. His initial (and best) explanation of this historical process is to be found throughout the
pages of The Great Thousand Years (Boston, 1918),
a slender book which was written (except for the
section entitled "Ten Years After") in 1908 and
published two years later in the journal Pax.
Scattered references to the process appear in almost all his later writings which are not primarily concerned with architecture.

25. Notice the scientific-like language with which he
once clothed his theory: "Like all the manifestations of natural forces, like the pulsing of
the life-blood, like life itself, history is a
system of vast vibrations, systole and diastole
beating eternally...." Ralph Adams Cram, Gold
Frankincense and Myrrh (Boston, 1919), p. 1. The
example is not atypical.

26. Louis H. Sullivan, Democracy: A Man-Search (Detroit, 1961), p. 17.

27. Alice Chandler, A Dream of Order: The Medieval
Ideal in Nineteenth-Century English Literature

(Lincoln, Neb., 1970), p. 11.

28. Ibid., pp. 10, 206.

29. Kermit Vanderbilt, Charles Eliot Norton: Apostle of Culture in a Democracy (Cambridge, Mass., 1959), p. 56.

30. Ibid., p. 205.

31. Peter Stansky, review of William Morris: Romantic to Revolutionary, by E. P. Thompson, in The New York Times Book Review, (May 15, 1977), p. 7. Thompson's biography supercedes his earlier one (1955) of the same title which even at that time was probably the most interesting and challenging of the various critical studies of this fascinating figure. See also, however, J. W. Mackail, The Life of William Morris, 2 vols. London, 1899.

32. William Morris, "The Hopes of Civilization," The Collected Works of William Morris, XXIII (New York, 1966), pp. 77-78.

33. Ralph Adams Cram, Editorial in Christian Art, I (October, 1907), 54.

34. Cram admired Thomas Aquinas as a dialectician and debater, but viewed his overall philosophy with reservations. His particular favorite among the scholastics was Hugh of St. Victor. Ralph Adams Cram, Introduction to Historia Calamitatum, the Story of My Misfortunes, an Autobiography by Peter Abelard, trans. Henry Adams Bellows (St. Paul, Minnesota, 1922), pp. vii, xx-xxi.

35. Cram, Great Thousand Years, pp. 56-62. He anticipated that a monastic saint was shortly to appear in the West. Ralph Adams Cram, The Ruined Abbeys of Great Britain (New York, 1905), p. 281.

36. Letter of Ralph Adams Cram to Louise Imogen Guiney, April 1, 1907, Guiney Papers.

37. Ralph Adams Cram, The Significance of Gothic Art (Boston, 1918), p. 13.

38. Cram, Great Thousand Years, pp. 30-31.

39. Ralph Adams Cram, "On the Religious Aspect of Architecture," The Architectural Record, II (January-March, 1893), 353.

40. Cram, Ministry, pp. 148-152, passim.

41. Ibid., 154-163, passim. Cram had a special aversion for the division of labor. To avoid it, he was willing to accept an inferior but honest piece of work, thereby achieving unity of both design and execution.

42. Ralph Adams Cram, Architecture in Its Relation to Civilization (Boston, 1918), p. 21.

43. Cram, The Ruined Abbeys of Great Britain, p. 283.
44. Cram, Ministry, p. 89; Cram, Gothic Quest, p. 159. He thought, in fact, that great art, due to what we would call a cultural lag, reached its zenith usually after "the great impulse that created it has broken down and yielded to inevitable degeneration." In this manner he was able to account for the relatively late blooming of Gothic architecture, as well as for Shakespeare and the painters of the Renaissance. Cram, "Architecture As an Expression of Religion," 210.
45. Cram, Ministry, p. 91; Cram, Gothic Quest, p. 47.
46. Cram, Ruined Abbeys, pp. 288-289.
47. Ibid., p. 286.
48. Cram complained, however, that even after Calvinism itself had declined, materialist and rationalist philosophers assured the predominance of its "un-Christian" thought. Ralph Adams Cram, Towards the Great Peace (Boston, 1922), p. 36.
49. Cram, Gothic Quest, p. 101.
50. Cram, Ministry, p. 230.
51. Cram, Ruined Abbeys, pp. 2-26, passim. He noted (p. 9) that while religious corruption existed, the monastic orders themselves were not corrupt.
52. Cram, Ministry, p. 230.
53. Ibid., p. 93.
54. Cram, "Architecture As an Expression of Religion." 214.
55. Ralph Adams Cram, The Substance of Gothic (Boston, 1917), pp. 36-37.
56. Cram, Gothic Quest, pp. 43-44.
57. The title "Doctor" refers to the honorary degrees Cram received from Princeton (Litt. D. -1910), Yale (LL. D. -1915), Notre Dame (LL. D. -1924), and Williams (Litt. D. -1928). Thomas Tallmadge, The Story of Architecture in America, 2nd ed., rev. (New York, 1936), p. 258. Tallmadge noted (p. 259), nonetheless, that Cram, whom, along with Goodhue, he considered second in importance only to McKim in the years between 1893 and 1917, had served a useful purpose in drawing attention to architectural beauty and possibilities: "Cram, in his architectural ceremonials, thundering forth anathemas and interdicts on carpenter-architects and purblind building-committees, like some crusading Innocent, did what no other man could do in effecting a reformation--a word, by the way, for which I beg his pardon."

58. Cram, "On the Religious Aspect of Architecture," 354; Cram, Ministry, p. 23.
59. Ralph Adams Cram, Impressions of Japanese Architecture and the Allied Arts, 2nd ed., rev. (Boston, 1930), p. 60.
60. Ibid., pp. 53-54, 71-73.
61. Ibid., p. 208.
62. Feudalism has not been a special preserve of western Europe. It has prevailed at various times in such diverse civilizations as those of Mesopotamia, Egypt, Byzantium, India, China, and Japan, as well as Russia. For helpful insights into the feudalism (or quasi-feudalism) of these societies, see Rushton Coulborn (ed.), Feudalism in History (Princeton, N.J., 1956).
63. Cram, Impressions, pp. 80-81.
64. Ibid., p. 149.
65. Ibid., p. 22.
66. For a masterful critique of Adams' "scientific" history, see William Jordy, Henry Adams: Scientific Historian (New Haven, Connecticut, 1952). The quest for a scientific history, of course, was not Adams' sole preoccupation. As Jordy points out (p. 276), "this inner battle between his aesthetic and his scientific predilections can be traced throughout Adams' life."
67. Henry Adams, The Degradation of the Democratic Dogma (New York, 1969), pp. 189-190.
68. The only "scientific" history that Adams wrote before 1908, the year Cram first publicly enunciated his theory, was "The Tendency of History," which appeared in 1895. In this brief article Adams called attention to the possibilities of treating history as a science but failed to offer any specific theories of his own.
69. Ralph Adams Cram, My Life in Architecture (Boston, 1936), pp. 5,147.
70. Ibid., p. 145.
71. Henry Adams, Mont-Saint-Michel and Chartres (Boston, 1913), p. 179.
72. Ibid., p. 381.
73. Cram, My Life, pp. 226-227.
74. Ralph Adams Cram, Introduction to Chartres, p. vi.
75. Cram, My Life, pp. 227-228.
76. Letter of Henry Adams to Elizabeth Cameron, December 17, 1912, Worthington Chauncey Ford (ed.), Letters of Henry Adams, II (Boston, 1938), p. 608.

77. Letter of Henry Adams to Ralph Adams Cram, January 30, 1913, Harold Dean Cater (ed.), Henry Adams and His Friends: A Collection of His Unpublished Letters (Boston, 1947), p. 753.
78. Letter of Henry Adams to Elizabeth Cameron, November 24, 1913, Ford, Letters, p. 619.
79. Letter of Henry Adams to Charles Milnes Gaskell, February 19, 1914, ibid., p. 621.
80. Letter of Henry Adams to Charles Milnes Gaskell, March 13, 1914, ibid., p. 623. Three years after Chartres was published, Adams was still lamenting his fate: "I have not published anything since 1890. Other people like Cram and [Henry Cabot] Lodge have sometimes done it--to please themselves, not me--and I have privately printed, but never published, nor shall I ever again do it...."Letter of Henry Adams to William Roscoe Thayer, February 6, 1916, ibid., p. 637.
81. Letter of Ralph Adams Cram to Louise Imogen Guiney, January 23, (?), Guiney Papers. Adams turned over his profits from the book to the American Institute of Architects for the purpose of giving copies of Chartres to impecunious students who otherwise might not be able to afford them. So great were the royalties, however, that the Institute soon was able to offer various prizes and to finance projects of which Adams supposedly would have approved. It also was able to establish the Henry Adams Lectures. Cram, My Life, pp. 228-229.
82. A. D. F. Hamlin, "Gothic Architecture and Its Critics: Part I, The Lure of Gothic," The Architectural Record, XXXIX (April, 1916), 354.
83. Agnes Addison, Romanticism and the Gothic Revival (New York, 1938), p. 138.
84. Cram, Ministry, p. 53.
85. Ibid., p. 55.
86. Ibid., p. 44.
87. Ralph Adams Cram, "Style in American Architecture," The Architectural Record, XXXIV, (September, 1913), 239.

CHAPTER VI

THE ARCHITECT AS CITY PLANNER AND ACADEMICIAN

When World War I erupted, Cram was in his fiftieth year and very nearly at the height of his professional fame. Success and age notwithstanding, he
continued, à la Henry Adams, to regard himself as a
student whose "education" was far from completed.
The war offered new chapters for this education,
bringing him both bitter disillusionment with the
world and opportunities to experience certain rich,
personal fulfillments.
    After the birth of their second child, Ralph
Wentworth, in 1905, Cram and his wife began to look
for a home in the country. As he noted: "The sense
of land ownership was, for both of us, by inheritance
and instinct, something that had no rival, except the
allied desire for children." "A suburban apartment,
a city domicile," he further explained, "could never
take the place of land--land in the country...."[1]
After several years of fruitless searching, the Crams
found almost exactly what they had been seeking in the
form of a large old house situated on one hundred and
sixteen acres of land in Sudbury, only a few miles
from Boston. This Colonial mansion in which George
Washington purportedly had slept, as well as the surrounding barns, now badly wanted repair, a task which
the family willingly assumed.[2] Over the years they
continuously found things to fix and busied themselves
with adding entire new sections, including an extensive library, to their home. Each year they also
worked the soil so as to produce a wide variety of
fruits and vegetables for their own use. Self-sufficient to a large degree, Whitehall, as their estate
was dubbed, would probably have pleased Squire Blake
immeasurably. So, too, might the family coat-of-arms
which his grandson had made.[3]
    Yet it was neither the renovations nor the till-
ing of the soil which provided Cram's greatest satisfaction. The year after acquiring Whitehall, he began to build a private chapel on the grounds. While
the chapel expressed no specific architectural style,

145

it resembled those found generally in rural France and
was called the Chapel of St. Elizabeth of Hungary.
Completed just before the war broke out, it is indica-
tive of how seriously the architect was taking his
medievalism.[4] For example, he attempted to simulate
the localism of the Middle Ages by having only those
stones which were found on the estate used for the
chapel, which he, his family, and local laborers
built. Decorated with furnishings provided by various
friends, St. Elizabeth's was blessed by the Fathers of
the Society of St. John the Evangelist (Boston) and
was the scene of regular Sunday morning services
often presided over by various priests, including a
certain Father Papineau who was Cram's personal chap-
lain for ten years. Actually, some of the religious
services were non-denominational in character and
attracted family friends who drove out from Boston or
its environs.[5] Though small, the chapel could com-
fortably accommodate at least twenty-five persons.
Over the years it was the setting for the marriages of
the two Cram daughters (Elizabeth Strudwick, the
younger, was born at Whitehall in 1913) and the bap-
tism of the first grandchild. Small wonder that this
designer of so many splendid churches could refer to
his own modest place of worship as "perhaps, the most
satisfactory church I have ever built."[6]
     Having acquired Whitehall and its expansive
acreage, Cram in his autobiography was able to reflect: "Living in a rented flat or in a narrow slice
of house in a city block I was no better than a wage-
slave, a proletarian. Now at last I was a free man."[7]
Yet Whitehall, though near enough to Boston to com-
mute, was never more than a summer residence, a haven
from the oppressive heat of the city. For the remainder of the year he and his family continued to
live in their Beacon Hill home at 52 Chestnut Street.
The ambiguity here is more apparent than real, more
reflective of changes in attitude wrought by time.
In the years before the war he relished city life, at
least as viewed from Beacon Hill, too much to forsake
it.[8] What he did was merely anticipate the tentative
solution to the problems of urban living practiced by
many of today's urbanites. Unwilling to sacrifice the
undeniable pleasures and benefits of the city or to
become a commuter, he elected to build a summer retreat in the country as a safety valve for the pres-
sures of megalopolis.

While Cram's commitment to living in Boston remained constant, his commitment to the city itself increased visibly during the war years. Having earned a substantial reputation for his concern with civic problems, especially in his role as president of the Boston Society of Architects, in 1914 he was appointed chairman of the newly established City Planning Board, a position he continued to maintain until 1922.[9] The city had begun to realize that urban blight was not a minor, transient malady and was seeking to put urban development and expansion on a rational footing. Cram, who had spent many years privately thinking of possible solutions and improvements, rightly noted: "City planning was not then a matter of such wide interest as is now the case; every American city had been allowed to grow, and was still growing, on the Topsy principle, known in more dignified parlance as that of laissez faire, with defects that were becoming increasingly obvious."[10]

In this new capacity as city planner, Cram effectively demonstrated that his talent for organization and design was not limited to the more-or-less aesthetic pursuit of Gothic church building. After all, how many hours as a youth had he devoted to the construction of cardboard cities? It would be absurd, of course, to expect a life-long Gothicist to be transformed overnight into an expert on modern urban renewal. Yet for all his dedication to the medieval past, he was neither unsympathetic to nor ignorant of urban conditions. In truth, he now saw a splendid opportunity for fusing the old and new into a higher synthesis. One of the two major plans he conceived as chairmen of the City Planning Board involved the development of the Charles River basin along lines reminiscent of Paris' Ile de la Cité. Far from seeing the area as a permanent wasteland, he wished to save it by building a new city hall, cathedral and open-air theater on the island which lay within the basin. This imaginative and ambitious scheme never fructified, however, as more "practical" heads prevailed.[11]

Though the Charles River basin plan may have been infeasible, the report of Cram and the Planning Board concerning the city's North End was as practical as it was humane. Since the late nineteenth century large numbers of immigrants, particularly Italians and Greeks, had been settling there. Fairly soon a slum had grown in the place of what had been one of Boston's quaintest quarters. Cram, perceiving the deteriorating living conditions, called for ameliorative action and the restoration of the North End as a residential, as opposed to commercial, area. The answer, he felt, did not rest with additional anti-slum ordinances; the old ones were generally adequate but had not been strictly enforced. Instead, after a three-year study he and the other members of the Board had concluded that by opening up new streets, widening old ones, and removing dead areas from the interior, the quarter could be largely restored to its wholesome condition at the time of the immigrant influx.[12]

Cram's efforts to reestablish the North End, with its largely working class population, as a decent residential area underscores his abiding concern with the living conditions of the lower classes. Addressing the delegates to the Seventh National Conference of Housing in America, held in Boston in late November, 1918, he insisted that whatever one might think of natural rights in general (and Cram thought very little of them, at least as Rousseau had expressed them), there was one which was inalienable: "the natural right of every man to live decently and in an environment that has some elements of attractiveness, if not actual beauty." Hastening to reassure his audience that he was not a Bolshevik, he added: "Not that transformation of character can be effected through education and environment, as so fondly believed by the doctrinaire scientists of the 19th century. There is such a thing as inherent character--in an individual, a family, a race--and no amount of elaborate education or ingratiating environment can wholly change this. It is a fact, however, that along these lines something can be done and the most made of potential character." Speaking a scant two weeks after the Armistice had been signed, he concluded: "What is all this reformation of the living conditions of the workers in the community but a symbol of the reconstruction of the world that lies before us."[13] Wilsonian idealism had momentarily infected the head of the household at 52 Chestnut Street.

Over the years the city did move sporadically in the direction pointed to by the Board for the restoration and preservation of the North End as a residential quarter. Other Board proposals fared less successfully. In terms of its suggestions to construct arterial roads throughout the city, the municipal government was decidedly less responsive. Roads were constructed, but oftentimes were too narrow to accommodate the heavy flow of the traffic. The Board's other major proposal, which would have diverted busi-

ness from the predominantly residential Back Bay area
to the city's South End, fell on totally deaf ears.[14]
Yet everything considered, the Board, at least while
Cram was its chairman, was a qualified success.

Perhaps more important than the Board's tangible
achievements was its symbolic value. With the establishment and implementation of this agency, the concept of city planning had come of age in Boston. Cram
might well have taken pride in his contributions to
urban problem-solving, and, to an extent, he did. But
even as his group pushed ahead with its work he began
to understand "the radical absurdity--and worse--of
the great cities as these have come to be today...."
Though the Boston Planning Board and similar agencies
elsewhere were striving to save the nation's munici-
palities, he seriously wondered whether they were at
all worth saving.[15] Megalopolis had becom pathopolis.
By the time he resigned his official position in 1922,
he had become convinced that the only solution rested
with a mass human exodus from the cities to rural
areas. The Wilsonian idealism of his 1918 speech, as
it applied to both domestic housing and international
reconstruction, had become a thing of the distant
past.

In 1914, at approximately the same time that he
was debating whether or not to accept the chairmanship
of the Planning Board, Cram received an offer to head
the Department of Architecture at the Massachusetts
Institute of Technology. He was not really surprised
by the former offer; he was astounded by the latter.
As noted previously, he was virtually the only major
architect of his time not to have received some formal
education beyond high school. His estimation of
formal education, moreover, was never very high. Late
in life he was to boast: "Never have I been taught
anything of lasting value by a school or a professional teacher...."[16] He had had absolutely no teaching
experience, moreover, and apparently had never seriously contemplated having any. Still, the selection
of Cram for this position was not nearly as outré as
it might appear at first glance. In choosing him to
fill the position vacated by Professor James Knox
Taylor, M.I.T. was adding one of the nation's most
lustrous names in architecture to its already distinguished faculty. As a member of the Royal Geographical Society and the North British Academy of
Art, and as the senior partner in a firm responsible
for building the cathedrals of Toronto, Halifax, and
Havana, he was internationally respected. He also had

served for seven years as chairman of the Committee on
Education for the American Institute of Architects.
Possibly the most decisive factor weighing in M.I.T.'s
decision was the fact that for the past two decades or
so he had written at some length on the subjects of
American education in general and architectural education in particular. Some of his views may have been
mistaken; they were all unmistakable. The Architectural Record found no difficulty whatsoever in concurring with M.I.T.'s selection: "...there are few
architects at the present time who are as familiar
with and as well prepared to take up the problems of
architectural education as is Mr. Cram."[17]

Cram had looked at college and university education in the United States and had found it wanting.
As might be expected of a religious-minded critic, he
deplored the secularism that pervaded education.
Addressing the Royal Institute of British Architects
in 1912, he had lamented that "we still hold to the
damnable opinion that education may be divorced from
religion, and ethics inculcated apart from a dogmatic
religious faith, and having sown the wind of an insane
secularism, we are reaping the whirlwind of civic
corruption and industrial anarchy."[18]

A second general criticism which he leveled
against American higher education concerned the elective system. Ever since the 1870's, when President
Charles Eliot moved Harvard away from a strictly prescribed curriculum, the elective system had become
widely operative throughout the nation's colleges and
universities. Though he spoke without benefit of
firsthand experience, Cram was quick to condemn
Eliot's far-reaching innovation, which, unavoidably,
had the effect of encouraging specialization. He did
not call for an end to the system, but argued for a
more judicious blend of prescriptive and elective
courses which would occasion the cultivation of the
broadly educated gentleman rather than the narrow specialist. Like many educators who preceded and followed him, he believed that the cultivation of the well-
rounded humanist should be the transcendent goal of
education. His belief that the free elective system
eventually would disappear, however, has hitherto
proved as mistaken as it was fervent.[19]

Cram had strong convictions and prejudices concerning America's general system of higher education,
but his principal concern, understandably, involved
the teaching of architecture. His feelings on the
subject were, to say the least, ambivalent, and one

can sense that he was never quite convinced of the efficacy of college training for prospective architects. After all, he had reached the summit of his profession without benefit of any such training. Publicly, he did accept the desirability of formal instruction for architects, asking only that their education be conducted along sound lines. By the time he had enumerated these lines, however, he had managed all but to condemn existing schools of architecture.

At one point Cram flatly asserted that architecture was taught better in the United States than elsewhere. This seemingly high encomium implied a multitude of invidious comparisons, particularly the one which involved the École des Beaux-Arts. The architect, of course, did not fail to recognize the very real merits of the Parisian school. Since the mid-nineteenth century the École had been offering the most rigorous program of architectural studies in the world. It had attempted--and with success--to inculcate a sense of taste, beauty, refinement, and logic in its students. There were disturbing aspects nonetheless. While training at the École could impart discipline to headstrong students, the training itself was deficient. Cram believed, for example, that the École was much too academic and formal in its approach to its subject matter. More specifically, he resented the fact that the Classical style had become entrenched there and the Gothic scorned. Satisfactory for public buildings, training at the Parisian school tended to neglect, if not actually deprecate, the building of churches and private residences. If a fledgling architect were bent on attending the École, advised Cram, he should first receive some practical and diverse training at home.[20]

American schools of art and architecture, unlike the École, were more open-minded in their general approach; that is to say, they were not wedded--despite undeniable proclivities--to the Classical form of expression. Cram, never easy to please, believed that despite relative tolerance, they erred in one of two directions--that of the dilettante or that of the narrow specialist. Art education increasingly had been taking its place in the schools' curricula, and he sneeringly likened this training to "schools of gastronomy, lectureships on the art of sleep, academies of inhalation and exhalation," choosing meanwhile to blame its flowering on "the strange madness we call the Renaissance." Art, as he repeatedly insisted, was neither "an industry nor a product; it is a mystery, a manifestation, and a result."[21] Castigating both the nouveaux riches and the narrow professional in terms which would have delighted a Thorstein Veblen or an advocate of the liberal arts, he added: "Art is not a possibly desirable amenity of life, to be acquired as a gloss to a commercial and industrial supremacy; neither is it a series of highly specialized professions."[22] Art, in sum, had become the special preserve of the chosen few: the amateur and the professional. But since, in Cram's opinion, it was primarily spiritual, it could and should be the domain of the spiritually endowed. The masses in the Middle Ages who built and admired both humble churches and soaring cathedrals were spiritually gifted, though neither dilettantes nor professional artists. This, at heart, was the fundamental reservation he held concerning university training for the artist and the architect.

Why, then, should aspiring artists and architects attend any professional school whatsoever? Certainly church builders had gained both knowledge and experience "without the slightest aid from the schools of architecture." Cram answered his own question by noting that while such formal training was not necessary for geniuses like H. H. Richardson, John Singer Sargent, and Augustus Saint-Gaudens (and, implicitly, himself), it was useful for most.[23] A sort of cultural Tory, Cram did insist, however, that truly great art resulted from the combined efforts of gifted artists and the faceless, nameless mass of spiritually enriched common people. Neither the mediocre artist nor his camp followers fostered this art.

Having explained what a professional school should not be, he then defined what it should be: "A true school of architecture should be half college and half monastery, set in the midst of beautiful surroundings and beautiful in itself. Rule and order and implicit obedience should be the primary essentials, relaxing slowly as the lesson is learned until at the end liberty and the feedom of personal development come as the reward of faithful service."[24] If the description leaned more towards the monastic than the academic, Cram would not have protested since he believed the fundamental concern of higher education, its sine qua non, inexorably must be character formation. Though, like other environmental factors, education could not radically change character, it

could aid in its development and refinement. Education added nothing to character, but as its etymology implies, it drew out.
Heavily armed with a set of pedagogical opinions but with no practical experience, Cram accepted M.I.T.'s offer to serve as a profesor in the Department of Architecture at an annual salary of four thousand dollars.[25] He agreed to the offer with one stipulation: he must have the title, "Head of the Department." For a man who, if anything, underplayed his important achievements when writing his autobiography, this outburst of egotism seems strange. Yet as he explained to Richard C. Maclaurin, President of M.I.T. from 1909 until 1920, he could not be chairman since Professor W. H. Lawrence was currently filling that position, and to be or even to appear to be subordinate to anyone in the department would be demeaning for a man of his professional stature.[26]
Cram concerned himself with more than mere titles, however. Freed from the cumbers of administrative duties, through his courses and his counsel he made genuine contributions to the department and, more importantly, to his students. After only a few months at the school, according to a report of the department, he had kindled a "keen enthusiasm of the students and the increased use of our library by them."[27] His achievement seems ironic when one considers that he was doing his best to discourage these neophytes. The pre-World War One years had witnessed a growing need for architects and a corresponding increase in the popularity of architecture as a profession. Yet Cram was convinced that a full sixty per cent of his students were not qualified to become either architects or draftsmen.[28] He wanted only the finest students, and if the mediocre ones chose to remain at M.I.T., it was not through his encouragement.
There were more positive contributions. For example, he made a specific point of assigning projects which involved church design, a field abysmally neglected by the secular-minded instructors at the school, who shared their prejudice with confreres at the École des Beaux-Arts. Everything considered, Cram was gratified by the religious designs he received. A second innovation which he effected was the introduction of senior theses demanding a well-written presentation which went beyond the accustomed scope of architectural projects. Disgusted by two-dimensional renderings, a practice which had been sanctified by the École, he also forced his students

to move from these two-dimensional representations to exact perspectives. Finally, he introduced and taught a course, the Philosphy of Architecture, which was intended to broaden the vistas of students by placing their chosen discipline in the larger context of artistic and historical forces.[29]

From the standpoint of his students, whether or not Cram was a successful teacher remains an unanswerable question for want of direct evidence. The department thought he was successful, and he personally enjoyed his teaching experience at M.I.T. from 1914 until his resignation in 1921. One may safely infer that as a speaker he was superb, his services having been engaged regularly since the 1890's both at home and abroad and for a variety of professional organizations and commencement addresses.[30] Having enjoyed a light teaching load, he gave two courses on a regular basis: Architectural History and the aforementioned Philosophy of Architecture.[31] According to his lecture notes, he outlined and taught the former on a straightforward, traditional basis, covering the highlights of architectural development from earliest times to the present. Broad in its definition and boundaries, the course on the Philosophy of Architecture, by affording the opportunity to expatiate at greater length on his own views, was probably more to his taste. This was a course, he wrote, "in which I tried to coordinate the very admirable teaching in other departments, indicating the nature of the architectural synthesis, its relation to history, culture, and the other arts, as well as some of my own ideas as to the theoretical principles of composition, planning, and the somewhat baffling quality of abstract and concrete beauty."[32] Like many a teacher, Cram had a decided proclivity for assigning his own works--in his case, no fewer than five books.[33] Most of the other works he assigned pertained to the Middle Ages. Henry Adams' Mont-Saint-Michel and Chartres, for example, was listed as suggested reading; two classics of medievalism, Henry Osborne Taylor's The Mediaeval Mind and H. W. C. Davis' Mediaeval Europe, were included as required reading, as was Ruskin's Stones of Venice.

In his classroom lectures (assuming that he followed the notes which he had prepared) Cram reiterated the themes upon which he had been expounding over the past twenty years. In the introductory lecture for the Philosophy of Architecture course, for example, he emphasized that the purpose of art went well beyond furnishing fashionable products for those who could afford them, and he lamented: "Society a chaos, no unity, only individualism." In a subsequent lecture he warned students: "Forget Renaissance idea of architect as exponent of amateur and sole arbiter of taste, and get back to Byzantine and Gothic idea of architect as 'primus inter pares.'" Beauty, as he complained in another address, was no longer instinctive, having gradually become moribund since the Renaissance. As for the École des Beaux Arts: "Bad taste and ugliness."

When Cram reached the modern age in his lectures, his fulminations became more mordant. Decrying the proliferation of public buildings which had resulted from pork-barrel politics, he observed, "At present government in contempt. Result of democratic methods," and warned of the "Precedent of Rome," In one of his most exhortatory addresses, he intoned: "Only highest ideals can save day. Stand for eternal truths represented by home, school and church. Emphasize sanctity of individual, but also the fact that society is greater than units. Bring back human scale in all things. In state above all." If Cram seemed even more somber than usual, it was understandable--the lecture notes read "1918." Fittingly, he asked on one of his exams for the spring of that year: "What influence will the Great War have on the future development of architecture in America, (a) if the Teutonic Powers win and establish their authority of force, and their system of Kultur over the civilized world, (b) if the Allies win the battle for liberty and local nationalism (c) if the war ends in a compromise and a temporary peace of exhaustion, injurious to all nations concerned?" Beyond its concern for architecture, the question could have been asked of mankind at large.

All of Cram's experiences at M.I.T. were not solemn or, strictly speaking, academic. In 1916 the school chose to celebrate the fiftieth anniversary of its establishment as well as its forthcoming move from Boston to its present location in Cambridge. President Maclaurin promptly selected Cram to conceive and direct the festivities. The resulting pageant, which its ambitious director said was to demonstrate "the eternal contest between man and the forces of Nature," could easily have been the prototype for a Hollywood extravaganza.34 Given a budget of twenty thousand dollars and the unlimited use of the M.I.T. student body, his imagination began to take fanciful flight. For several months he labored on preparations whose denouement would be reached during the Reunion Program of June 11th through the 14th. At one point he became infuriated with the staid Maclaurin, who, correctly anticipating what was to come, declined to appear at the pageant. Cram reminded the president that he had forced him to take charge of the time-consuming preparations even though he was a very busy man.[35] Besides, the governor of Massachusetts and the mayors of Boston and Cambridge had agreed to be present at the ceremonies. It is not known whether Maclaurin yielded on this point.

Cram personally conceived the idea of transporting the school's archives and some of its officials and teachers by water from Boston to Cambridge. To carry out, as he conceded, this "somewhat ill-advised idea," he purchased a decrepit ferryboat, which had seen all of its best days, for twelve hundred dollars. One hundred feet long, painted white, and "with a liberal camouflage of plaster-of-Paris and papier-mâché," it was christened the Bucentaur in honor of the official state barges the Venetian doges had sailed upon for the rituals in which they wedded their city to the sea. To an age which had never heard of "participatory democracy," it did not seem strange that teachers and college officials should ride the Bucentaur while twenty-five students plied the oars. After all, Cram had decreed that students should compete for this honor! To be sure that those watching the spectacle would not fail to sight the ship, the Bucentaur was bedecked with some five hundred sculpted figures. On her trial voyage she lost two of her cast cupids, and the local newspapers began to voice grave doubts as to whether she would make it from one side of the Charles River to the other. Fortunately for Cram, the twenty-five honored oarsmen, and a host of collegiate dignitaries, she did.

The Bucentaur episode was only the beginning of festivities. A court with classical facades on three sides was constructed to seat more than ten thousand persons; rooftops and nearby windows afforded a view to another five thousand; and arrangements for aquatic and lighting effects were devised. The governor and the mayors of Boston and Cambridge were ensconced on thrones, as were persons representing Earth, Air, Fire, Water, Steam, Electricity, and Time Spirit. Cram meanwhile had induced the governor to call out a troop of lancers for the occasion, and, suppressing what feelings one can well imagine, they stood at respectful attention. Once the masque had commenced, more than a thousand persons, mostly students, proceeded to stage twelve episodes, including the "Procession of the Ages," which portrayed man's development from primitive times to the present. Clad in appropriate costumes, groups reenacted historical scenes depicting the Egyptians, Chaldeans, Greeks, Romans, Moslems, Carolingians, Byzantines, Crusaders, and Chinese, among others. The careful observer could see such personages as Prometheus, Augustus Caesar, Justinian, Columbus, and--since Cram certainly was not about to overlook the Middle Ages--Charlemagne, Richard the Lion-Hearted, and Saladin. If all that were not enough to capture the audience's fancy, Envy, Hatred, War, Selfishness, Vainglory, Earth, the Alma Mater, and the several Liberal Arts capered nimbly to the pipings of the M.I.T. band. At the conclusion of the pageant the participants paraded around the court and chanted, "Peace without Victory," a grim reminder, however tinged with optimism, that the evening's revelry would yield in the morning to the stark fact that the world was at war. Extravagant as it was, the spectacle would have been disappointing had its guiding spirit not appeared. Cram wished to disappoint no one. He came as Merlin.

The years spent teaching at M.I.T. were happy and fruitful ones for Cram, despite occasional disappointments such as the unwillingness of the school to permit him to offer a course on city planning.[36] With the end of the war, however, he had begun to loosen academic ties. In August, 1919, he requested a leave of absence from the early portion of the fall semester in order to go to France for the possible construction of a votive church to Joan of Arc which was to be built with funds contributed by English-speaking people.[37] That same year he relinquished his regular position as Professor of Architecture, but continued to offer his courses on the History of Architecture and the Philosophy of Architecture, as well as occasional lectures. Two years later he severed all connections with the school.

Cram's reasons for terminating his teaching were diverse. First of all, he had become less able to countenance architectural training through the academic system.[38] In his pre-teaching years he had mistrusted such training; after several years of firsthand experience he was not inclined to reverse his judgment and had lost virtually all patience with the

concepts and practices of general formal education.
Free, compulsory, universal, and secular, education
was guilty of catering to mediocre rather than gifted
students. Moreover, voicing his oft-repeated contention that education could develop but not create
potential, he argued that schools should concern
themselves with the education of the Christian gentleman, "not the stall-feeding of intellect," or "the
practical preparation for a business career."[39]
Since current pedagogical practices in terms of
character development were "probably the worst ever
devised," schools, particularly the colleges, must
drastically reform their ways.[40] They should, for
example, offer fewer courses in the sciences and more
in history and English literature, which should be
taught for their humanistic values rather than as dry
recitations of facts and dates. Though he had earlier
posited cyclical laws as a basis for history, he now
denounced the application of scientific criticism to
the known past. "The true history," he argued, "is
romantic tradition; the stimulating thing, the tale
that makes the blood leap...."[41] Like George Santayana, Cram believed that the actual experience of living
in a college ultimately counted for more than the
college's curriculum. To produce optimum living conditions, however, the college, like the rest of
society, should be a small, self-sufficient community
--a "community of scholars," as Paul Goodman was to
call it some forty years later.[42] Any college with
a student body of more than five thousand was "a mob,
not an organism, and as a mob it ought to be put
down."[43]

Part of Cram's decision to abandon teaching also
stemmed from practical considerations. During the
war years there had been diminished opportunities for
architects, even ones as esteemed as Cram. Economic
priorities and uncertainties, both before and during
the nation's involvement, had militated against normal architectural activity. In the fall of 1919 Cram
was complaining that he had nearly gone bankrupt
since the United States entered the war. He was still
attempting without the least bit of success to collect
the thirty-five thousand dollars which he felt West
Point and the government owed him and his former partner Bertram Goodhue. To make matters worse, work on
the Cathedral of St. John the Divine had temporarily
ceased, and the church had refused to pay him some
sixty-three thousand dollars until work should re-
sume. He further claimed that a Boston real estate

company had also reneged on its financial obligations, in this instance to the amount of twenty-five thousand dollars.[44] Once the war ended, however, a building boom began and work on St. John's was recommenced. With a wife and three children, Cram felt especially obligated to recoup his losses by devoting himself to his architectural work on a full-time basis.

Though his teaching experience had been satisfying, Cram left M.I.T. a far less happy man than when he had entered. The war had taken its toll on him. In preparing a concluding lecture for his Philosophy of Architecture course, he had noted: "Those who fight, do so in defence not of democratic mechanism, but for honour, truth, mercy, sanctity of promises, --all that is left us of the Old Christian civilization. On basis of victory, build up out of ruins of a false democracy, the true democracy, whatever its form may be. If we learn lesson we shall not have to worry about architectural style."[45] He was not at all sure, however, that the West had learned any lesson. If it had not, it was through no fault of his, for he had formulated in unmistakable terms just what that lesson should be.

1. Ralph Adams Cram, My Life in Architecture (Boston, 1936), p. 229.
2. The story of Washington, which may well be apocryphal, comes from my interview with Ralph Wentworth Cram, August 9, 1972.
3. Cram, My Life, p. 187.
4. The town of Sudbury itself offers an example of a fanciful and picturesque return to the past. Henry Ford, another nostalgic (though of a quite different variety than Cram), financed the recreation of several Colonial buildings (the Wayside Inn, for example), modeled, in part, after his Greenfield Village in Dearborn, Michigan.
5. Helen Howe, daughter of Harvard professor Mark De Wolfe Howe, recalled how her parents once attended these services. Though not dwelling at length on the incident, she implied that Cram took himself much too seriously. Helen Howe, The Gentle Americans, 1864-1960: Biography of a Breed (New York, 1965), pp. 117-118. More recently, the chapel has become a tourist site for visitors to the Boston area. Interview with Ralph Wentworth Cram.
6. Cram, My Life, p 233.
7. Ibid., pp. 231-232.
8. Cram took particular delight in the Christmas seasons on Beacon Hill. Disappointed with his neighbors' lack of Yuletide spirit, he inaugurated the practice of carol singing sometime around 1906 and took delight in its subsequent adoption throughout the country. Ibid., pp. 220-222.
9. For details of two of the Board's major proposals made while Cram was chairman, see East Boston, A Survey and a Comprehensive Plan, A Report of the City Planning Board of Boston, Massachusetts (Boston, 1915), and The North End, A Survey and a Comprehensive Plan, A Report of the City Planning Board of Boston, Massachusetts (Boston, 1919).
10. Cram, My Life, p. 201.
11. Ibid., p. 204.
12. Since Cram's day the North End, still predominantly Italian in its ethnic composition, has been used as a model problem to test the wits of Harvard and M.I.T. architectural students. While "officially considered Boston's worst slum and

civic shame," it has remained, in Jane Jacobs' opinion, a viable community, resisting the disintegration which has afflicted so much of urban America. Jane Jacobs, The Death and Life of Great American Cities (New York, 1961), pp. 8-9. At one point Cram suggested replacing the city's three-tiered tenements with cottages which would rent for fifteen dollars per month. New York Times, September 23, 1942.

13. Ralph Adams Cram, "Scrapping the Slums," The American Architect, CXIV (December 25, 1918), 761-763.

14. Cram, My Life, pp. 201-203.

15. Ibid., pp. 203-204.

16. Ibid., p. 56.

17. "R. A. Cram, Professor of Architecture at Boston 'Tech.,'" The Architectural Record, XXXVI (August, 1914), 175. The journal expressed its belief (p. 176) that Cram would provide a healthy infusion of fresh views for a faculty, most of whose members had been graduates of either the École des Beaux-Arts or M.I.T. itself.

18. Ralph Adams Cram, The Ministry of Art (Boston, 1914), pp. 170-171

19. Ibid., p. 172; Ralph Adams Cram, Gothic Quest (New York, 1907), pp. 324-325. Cram particularly wished to restore Latin and logic as prescribed courses. Ralph Adams Cram, Towards the Great Peace (Boston, 1922) pp. 184-185.

20. Cram, Gothic Quest, pp. 327-328, 297-319, passim.

21. Ralph Adams Cram, Ministry, pp. 67,70.

22. Ibid., p. 79.

23. Ralph Adams Cram, Editorial in Christian Art, II (March, 1908), 306.

24. Cram, Gothic Quest, pp. 342-343. Cram deemed the late Gothic style of English architecture, with its beauty and the ideals it reified, as most appropriate for modern colleges and universities. Cram, Ministry, p. 174.

25. Letter of Richard C. Maclaurin to Ralph Adams Cram, June 20, 1914. M.I.T. Office of the President. (AC 13) Institute Archives and Special Collections, M.I.T. Libraries, Cambridge, Massachusetts. (Hereafter referred to as "AC 13.")

26. Letter of Ralph Adams Cram to Richard C. Maclaurin, June 22, 1914, ibid.

27. Bulletin of the M.I.T.: Reports of the President and Treasurer, (January, 1915) pp. 73-74.

28. Cram, My Life, pp. 208-209.

29. Ibid., pp. 210-212.
30. John T. Doran, who knew him well, tells of Cram's mesmerizing charm with his clients. An appointment with Cram almost invariably resulted in his doing most of the talking. Interview with John T. Doran, August 8, 1972.
31. Cram's unpaginated lecture notes and exams for these two courses for the years 1917, 1918, and 1920 are to be found in the Rotch Library, M.I.T. Libaries, Cambridge, Massachusetts.
32. Cram, My Life, p. 211.
33. The books were: The Ruined Abbeys of Great Britain, The Ministry of Art, Heart of Europe, The Substance of Gothic, and Walled Towns. He also assigned The Substance of Gothic as required reading for his History of Architecture course.
34. Descriptions of the pageant upon which I have drawn (unless otherwise indicated) are to be found in Cram's My Life, pp. 213-217, and "Technology Pageant," 1916 papers. (ASC 15) Institute Archives and Special Collections, M.I.T. Libraries, Cambridge, Massachusetts. (Hereafter referred to as "ASC 15.") Local newspapers--the Boston Transcript, Boston Globe, Boston Herald, Boston American, Boston Post, and Cambridge Daily Standard--devoted a good deal of coverage to the progress of this event.
35. Letter of Ralph Adams Cram to Richard C. Maclaurin, May 5, 1916, AC 13.
36. Letter of Ralph Adams Cram to Richard C. Maclaurin, May 21, 1918, ibid.
37. Letter of Ralph Adams Cram to Richard C. Maclaurin, August 25, 1919, ibid. On September 3, Cram again informed Maclaurin that he had a possible job in constructing this church. Apparently he did not obtain the leave of absence since his visit to France did not come until the winter months. Cram, My Life, p. 136. Nor did he offer any further allusion to building the French church.
38. Cram, My Life, pp. 212-213.
39. Cram, Great Peace, p. 187.
40. Ralph Adams Cram, The Nemesis of Mediocrity (Boston, 1919), p. 31. In insisting that schools had neglected their duty to inculcate "learning, culture, manners and character," in order to act as "feeders for the supreme domains of business, finance, applied science and (through law) practical politics," Cram anticipated the criticisms

162

of numerous modern educators. Ralph Adams Cram, The Sins of the Fathers (Boston, 1919), p. 55. For a brilliantly trenchant critique of business influence on higher education which paralleled Cram's, see Thorstein Veblen, The Higher Learning in America: A Memorandum on the Conduct of Universities by Business Men (New York, 1918).

41. Cram, Great Peace, pp. 172-175. He also insisted upon having young people taught about knights and knighthood during their formative years.

42. Paul Goodman, The Community of Scholars (New York, 1962). In this work Goodman uses the medieval concept of the university as a model for contemporary education.

43. Cram, Great Peace, pp. 186-187. For a fuller denunciation of the emphasis on quantitative rather than qualitative education, see Ralph Adams Cram, "Education and the Qualitative Standard," Educational Review, LVII (April, 1919), 304-311.

44. Letter of Ralph Adams Cram to Louise Imogen Guiney, September 30, 1919, Louise Imogen Papers, Holy Cross College.

45. Cram, "Lecture Notes for The Philosophy of Architecture," n.p., Rotch Library, Massachusetts Institute of Technology.

CHAPTER VII

WORLD WAR I: THE ARCHITECT AS JEREMIAH

Inveterate travelers, the Crams had planned to pass the winter of 1914-1915 in Europe, visiting friends in England and making pilgrimages to various cathedrals and churches in France and the Low Countries. When Ralph Cram received and acceded to the teaching offer from the Massachusetts Institute of Technology, he and his wife revised their plans to accommodate a brief summer sojourn. Booking passage on the Cunard line, they hurriedly prepared for their departure from Boston on August 4, 1914. For obvious reasons they did not sail on that historic day. Five years later when they did take their trip to Europe, they were still able to visit their friends, but many of the great religious shrines--Reims, Soissons, Noyon, Ypres--now lay in ruins, the result of the Great War.

There was never any real doubt in Cram's mind as to which side was "right" and deserved the victory. Through heritage and conviction he had always been a confirmed Anglophile, repeatedly stating that the United States was bound to Great Britain by the strongest ties of blood, sympathy, and tradition.[1] As he wrote to Louise Guiney in 1910: "Oh, but wasn't it good to set foot on British soil again? Why does one ever go elsewhere!"[2] Respect for its people, history, and institutions, and a love bordering on veneration for its Gothic architecture, had convinced him that Britain had achieved the highest civilization in the modern world. Shortly after the war broke out he did admit that "the skirts of no nation were clean."[3] Hostilities had resulted from certain conditions of modernism, to which, much to his distress, even Great Britain had fallen prey. Yet if each European nation shared in the making of this catastrophe, Germany alone ultimately deserved the blame.

In a public address delivered less than two months after the fighting started, Cram announced that "the whole world was threatened with the reign of Anti-Christ and the armies [were] now assembling for Armageddon. On the one side were all the powers of a

165

godless materialism, on the other all those forces that were ready to rise up in defense of Christian society.[4]   The land of the Antichrist was Germany, and, having desired the war, Kaiser Wilhelm was the Anti-Christ incarnate.   Actually, when he chose to be specific, Cram blamed the war on Prussia, not on the entire German nation.   Esteeming the culture of medieval Germany, he carefully noted that at that time Prussia was no more than a pagan, semi-civilized state.[5]   The Protestant Reformation and Prussian expansion had wrenched Germany from the path of high civilization and towards that modernism which had culminated in the grandiose imperialism of the German Empire.   "It was a dream of empire such as appeals to the parvenu," he wrote, "for Prussia is essentially a parvenu, with no ancient history, no cultural tradition comparable with those of the nations that surround her...and the heart of this Satanic dream was material supremacy founded on force and the denial of abstract right and wrong."[6]

The early events of the Great War merely confirmed the architect's passionate antipathy towards Germany.   First came the brutal violation of Belgian neutrality, whose legal guarantee her invaders had deemed "a scrap of paper."   Reports of susequent atrocities perpetrated on the civilian population only intensified his disgust.   When the great Cathedral of Reims was almost totally destroyed, he began to fear that the armed juggernauts of both sides would be unwilling to spare the religious art lying within the area between northern France and western Germany.   Nonetheless, from the outset of the war he decided that anything short of Germany's   unconditional surrender would constitute "treason against civilization."   Once the Central Powers were defeated, Germany, as well as Austria-Hungary, should be carved up until their very names disappeared from the map.   Only then could the West even dream of "a new salvation" and "an era of true enlightenment and of Christian living."[7]

Like Theodore Roosevelt, whom he greatly admired,[8] Cram chafed at the United States' refusal to become involved in the war.   Though confident that Germany would be defeated in any case, he lamented "the Great Refusal" to join the Allies.[9]   Worse, the war, in his estimation, had "produced not one man who can lead, when the world howls for leadership."   For example, he assailed the papacy for its neutrality and failure to offer any practical intervention.   He deeply feared that the fighting, if not soon terminated, would lead mankind directly into a new dark

ages.[10] By the early spring of 1916, the architect
had reached the height of his rage. Writing to Louise
Guiney, he complained: "I went on the other day for
the consecration of St. Thomas' Church, and that and
the work at the Cathedral [St. John the Divine] all
seemed to me of a piece, which is money, materialism
and expediency. Nothing more than the shreds and
patches of a real religion that has broken down through
the wickedness of man."[11] At the same time, he was so
disgusted with the nation's neutrality that he expressed a desire to leave the United States. Though
afforded the opportunity of buying a house in England,
he was beginning to believe that life in that country,
with its stumbling prosecution of the war (a condition
which he attributed to parliamentary government and
democratic practices), might not be as attractive as
he had formerly conceived. Meanwhile, as he informed
the poet, he and his wife were occupying themselves
with a variety of war relief agencies. He also admitted that his students at M.I.T., "with their idealism and their infinite possibilities," did somewhat
relieve his gloom.[12] A year later when President Wilson successfully obtained from Congress a declaration
of war against the Central Powers, Cram exulted. "At
last," he wrote Guiney, "I feel that without blushing
I can write to my friends in England. For months I
have been unable to hold up my head, my sense of national humiliation has been so great, but now even
though it is at the eleventh hour, the President has
acted magnificently and as he should have done long
ago. Congress and the whole country follows [sic]
suit and once more I feel that I belong to a nation
that is really my own."[13] A year and a half later he
learned of and applauded that unconditional surrender
of Germany that he had so vociferously demanded.
    On one level, one can view Cram simply as a
staunch partisan of the Allied cause. Casting the
drama of World War I in absolute terms of morality and
immorality, he denigrated pacifists and neutralists
alike, and found cause to rejoice only with the total
defeat of the Central Powers. This level of interpretation, while accurate, misses the richer complexity
and nuances of his thought. In addition to a variety
of articles and pamphlets, his restless pen (he refused to use a typewriter) accounted for no fewer than
six books dedicated to the questions of war and
peace.[14] What caused the war? What changes had the
war effected? What, if anything, could be salvaged
from the ruins of the holocaust? These were the ques-

167

tions which intrigued him and for which he attempted
to find answers. As the war, in his judgment, was not
a fortuitous aberration, so his views concerning it
were not isolated from the mainstream of his general
thought. To understand his mind more fully, it becomes necessary to examine those views.

Construing events narrowly, it is possible to explain the outbreak of World War I by the assassination
of the Archduke Francis Ferdinand and by the ensuing
machinations and miscalculations of so-called statesmen. Cram disagreed completely. He saw the war as
"no casual and untoward event, [but] the rash precipi-
tation in time and space of the insane illusions of
paranoiacs, the accident of industrial war, the catastrophe that might have been escaped."15 For him, the
war took on a certain air of inevitability, fittingly
having erupted at the end of one of his five-hundred-
year historical cycles. Just as the fall of Constantinople in 1453 bore dramatic witness to the end of
the previous cycle, so had World War I marked   the
culmination of the present one. It might be argued,
of course, that to liken the capture of Constantine's
city to the cataclysm of 1914-1918 was to posit a
strained analogy. Confronted directly with this objection, Cram might well have agreed, for he did admit that "nothing exactly like it [World War I] has
ever happened before...." Yet he quickly added:
"...but nothing even remotely like modern civilization
has ever happened before."16 Simply stated, a poison-
ous modern civilization had occasioned the Great War.

Cram's catalogue of what comprised modernism made
Pius IX's Syllabus of Errors seem pale in comparison.
At various times the architect included in his definition of the term: democracy, imperialism, collectivism, materialism, science, evolution, pragmatism, determinism, secular education, current styles of art,
and, certainly not least of all, Protestantism. It is
senseless to attempt to ascertain which of these manifestations he most detested--he detested them all and
saw them as interrelatedly forming a noxious whole.
As part of a single malady, moreover, they occasionally abraded one another. Indeed, it was precisely such
friction which had ignited the war:

> When, therefore, modernism achieved its
> grand climacteric in July, 1914, we had
> on the one hand an imperialism of force,
> in industry, commerce, and finance, ex-
> pressing itself through highly developed
> specialists, and dictating the policies

and practices of government, society, and education; on the other,
a democracy of form which denied,
combatted, and destroyed distinction
in personality and authority in thought,
and discouraged constructive leadership
in the intellectual, spiritual, and artistic spheres of activity. The opposition was absolute, the results catastrophic. The lack of competent leadership in every category of life finds a
sufficient explanation in the two opposed forces, in their origin and nature, and in the fact of their opposition.[17]

At this point one is sorely tempted to dismiss
Cram as a kind of Miniver Cheevy, a man who, like the
poet Edward Arlington Robinson's character, deplored
the present as he sighed for the past, particularly
the medieval past. His convictions--prejudiced and
overstated sometimes to the point of near hysteria--
violently run counter to the mainstream of modern life
in which we all, to one extent or another, are im-
mersed. Yet beneath the shrillness of his tirades re-
sides a certain noteworthy perception and cogency, by
no means irrelevant to the twentieth century. The
warnings and advice of a Jeremiah are neither popular
nor, by definition, heeded. Still, such a person
might have something useful, even vital to say.

For Cram, the Middle Ages was the touchstone by
which one compared and judged societies, past and
present:

During the Middle Ages, when the ideal
of democracy was at its highest point,
and when it was most nearly achieved, it
was held as incontrovertible that the
purpose of political organization was
primarily ethical and moral, and that
its function was the achievement of
righteousness and justice. Authority
was from God, and the power also to enforce that authority, but both were
held operative only when they were used
for right ends....
Equally unquestioned was the fact that
law was not made, but was the concrete
expression of that morality, right and
justice that had grown with the life of
the community, exactly expressing the

169

needs of society, and with the moral
sanction of communal life behind it.[18]
Further contrasting the medieval ethos with that of
the modern age, he reflected: "The Middle Ages had
nothing of imperialism about them; Cecil Rhodes or
J. P. Morgan or Kaiser Wilhelm would have perished of
inaction and lack of employment. Bigness was not an
obsession, rather the reverse, and they possessed the
secret of making the materially small thing spiritually great...they had sense of scale, and scale is proportion, and proportion is a just estimate of comparative values,--the thing above others in which Medievalism excelled."[19] The Middle Ages had indeed been
nothing less than the pursuit of perfection.

With the advent of the Renaissance and Reformation, however, the seeds of modernism were planted and
the pursuit of perfection as an end in itself yielded
to pleonexia--the insatiable, relentless drive for
sheer power. For Cram, Machiavelli and Luther, sym-
bols of these historical forces, "invented and justi-
fied and popularized autocratic government, so destroying the old Medieval democracy."[20] Tainted as it
was, he could at least accept the art of the Renaissance and dismiss its immorality as but a materializa-
tion of its inherent paganism. His special wrath he
reserved for the Reformation, maintaining that it had
undermined the spiritual and material unity of Christendom. Subverting the sacramental system, foisting
the concept of predestination upon the masses (he apparently failed or was unwilling to understand that
there had been and are still Catholics who willingly
accept this doctrine), and diminishing the theological
legitimacy of good works, Protestantism represented
the greater evil. Moreover--and here he accepted the
theses advanced by Max Weber and R. H. Tawney--it had
been responsible for capitalism's birth and growth,
and its subsequent perversion of manufacturing goods
for profit rather than consumption. Material things
were once subordinate to ideals; now the situation was
reversed, as evidenced by the present state of schools
and churches. "The material end, the material means,
and the surrender to materialism," he wrote, "are the
finally distinguishing marks of modernism."[21] Should
particularly dull-minded readers have failed to see
any causal connection between Protestantism and World
War One, he reminded them that Germany had been the
home of the Reformation. Proving that his prejudices
were by no means confined to Protestants, he added:
"It is the Protestant nations and their enclaves of

170

Jews that built up that materialistic civilization that in its bloated triumph finds its own nemesis in the war of the last five years...."[22]

Closely related to the twin evils of capitalism and materialism was that of imperialism, "the fruition of the quantitative in all things," and the last and most perfect expression of the current historical cycle. Imperialism was not a new phenomenon --Cram actually admitted that even the Crusaders had been guilty of it--but in its modern context, dating, in his opinion, from the late eighteenth century, it had become particularly pernicious.[23] It represented, moreover, the exact antithesis of democracy. As he explained: "The essence of imperialism is aggregation, with the working downward of delegated authority from a high and omnipotent source. The essence of democracy is differentiation, local autonomy, and a building up of authority from primary units."[24] Posed in these therms, the two were inveterately opposed to one another. Yet this "comparatively real democracy" expounded by Hampden, Rousseau, and Jefferson "long ago became merely a collection of literary remains, an archaeological abstraction" and has given way to a false democracy, guilty of perpetually trying to make itself more democratic.[25] As imperialism was the antithesis of what Cram called "the democracy of the ideal," the true democracy, the latter, in turn, was the polar opposite of what he termed "the democracy of method," the false democracy. Modern times had witnessed the unholy alliance between imperialism and "the democracy of the unfit." But this false democracy was at once the succor and bane of imperialism. Misguided in its assumption of the wisdom of the masses, it sometimes blindly supported and augmented imperialistic tendencies, but on other occasions balked at accepting the leadership of an (imperialist) elite. The synchronizing of these two malignant forces, claimed Cram, went far to explain the outbreak of the war.[26]

As applied to Cram, "anti-democrat" is an epithet easily understood by a cursory reading of some of his works. Yet he considered himself a genuine democrat, at least within the terms of his definition. Far from refuting it, he considered the right kind of democracy to be "the noblest ideal ever discovered by man or revealed to him."[27] This democracy consisted of three elements: (1) the abolition of privilege, (2) equal opportunity for all, and (3) the utilization of ability. (His belief that these ele-

171

ments comprised the "democracy" of the Middle Ages, of course, was one of his grossest historical distortions.) Once this was clearly understood, the particular form of government adopted by a society was relatively unimportant. Unfortunately, the modern world had failed to differentiate between democracy as a means and democracy as an end: "One of the chief faults with what we call our democracy is our stolid failure to understand that there is a democratic ideal and a democratic method, that there is not necessarily any connection between the two, and that generally speaking the democratic method (unstable, constantly changing its form) is incapable of accomplishing the democratic ideal."[28] With the demise of this ideal in the mid-nineteenth century, the Western world increasingly turned to representative government, the party system, the secret ballot, the popular election of senators, rotation in office, female suffrage, and the initiative, referendum, and recall. Repeating Emile Faguet's acute observation that the French Revolution had replaced "<u>Votre Majesté</u>" with "<u>Votre Majorité</u>," Cram insisted that not one of these would-be reforms had hastened the second coming, as it were, of the ideal democracy. On the contrary, they were counterproductive, and governments had become more irresponsible.[29] "'The world must be made safe for democracy' is a noble phrase," he readily assented, "but it is meaningless without its corollary, 'democracy must be made safe for the world.'" "For exactly one hundred years," he concluded, "democracy has suffered a progressive deterioration until it is now not a blessing but a menace."[30] His explanation and elaborations notwithstanding, it is not difficult to understand how Cram won his reputation as a foe of democracy.

Related to the problem of democracy was the one posed by leadership. Indeed, the two were linked inextricably since the ideal democracy could not function without strong leadership. Since he insisted on the primacy of this leadership, one can readily understand the usual classification of Cram as an elitist. The masses had their rights, to be sure; but these rights could only be secured through the assistance and tutelage of virtuous, gifted leaders. The architect argued that each cycle of history had at its inception but a limited amount of spiritual, that is to say, positive energy. Much of this energy was embodied in great leaders, who then somehow refined and transmitted it to the masses and led them toward de-

172

sirable goals. As the five-hundred-year epoch waned, so, too, did its spiritual energy, and with the dissipation of this energy came degeneracy and ultimate dissolution, culminating in the birth of a new era and a new dominant wave of forces. As the present epoch was drawing to its violent close, Cram saw that "in spite of academic aphorisms on Equality, a dim consciousness survives of the fundamental truth that without strong leadership culture and even civilization will pass away."[31]

Cram denied the contention that the masses, by definition, rejected all forms of leadership. What they rejected--and quite rightly, he thought--was the inferior leader, the "specious demagogue," the "unscrupulous master of effrontery." Still, when left to their own devices (the democracy of method), they did choose leaders who were more or less in their own image. For some reason, he felt that the West between 1880 and 1905 had been filled with outstanding leaders--"immortals," as he called them. Ten years or so later--and here his judgment defies understanding--the masses had brought to power the likes of Giolitti, MacDonald, Caillaux, La Follette, and Lenin. Most of the qualified leaders, meanwhile, had entered business rather than politics or statecraft, thus further depriving a world woefully in need of moral direction. While admitting that the war probably could not have been averted in any case, he warned: "When, as now, the greatest crisis in fifteen centuries overpasses the world, and society sinks under the nemesis of universal mediocrity, then we realize that the system has doomed itself, since, impotent to produce leaders, it has signed its own death warrant."[32] Though the chemistry of war eventually was bound to produce new leaders, he wondered whether the world could wait that long.[33]

One might legitimately ask at this point how the Allies could possibly have won World War I while laboring under a system which had failed to produce proper leadership. For Cram, the answer was simple (much too simple, in fact). They had emerged victorious because they had sloughed off the democracy of method--the method guaranteed to secure second-rate leaders--in favor of "a pure and perfectly irresponsible absolutism," either of one man or of a coterie. Even Great Britain and the United States, the most democratic of the world's nations, had turned to autocracies "that would make Constantine, Henry VIII and Louis XIV hang their heads...."[34] While the case of the United States was instructive in illuminating how little the war had augmented leadership, President Wilson had provided the exception to the rule. Having followed the muddleheaded vagaries of majority rule which had dictated a policy of neutrality for nearly three years, he gradually bypassed a debilitating democratic method in favor of an efficacious personal leadership. Writing of Wilson in 1917, Cram predicted: "If he wills he may become the coordinating, the directing, and the constructive force in the world, Arbiter of Democracy, re-creator of the true democracy of ideal." In a postscript written two years later he continued to cast the president as Superman: "...for the moment at least--all issues have been pooled in one extraordinary Personality who has become a kind of super-leader, universal dictator, Manager of the World --the adequate phrase does not suggest itself."[35] The Allies, saddled with an unholy alliance between a deficient democracy and an ersatz dictatorship, had somehow managed to win the war. It remained to be seen whether or not they could win the peace.

Almost as soon as the war had begun, Cram put forth his ideas for a just settlement. Germany and Austria-Hungary were to be truncated into smaller units, with territorial manipulations made on the basis of national and religious considerations. Turkey would cede Constantinople to Russia, and Poland, having existed only as a geographical name since the late eighteenth century, would be reconstituted as a kingdom. As he euphorically exclaimed in a public address: "The Kingdom of Poland lives again." Indeed, one of his principal projections was the future establishment of kingdoms, as opposed to republics. Appealing to current American prejudices, he cited the case of Mexico, then in near chaos, to buttress his argument.

As the war drew to its conclusion, Cram's views regarding the settlement, though broadened, remained substantially the same, except that Russia, on the verge of falling to the Bolsheviks, was no longer to receive Constantinople. The crux of the problem remained Germany and Austria-Hungary, and he continued to envision partition without annexation as the only means of avoiding another holocaust. First, however, these two defeated powers must relinquish certain territories to which their claims were not clearly justifiable: Alsace-Lorraine, Schleswig-Holstein, and Trentino. The architect was in full agreement with President Wilson's concern that the principle of self-

determination for subject-nationals be respected.
Afterwards, the two Central Powers would be divided
into five autonomous states.   This partition, argued
Cram, did not reflect a vindictive spirit; it represented future security for both the winners and the
losers of the war. A fragmented Germany--he was less
concerned with the military potential of Austria-
Hungary--was a Germany unable to wage aggressive war.
While the statesmen at Versailles, for all their re-
vanchist feelings, did not arrive at this extreme conclusion, those who made the peace after World War II
did. For Cram, the model for a reconstructed Central
Europe, moreover, was to be either the Holy Roman
Empire of the Middle Ages or the German Confederation
which succeeded the Empire in the nineteenth century
but which preceded Prussia's most flagrantly expansive
thrusts.   In place of autocracy, <u>Mitteleuropa</u> was to
consist of "small, compact, self-contained and autonomous states conceived in human scale."[36]
     To supervise the settlement and to attempt to pre-
serve the peace, Cram called for the establishment of
an international body, similar to, but not identical
with, what emerged as the League of Nations.   While it
struggled with the economic and social problems that
beset war-torn Europe, this "Congress of Ambassadors"
concomitantly would formulate and enforce international law.[37] As to just how much actual power the Congress was to exercise, he equivocated.   In 1918 he
believed that it should be able to arbitrate, though
its decisions would not be binding, and might "inter-
vene"--though this is left vague--if one or another
state acted criminally. The following year he seemed
more willing to give the right of military intervention to the Congress.[38] His hesitation in according
effective, that is, military power to an international body reflects his fear of bigness. Defending the
ideal of nationalism, despite his recognition that
nationalist aspirations had contributed mightily to
fomenting the war, he decried the establishment of any
body which would diminish the autonomy of smaller,
localized political units. To invest all military
power in such an agency would precipitate tyranny and
"Super Imperialism." With territorial units not ex-
ceeding fifty million people or two hundred thousand
square miles (a situation possible should civil war
and anarchy leave Russia decentralized), and with
these states abolishing their standing armies in favor
of programs of universal military training, there
would be no need further to diminish local sovereign-

ty.[39] After all, he argued: "The world is not to be remade by a shuffling and new disposition of old material; it is not to be remade even through the discovery of some new principle or the fabricating of a new set of mechanical toys; it is to be remade, if at all, only through the releasing of old spiritual energies."[40]

No matter what kind of Congress or League of Nations was established, Cram had no expectation that future wars would not take place.[41] For the immediate future he was most pessimistic, seeing the Allied victory as quite inconclusive. The Treaty of Versailles, far from having secured a lasting peace, had created "a condition of unstable equilibrium constantly tending by its very nature to a point where dissolution is apparently inevitable."[42] Sensing that the world was currently dominated by the equally malefic but opposed forces of reactionaries and Bolsheviks, he warned: "The best that one can say, if peace really comes again and man returns once more to his old ways of life, is that the return will be for the briefest of periods. The war is only the first of a series, for one war cannot undo the cumulated errors of five centuries."[43] He anticipated another major war very shortly, one whose casus belli would be the injustices wrought by the capitalist system. Immediately following or perhaps even merging with this second global conflict would be a third war fought between the forces of the false democracy and what remained of the true democracy, the democracy of the ideal. "From these three visitations," prophesied Cram, who now had indeed become a Jeremiah, "there is no escape."[44] Actually, he held out one slim hope that the world (meaning the West) could be saved from "a fate it richly deserves": it must uproot and utterly destroy the pernicious effects of modernism.[45]

Even before its outcome had been assured, he concluded that the Great War would mean two things: "that the world after the war will be, for good or ill, an entirely new world; and second, that every preconceived idea of the man of the nineteenth century must now submit itself to the process of re-estimation."[46] Less concerned with any peace settlement that would conclude the war, he stressed the dire necessity of reevaluating and transvaluating the cherished ideas, institutions, and practices which had characterized the West on the eve of the fighting. If to be a radical implies going to the root of the matter, that label fit Cram very well.

176

One of the major changes he believed the war had effected was to undermine faith in evolutionary philosophy. The change was a welcome one, for the carnage had proved evolution to be a "fable," the notion of progress a "delusion," and the concept of human perfectability a "dream."[47] A general and misplaced faith in the truth and efficacy of evolution had prevented man from perceiving the dangerous drift of events and, because he tended to accept progress as inevitable, from being able to distinguish clearly between good and evil. Social Darwinism, moreover, had fostered a bloated sense of material values, a cynical philosophy of might makes right, and a general acceptance of so-called enlightened self-interest. All of this, in turn, was related to the dangerous conviction that mass, secularized education would necessarily yield ameliorative fruits. Had Social Darwinists known what Hanry Adams (and Cram) had known about the dissipation and degradation of force and energy--that it rendered evolution impossible--they would have saved themselves and the world a good deal of trouble.[48]

With his strong attacks on Social Darwinism, as well as persistent barbs against eugenics,[49] one might logically suppose that Cram would have inveighed against the omnipresent racism of his time. The contrary was true. Judging from his scattered references to the subject, he seems to have imbibed some of the prepossessions of a Madison Grant or a Lothrop Stoddard.[50] From the 1890's until approximately the outbreak of the war, he can best be described as an Anglo-Saxon culturalist; with the war, however, he, like so many of his countrymen, fell prey to a growing prejudice based on race.

In the midst of the war, Cram began to despair that with the recent influx of the New Immigrants and mixed breeding, "just and normal barriers of race" were being destroyed. "Continued for another generation or two," he warned, "the result can only be universal mongrelism and the consequent end of culture and civilization." There was no way of avoiding the facts: genes were destiny. Sympathetically but stridently as well, he wrote: "There is no tragedy greater than that of the human soul full of promise and potency and desire of good things, imprisoned in the forbidding circle of mongrel blood, inimical inheritance and pernicious environment against which it desperately rebels, but from which there is no possibility of escape except through the power of supernatural

177

assistance on which it no longer possesses the impulse or will to call."[51] Freely admitting that his views flaunted humanitarian sentiments, democratic thought, and, unless properly understood, Christianity itself, he singled out various racial and ethnic groups as being "static" or "retrogressive": the Hottentots, Malays, American Indians, and mixed bloods such as the Mexican peons and Mongol-Slavs. They did, however, as he gratuitously observed, have souls.[52] For these people, he appears to have had more pity than contempt; for Jews, the reverse held true. It was not that Jews lacked ability--far from it. It was the uses to which they put their ability. Thus, when he raged against "the pacifist-internationalist-Israelitish 'League of Free Nations'" and "the clutching fangs of imperial finance and Jewish internationalism," he was castigating that group for its supposed immorality, not inferiority.[53]

Though mongrelization and the "low mentality and character-content of millions of immigrants and their offspring" had already adversely affected the nation, it was not too late to act.[54] Cram suggested that certain races and classes of persons--which ones he did not specify--be excluded from entering the country. Towards this end he proposed strengthening naturalization laws. With the blessings of the architect and countless others, Congress did enact a series of bills during the 1920's which had the effect of slamming shut the doors of entry to millions of prospective immigrants from southern and eastern Europe. Congress, however, stopped short of enacting one of Cram's most extreme proposals, the prohibition of intermarriage for certain (but unspecified) racial groups. Nor did they accede to his suggestion that persons not be allowed to conceal their ethnic identity by changing their names. As far as Cram was concerned, Leon Trotsky should have remaind Lev Bronstein.[55]

Cram's overall theory of social organization rested precariously on the acceptance of inherent and inherited differences between groups as well as individuals. Environmental influences counted for little in comparison to the innate inequality in human potential. In this age of the false democracy it was imperative for a true aristocracy, an "aristocracy of character," to assume leadership. While he admitted that the Christian influence was paramount in forming such character, he also insisted that the racial factor was by no means unimportant.[56] Having begun by attacking the general tenets of the Social Darwinists,

178

he ended by espousing their racism. The fact that
these views were shared, in all likelihood, by a ma-
jority--probably even by a majority of the educated--
cannot negate the conclusion that, from an intellectual and moral standpoint, they did not form one of
his finer efforts.

Harmful as its suppositions and results had been,
Social Darwinism was only a sympton of the more deeply
rooted maladies of imperialism and capitalism. Though
Cram could not conceive that Europe and the United
States would freely give up the reality and aspirations of empire, he warned: "Democracy--vital and
righteous and constructive democracy--is incompatible
either with imperialism or with 'big business and high
finance.' Either imperialism must go, in government,
in industry and in finance, or democracy in any form
must be abandoned."[57] He added: "...'class consciousness' is the direct and inevitable result of the
imperial scale in life which has annihilated the social unit of human scale and brought in the gigantic
aggregations of peoples, money, manufacture and la-
bourers, where man can no longer function either as a
human unit or an essential factor in a workable society." Society now had two alternatives: it could
continue to grow and ultimately destroy itself, or it
could return to a smaller state of organization, the
"human scale."[58]

In considering the current state of the world,
Cram could find little evidence of an operative human
scale. On the contrary, he discerned the predominance
of intensified bigness or collectivism in state socialism, the League of Nations, and Bolshevism. In
his opinion--an opinion shared by few critics--even
the United States seemingly had become a convert to
state socialism. Having shed almost all remaining
vestiges of democracy, either of the "true" or "false"
variety, the nation during the war had embraced an un-
wholesome form of collectivism and had established an
imperial government with a dictator at its head.[59]
As for the League, while agreeing to the necessity of
some form of supranational agency to maintain international law, he regarded it as essentially a perpetra-
tor of the very evil--imperialism--it purported to
attack. He tersely reasoned: "Collectivism is imperialistic in its essence and imperialism is its
goal."[60]

Though the state socialism of the United States
and the collectivism of the League of Nations were
bad, Bolshvism was worse. Cram had been horrified by

179

the deposition of the Czar and the subsequent turmoil in Russia which had eventuated in the success of the Bolsheviks. Any revolution which first destroyed society's fabric and then thrust forward "the ingenious substitutes of ambitious and presumptuous Frankensteins," was dreadful, but the Russian Revolution seemed particularly so.[61] The victors had established the "Servile State" and had denied all law, both human and divine. They had begun as revolutionaries by rightfully warring against the non-human or large scale of life, but then had failed completely to recognize individual differences, to respect rights of property, or to interest themselves in non-quantitave, that is to say, spiritual matters. Further, by enthroning "the autocracy of the proletariat," they merely had brought forth another variant of imperialism.[62] Cram feared that the West was being impaled on the horns of a dilemma: either it must return to the status quo antebellum and thereby exacerbate political, economic, and social conditions, or it must ultimately move from state socialism to Bolshevism.[63] Fearful of Bolshevism, he became increasingly concerned with the rash of strikes which erupted throughout the United States in 1919. He thought that "Massachusetts did well" in crushing the Boston police strike of that year and hoped that "what happened here stiffened the whole country." In a letter to his friend, the retired army general Rush C. Hawkins, he voiced his opinion that "the administration at Washington has become conscious of the peril that overhangs us, and I personally believe (though I have little sympathy with Woodrow Wilson,) that they will fight the thing through to a finish."[64] Cram need not have worried. Attorney General A. Mitchell Palmer was already conducting the first of his infamous raids on suspected subversives. The Red Scare was in full swing.[65]

While condemning both state socialism and Bolshevism as a false paradise for labor, Cram was fully cognizant of the damage inflicted on the workingman by capitalism. In this respect his views often seemed remarkably similar to those of another trenchant critic of the capitalist system, Thorstein Veblen.[66]

While Cram pointed to the Middle Ages as the optimum period for the workers, Veblen looked toward an earlier primitive stage of development. During this period, the economist argued, simply organized, self-sufficient groups, though poor, enjoyed the fruits of peace and managed to avoid most of the violence and aggression which characterized later societies. Their

180

lives, like those of Cram's serfs, were marked by a
certain innocence. Neither Cram nor Veblen was arguing that the twentieth-century worker would do best
to return to serfdom or primitivism. They were suggesting, however, that the modern labor problem had
become critical. Both saw at the heart of this problem
the sheer boredom and meaninglessness of the industrial worker's efforts. What was lamentably lacking in
a technologically oriented society was for the architect the "holiness and joy of work," and for the
economist "the instinct of workmanship." Both saw
clearly the link between labor-saving machinery and the
economic expansion which had resulted in imperialism.[67]
Though Cram unreservedly detested the machine, while
Veblen was ambivalent,[68] the two also concurred in
their denunciation of production for profit only.
Cram strongly seconded Veblen's castigation of conspicuous consumption and conspicuous emulation,[69] and
called for an end to the proliferation of non-essen-
tial goods in a society, many of whose members suffered
from abject poverty. In the architect's opinion, only
a quarter of the nation's total labor force were engaged in the production of necessities.[70] The respective positions of both Cram and Veblen are vulnerable
to attack from a variety of points of view. Neither,
however, can be faulted for the sincerity and timeli-
ness of his attacks on the modern problems of capital
and labor.

Cram viewed the capitalist system as ultimately
"wasteful, artificial, illogical, unsocial, and therefore vicious." He thought (and hoped) that "imperial
industry" was toppling from its own deficiencies of
overproduction, too much credit, and internecine class
warfare. Anticipating the frightful results of the
1929 crash and ensuing Great Depression, he predicted
in the early 1920's that the collapse was imminent,
that it would affect the entire world, and that it was
currently prevented only by a false sense of optimism.[71] The sole means of averting a worldwide economic catastrophe, he warned, was a return to small,
self-sufficient units of economic production akin to
those of the medieval manor. Emphasizing the need for
the human scale, he wished to reduce modern man's de-
pendency on the factory, the machine, and the division
of labor. Since state socialism only exacerbated existing problems by adding to economic bigness and
contravening ideal democracy, he proposed the resuscitation of the guild system as a prelude to the abolition of usury, private banks, and insurance companies,

all pillars of capitalism and exploitation. He stressed, however, that the guilds themselves must be established on the human rather than imperial scale, fearing that large guilds might develop into facsimiles of modern trade unions, which he deplored almost as much as he did the businessmen who had built and sustained the present system of economics. As he mordantly noted: "Trade unionism is fighting for its life and thereafter for world conquest."[72] Until the nation fully rejected capitalism, Cram urged, in addition to guilds, such related measures as the increased use of consumer cooperatives, an improvement in union leadership, and something which would gain greater popularity in the 1930's, a return to rural living and agrarian pursuits.[73]

Despite all the detailed advice he offered gratis to a troubled world, Cram continued to despair for its prospects. Tinkering with the system simply was not sufficient. What must change was the fundamental way one looked at matters: "The whole of our world today is rooted and grounded in intellect. Our machinery, our institutions, our great systems, the entire body of enterprise is governed by brains."[74] Since Cram himself was an intellectual, this outburst of anti-intellectualism requires some explanation. He by no means objected to the life of the mind. What he did remonstrate against--and here he was in good company-- was the belief in the unlimited effectiveness of reason. The intellect, functioning without such non-intellectual components as faith, intuition, and feeling, was too limited.[75] More specifically, what he desired was a wholesale return to religion, specifically, to a unified Christianity. If the world were to be saved at all, he flatly declared, Catholicism would have to be "the saving motive."[76] However, while proffering the means of redemption to the individual, Catholicism had been a negligible force in society and politics since at least the end of the Renaissance and Reformation. Its failure to assume a powerful public role had constituted the world's greatest disaster since the fall of the Roman Empire.[77]

If Catholicism were "the saving motive" for the world, monasticism was to operate as its "divine agency."[78] Historically, monasticism had developed along clearly discernible lines of organization. It had been personified initially by individuals (hermits), and then, growing more institutionally complex, in the forms of the family (Benedictines), the state (Cluniacs and Cistercians), and the army (Jesuits).

182

Moreover, the appearance of these more complex examples, by synchronizing with the ebbing of successive five-hundred-year cycles, seemed to sustain Cram's vibratory theory of history. With another cycle about to end, he posited a recrudescence of monasticism, hoping that one of the positive results of the war might be a greater willingness on the part of society to accept the traditional monastic vows of poverty, chastity, and obedience, as transmogrified by him for use in secular life.[79]

One of Cram's greatest fears--one which has subsequently metamorphosed into reality--was that of mass society. Both imperialism, with its inherent expansionist drives, and that kind of democracy, the democracy of method, which failed to take cognizance of individual differences, increasingly were destroying localized and primary units of human association and forcing people to become parts of mass aggregations. Put simply: urbanization was accelerating. To reverse this process of accretion and also to encourage the social practices of Christianity, the architect urged the Christian family to exile itself to a "voluntary concentration camp."[80] For the Christian who was beset by the evils of modernism, it was time to retreat to Walled Towns.

While walled towns formed a familiar scene in the landscape of the Middle Ages, Cram's advocacy of their use as a refuge against modern conditions was novel.[81] His Walled Towns, published in 1919, remains one of his most significant contributions to the intellectual history of the wartime period, as well as one of the more important of all his books.[82] Part of the inspiration for these self-sufficient communes resulted from an inspired conception, based both on fact and fancy, of what had constituted a typical medieval walled town; the rest stemmed from his intense dissatisfaction with modern life. Nostalgically recalling the youthful days spent at his grandfather's farm and "the old patriarchal life of the New England countryside...before the juggernaut that crushed wholesome society and sane living had begun its fatal course," he rebelled against the growing urbanism which was both cause and symptom of the modern condition.[83] Even those who did not share his medieval bias, so he believed, would be attracted to the idea of a walled town, whose appeal "will be primarily social, the revolt of man against the imperial scale, against a life of false values impregnably intrenched behind custom, superstition and self-interest, against the quantitative standard, the tyranny of bulk, the gross oppression of majorities. It will echo a demand for beauty in life and of life, for the reasonable and wholesome unit of human scale, for high values in ideal and in action, for simplicity and distinction and a realization of true aristocracy."[84]

The history of communistic societies in the United States, while not an unqualified failure, has scarcely been one of success. From the religiously oriented establishments of the Shakers and Rappites to the secular, anti-capitalist ventures of Robert Owen at New Harmony, the Roycrofters in upstate New York, and the Ruskin Commonwealth in Tennessee, American communes have evoked neither a true utopia nor the millennium.[85] Cram was aware of the disappointing yield from these harvests, but was not discouraged. In the first place, unlike most of these previous societies, his walled towns would scrupulously respect individuality, the integrity of the family, and private property. In addition, while various Christian denominations might people these towns, sacramentalism would be exalted in order to act as a unifying force among these various religious groups. This was another way of saying that ultimately Christians would find reunion within a reformed Roman Catholic Church.[86] Given these special secular and religious twists, there seemed no reason why the towns should not prove successful.

Walled towns were expected to fulfill their several obligations to existing levels of government--taxes, military service, jury duty, for example. Yet they would also be responsible for organizing their own local and independent systems of government and education, which would presumably reflect the ideas and values which Cram had advanced so painstakingly in his writings and lectures. Above all, they would serve as havens for those who wished to pass safely through the Scylla of capitalism and the Charybdis of Bolshevism. Appalled by its growing radicalization, Cram feared that labor was turning in desperation to Bolshevism, not realizing that this "cure" would eventually prove worse than the capitalist disease itself. On the other hand, should workers reject Bolshevism, a strong possibility of economic and social collapse would still remain. By setting up a system of production geared to utility rather than profit, as well as a guild system, walled towns appeared to be man's best hope for the foreseeable future. Summing up his arguments, Cram, the architect acting as Old Testament

184

prophet, exhorted: "Evil imperial in scale cannot be blotted out by reforms imperial in method. The old way was the good way, the way of withdrawal and of temporary isolation. 'To your tents, O Israel!'"[87] Buoyed by the force of his impassioned arguments, he fully anticipated that the tents would soon be filled.[88] However, his prophetic call was answered only by its own echo. Well, not quite. At least one voice--and a strong one at that--could be heard in support of his plea. In 1912 the vagabond poet Vachel Lindsay traversed the country, spreading his "Gospel of Beauty" and messianically calling for a better way of life. Some years later he espoused a "New Localism," which was supposed to engender self-sustaining economic communities and be conducive to an arts and crafts movement. In "Springfield's Ancient Mariner" (Lindsay himself was the Mariner), which forms an important part of his 1920 futuristic novel, The Golden Book of Springfield, he acknowledged his indebtedness to Cram.[89] Springfield, Lindsay's mythical city, was to be a bastion of civilization protected from evils outside by a series of star-shaped double walls, one set of which was named for Cram. Intending Springfield as a model for future American cities, the troubador poet, like Cram, included in his blueprints for his walled town a gigantic cathedral as a symbol of man's highest aspirations. There is no indication that Cram was ever aware of the influence he exerted on Lindsay. More unfortunate, a poet does not a quorum, much less a majority make. Neither immediately after the publication of Walled Towns nor during the remainder of his lifetime was the architect to see the development of any substantial communitarian society.

The war was over, and perhaps the best that could be said for a shattered West was that it survived. Yet as far as Cram was concerned, much of what survived should have perished. Imperialism seemed not only to have remained intact, but actually to have grown. The war, moreover, had given an impetus to state socialism and had made possible the fruition of Bolshevism in Europe's largest country. In the United States, much to his disgust, the people, while at least temporarily rejecting state socialism and Bolshevism, appeared to have hailed and followed their president in a return to normalcy. Though he announced "the great World's Fair of multiplied, ingenious mechanisms we have called 'modern civilization'" to be "at a point of practical bankruptcy,"[90] the forces of modernism everywhere remained ascendant. Jeremiah's

warnings had proved feckless, for like the Bourbons,
the West seemingly had learned and forgotten nothing.

NOTES

1. Ralph Adams Cram, "The Influence of the French School on American Architecture," The American Architect and Building News, LXVI, (November 25, 1899), 66; Ralph Adams Cram, The Ministry of Art (Boston, 1914), p. 176.
2. Letter of Ralph Adams Cram to Louise Imogen Guiney, August 17, 1910, Louise Imogen Guiney Papers, Holy Cross College. Always the Francophobe, he added in this same letter: "And why, of all places, does one ever go to this shattered and crumbling France, toppling on the perilous edge of deep damnation?"
3. Ralph Adams Cram, The Significance of the Great War (Boston, 1914), p. 12.
4. Ibid.
5. Ralph Adams Cram, Thomas Hastings, and Claude Bragdon, Six Lectures on Architecture (Chicago, 1917), p. 26.
6. Cram, Great War, pp. 10-11.
7. Ibid., pp. 16, 18-19, 22; Ralph Adams Cram, "Cathedrals Under the War Cloud," Everybody's Magazine, 31 (December, 1914), 782. For a later and fuller lamentation of the destruction of European art and architecture wrought by the war, see Ralph Adams Cram, Heart of Europe (New York, 1915).
8. In 1910 Cram wrote that Roosevelt had been attempting to do for national self-consciousness what he was attempting to do for artistic expression--namely, to induce a spiritual regeneration. Ralph Adams Cram, "The Relation of Architecture to the People," Supplement to Art and Progress, I (July, 1910), 19.
9. Cram, Heart of Europe, pp. 11-12.
10. Letter of Ralph Adams Cram to Louise Imogen Guiney, October 22, 1915, Guiney Papers.
11. Letter of Ralph Adams Cram to Louise Imogen Guiney, May 12, 1916, ibid. Workers were beginning to break ground for the nave at St. John's, but he did not believe that the work would progress very far.
12. Ibid.
13. Letter of Ralph Adams Cram to Louise Imogen Guiney, April 7, 1917, ibid.
14. These books were: Heart of Europe (1915), The

Nemesis of Mediocrity (1917), Gold, Frankincense
and Myrrh (1919), The Sins of the Fathers (1919),
Walled Towns (1919), and Towards the Great Peace
(1922).

15. Ralph Adams Cram, The Sins of the Fathers (Boston,
    1919), pp. 2-3.
16. Ralph Adams Cram, The Substance of Gothic (Boston,
    1917), p. 12.
17. Ralph Adams Cram, Towards the Great Peace (Boston,
    1922), p. 20.
18. Ralph Adams Cram, The Nemesis of Mediocrity (Bos-
    ton, 1919), pp. 27-28. Cram's call for excellence
    in this book did not go entirely unheeded. At the
    end of his pamphlet, The Significance of Gothic
    Art (Boston, 1918), there appears the following
    praise from Senator Albert J. Beveridge: "I wish
    the 'Nemesis of Mediocrity' might be in the hands
    of every thoughtful man and woman, young and old,
    in the United States." At least one person, how-
    ever, who described himself as "an Obscure Medio-
    crity," strongly dissented from Beveridge's view.
    He sarcastically predicted, for example, that
    Cram's phrase--"Renaissance, Reformation and Rev-
    olution"--might become as egregious as "Rum, Ro-
    manism and Rebellion," the unfortunate expression
    offered by the Reverend Samuel Burchard which may
    very well have cost James G. Blaine the presiden-
    tial election of 1884. Frederick W. Stevens ,
    Observations by an Obscure Mediocrity, on a Re-
    cently Published Brochure Entitled "The Nemesis
    of Mediocrity" (Ann Arbor, Michigan, 1918), p. 8.
19. Cram, Significance of Gothic Art, p. 15. He ad-
    mitted on more than one occasion that medieval
    practices did not always live up to medieval the-
    ory, but insisted that the deficiencies were not
    as marked as those of other ages. See, for ex-
    ample, Ralph Adams Cram, "What Is Civilization,"
    The Forum, LXXIII (March, 1925), 357.
20. Ralph Adams Cram, Architecture in Its Relation to
    Civilization (Boston, 1918), p. 28.
21. Cram, Sins, pp. 102-103, 77-78.
22. Ralph Adams Cram, Gold, Frankincense and Myrrh
    (Boston, 1919), pp. 51-52, 84. For other in-
    stances of Cram's anti-Semitism, see The Nemesis
    of Mediocrity, pp. 10-16. Bigoted statements not-
    withstanding, his prejudice against Jews apparent-
    ly was not totally pervasive (see Chapter VIII).
    Like the Populists, he tended to stigmatize Jews
    not for their religion, but as symbols of capital-

istic exploitation.

23. Cram, _Sins_, pp. 46, 19.
24. Ibid., p. 17.
25. Ibid., p. 16. One should not be misled by his praise of these three men into thinking that he fully accepted the concept of natural rights. Partial to the theory of natural law favored by the Middle Ages, he was generally suspicious of natural rights, detesting them when supported and interpreted by individuals such as John Locke, Adam Smith, Jeremy Bentham, and the Manchester liberals. In the hands of the latter, natural rights had served to foster the voracious appetite of economic self-aggrandizement of both individuals and nations. Cram, _Great Peace_, pp. 115-116.
26. Cram, _Sins_, pp. 65-66.
27. Cram, _Nemesis_, p. 23.
28. Ibid.
29. Ibid., pp. 24-30, passim.
30. Ibid., p. 22.
31. Ibid., pp. 47-49, 5-6. In a phrase often used by Irving Babbitt, another "anti-democrat," Cram (p. 6) saw true leaders as exercising a "centripetal force" for the cohesion of society. He also uses the word "nemesis" in roughly the same context as the Harvard professor and New Humanist did.
32. Ibid., pp. 7-9, 31, 45-46.
33. Cram, _Walled Towns_ (Boston, 1919), pp. 24-25.
34. Cram, _Nemesis_, p. 24; Cram, _Sins_, p. 16.
35. Cram, _Nemesis_, pp. 18-20, 54. He also had some praise for the Allied military chiefs in general, but singled out Theodore Roosevelt, who had died in 1919, as a particularly gifted leader whose death was a terrible loss for the world (pp. 53-54). After his role in the failure of the United States to join the League of Nations, Cram's ardor for Wilson cooled considerably.
36. Ralph Adams Cram, _A Plan for the Settlement of Middle Europe on the Principle of Partition without Annexation_ (Boston, 1918), pp. 3-14, passim; Cram, _Sins_, pp. 29-32.
37. Cram, _Plan_, pp. 14, 16; _Sins_, p. 33. Though he hated imperialism, in his _Plan_ he also advocated the establishment of an "Imperial City" for the arts and sciences (p. 16).
38. Cram, _Plan_, p. 15; Cram, _Sins_, p. 33.
39. Cram, _Plan_, pp. 18-21.

40. Cram, _Sins_, p. 111.
41. Emphasizing that his Christian beliefs did not embrace pacifism, he did not, in fact, consider eternal, universal peace to be desirable. In light of the incessant warfare of his beloved Middle Ages and his bellicose tirades during World War I, one wonders for consistency's sake how he could have believed otherwise. Cram, _Plan_, p. 15. Then, too, he had expressed his chagrin at being too old to serve in World War I and kill Germans. Letter of Ralph Adams Cram to Dr. Herman T. Radin, June 24, 1918, Herman T. Radin Papers, New York Public Library.
42. Cram, _Great Peace_, pp. 2-3.
43. Cram, _Nemesis_, pp. 54-43.
44. Ibid., p. 44.
45. Ibid., p. 51.
46. Cram, _Substance of Gothic_, p. 3.
47. Cram, _Gold, Frankincense and Myrrh_, p. 1. Since the theory that acquired characteristics were inherited had been disproved, he thought that the scientific underpinnings for progress had been thoroughly undermined. At the same time, however, he admitted that his views on evolution were theoretical and not likely to gain acceptance from most scientists. Cram, _Great Peace_, pp. 161, 251-252.
48. Cram, _Great Peace_, pp. 17-21.
49. He insisted, for example, that "the insolent brutalities of eugenics are the Nemesis of wholesome humanity." Ralph Adams Cram, "Architecture As an Expression of Religion," _The American Architect_, XCVIII (December 28, 1910), 210.
50. Madison Grant (1865-1927) was a naturalist who won a good deal of popularity for his books on race, particularly his pseudo-scientific _The Passing of the Great Race_ (1916) in which he bemoaned the loss of dominance of Anglo-Saxons. Theodore Lothrop Stoddard (1183-1950) was best known for _The Rising Tide of Color Against White World-Supremacy_ (1920) and _Clashing Tides of Colour_ (1935), a book for which Grant wrote an introduction. Stoddard was also recognized for his several books on travel and a biography of the late nineteenth-century Tammany boss, Richard Croker.
51. Cram, _Nemesis_, pp. 35, 39, 41.
52. Cram, _Great Peace_, p. 71.
53. Cram, _Walled Towns_, pp. 14-15; Cram, _Gold_, p. 59.
54. Cram, _Great Peace_, pp. 149-150.

55. Ibid., p. 76.
56. Ibid., pp. 69, 76-77.
57. Cram, Sins, pp. 36-37.
58. Cram, Great Peace, pp. 61-62.
59. Cram, Sins, p. 42.
60. Ibid., pp. 40-41.
61. Cram, Great Peace, pp. 129-130.
62. Ibid., pp. 64, 41; Cram, Significance of Gothic Art, p. 27.
63. Cram, Sins, pp. 43-44.
64. Letter of Ralph Adams Cram to Rush C. Hawkins, November 13, 1919, Rush C. Hawkins Papers, Annmary Brown Memorial, Brown University. Born in Pomfret, Vermont, Rush Christopher Hawkins (1831-1920) served in both the Mexican War and the Civil War, rising to the rank of brigadier-general in the latter. In 1860 he married Annmary Brown of the Brown family which founded the university of that name. After his retirement from the Army, he became a renowned collector of incunabula, most of which can be found in the Annmary Brown Memorial at Brown University. Attracted by their mutual doomsday views, he and Cram maintained a sporadic but friendly correspondence during the war. Hawkins, who on one occasion had arranged for Cram to deliver a lecture, sent the architect several short papers--"Is Avarice Triumphant?" "Destruction of Art in America," "Brutality and Avarice Triumphant," and "Our Political Degradation," for example. Cram promised to read them and thanked the general for his "several contributions toward my intellectual and spiritual advancement." In turn, he sent Hawkins some of his works, including The Nemesis of Mediocrity. Letters of Ralph Adams Cram to Rush C. Hawkins, October 30, 1917, November 8, 1917, February (?), 1918, and November 13, 1919, Hawkins Papers. Hawkins was hit and killed by an automobile in 1920.
65. Unfortunately for the historian, Cram never made any further written allusions to the Red Scare. In 1922, however, two years after it had abated, he did refer to the government as "autocratic, inquisitorial, and largely irresponsible." Cram, Great Peace, p. 132.
66. There is no evidence to indicate that Cram or Veblen ever read each other's works. Moreover, Cram, who was fond of suggesting books for his readers, never listed any of Veblen's.

191

67. Veblen touched on this point throughout his writings. For its fullest examination and historical application, see his Imperial Germany and the Industrial Revolution (New York, 1915).

68. Veblen, for example, derided the high cost of hand-made goods in the face of more exact machine-made products. See his chapter, "The Pecuniary Canons of Taste," in The Theory of the Leisure Class (New York, 1899). More important, he was one of the first technocrats, envisioning a future society efficiently guided by engineers and technicians. See his The Engineers and the Price System (New York, 1921).

69. Cram was particularly disturbed by the spread of tastelessness and the flaunting of wealth in architecture. "An architect," he once moaned, "as we count him today, is a sign of inferior culture, necessary but regrettable." Cram, Six Lectures, p. 58.

70. Cram, Great Peace, pp. 84-93, passim.

71. Ibid., pp. 96-99.

72. Ibid., pp. 100-113, passim. As for the business community, he sneered at "the cynicism of trade fighting to get back to 'normalcy.'" (p. 27)

73. Ibid., pp. 114-115. For a fuller discussion of the "back to the land" movement, see Chapter IX. Having approached economic problems with intrepidness, Cram apparently convinced some of his readers that he was an expert in such matters. One of his fans, for example, a physician from New Jersey, asked for advice on the matter of taxation of state, county, and municipal bonds. Cram declined to give any, frankly admitting his ignorance of such technical matters. Letter of Ralph Adams Cram to Dr. S. C. Watkins, April 20, 1923, S. C. Watkins Collection, Yale University Library.

74. Cram, Great Peace, p. 226.

75. One cannot blame the war for Cram's disillusion with the intellect: he had been building a case against it since the 1890's.

76. Cram, Gold, pp. 13, 6.

77. Ibid., p. 64; Cram, Nemesis, pp. 33-34.

78. Cram, Nemesis, p. 6.

79. Cram, Walled Towns, pp. 32-36. Cram had been sensing this monastic revival since the 1880's, but believed that the events of 1914-1918 had given it a further fillip.

80. Cram, Gold, pp. 28-30.

81. Morton and Lucia White seem to feel that Cram saw in Henry Adams' Mont-Saint-Michel and Chartres "a blueprint of cities that Adams thought could be restored in America...." Cram, they assert, "exaggerated the practical significance" of Chartres, which was, in the final analysis, "an unrealizable vision of what civilization should be like." Morton and Lucia White, The Intellectual Versus the City: From Thomas Jefferson to Frank Lloyd Wright (Cambridge, Massachusetts, 1962), p. 73. How much influence Adams' book actually had on Cram's concept of walled towns is a moot point. Cram, after all, had been a student and advocate of medievalism for some twenty years before he read Chartres.

82. Cram admitted that his other wartime works were meant to be negative in tone, whereas Walled Towns represented a possible solution to the ills he had delineated in these previous works. He cautioned, however, that he was blueprinting no ultimate utopia, but only an interim placebo (p. 28).

83. Ibid., pp. 51-56. For an interesting example of what could constitute the life and character of a modern walled town, see his description of the mythical New England town of "Beaulieu," ibid., pp. 59-95. Cities whose population exceeded one million inhabitants he deemed criminal. Cram, Great Peace, p. 59.

84. Cram, Walled Towns, p. 97.

85. For a fuller discussion of American communistic societies, see John Humphrey Noyes, History of American Socialisms (Philadelphia, 1870) and Alice Felt Tyler, Freedom's Ferment: Phases of American Social History to 1860 (Minneapolis, 1944), pp. 68-224.

86. Cram, Walled Towns, pp. 36-40.

87. Ibid., pp. 41-48, 100-104, passim.

88. Ibid., p. 105.

89. The Golden Book of Springfield (New York, 1920) is an imaginative work set in the year 2018 A.D. Its main theme--one to which Cram, considering his racism (though he liked the Japanese), might have subscribed--concerns the attack on Western civilization by barbarous Asiatics. For brief accounts of Cram's influence on Lindsay, see Anna Massa, Vachel Lindsay: Fieldworker for the American Dream (Bloomington, Indiana, 1970), pp. 118-119, and David Howard Dickason, The Daring Young

<u>Men: The Story of the American Pre-Raphaelites</u>
(Bloomington, Indiana, 1953), pp. 193-197. It
should be noted that Lindsay's appreciation of
Cram's philosophy, at least with regard to his
walled towns, did not necessarily extend to his
architecture or architectural views. Unlike Cram,
he was a great admirer of both Louis Sullivan and
Frank Lloyd Wright.

90. Cram, <u>Great Peace</u>, p. 243.

CHAPTER VIII

CRAM ON MODERN ART AND RELIGION

The argument that a pessimistic world-view is
rooted in personal disappointment, frustration, or
dyspepsia falls to pieces in the instance of Ralph
Adams Cram. The personification of intellectual
gloom, until the last years of his life he enjoyed the
personal health, happiness, fulfillment and public
prestige often denied artists of a more optimistic
persuasion. The paradox is as puzzling as it is real.
     Much of Cram's private happiness derived from a
rich family life passed on Beacon Hill and at Whitehall. Devoted to his wife and children, he spent as
much time with them as his arduous public life as architect, speaker, writer, and active citizen would
permit. He also relished entertaining friends at both
his Boston and Sudbury residences. Mrs. Elizabeth
Wall, his niece, could recall her uncle as the center
of parties, especially when he chose to play croquet
or cards with visiting children.[1] Many of the visitors to Whitehall came especially for Sunday services
at the Chapel or to admire the landscaping, which was
probably Cram's favorite hobby. When he could not
persuade someone to play chess, the architect spent
most of his leisure time either cultivating his flow-
ers and shrubbery or his vegetable garden. Like all
of his ancestors since Colonial times, he was a tiller
of the soil, though in his case the act resulted from
pure volition. Gardening was the closest he ever came
to being an outdoorsman, however. A great lover of
animals--his black cat "Dammit" was his favorite--he
detested hunting and constantly discouraged his son
from taking adventurous safaris on their one-hundred-
and-sixteen-acre estate. In fact, he liked no out-
door sports whatsoever. Only his wife Elizabeth and
the children ever used the tennis court which they had
constructed. Nor did he care for anything involving
even a modicum of mechanical skill, a fact not surprising when one considers his pronounced aversion to
gunpowder, the printing press, and the internal combustion machine. Fittingly, he never even attempted

to learn how to drive a car.[2]

Interviewing the sixty-seven-year-old architect
in 1931, George H. Allen thought that he looked like
a man of fifty. Despite a cough which had persisted
for a quarter of a century--he was an inveterate pipe
smoker--he had enjoyed remarkably good health throughout his life. Never a heavy eater (he usually took
only fifteen minutes for a light lunch while at his
office), the barrel-chested, five-foot-seven-inch
Cram rarely weighed above his customary trim one hundred and fifty pounds. Of course, his abstinence never precluded occasional gourmet meals or a hearty zest
for imported wines. Dressing conservatively and spec-
tacled with a pair of horn rims to which he had
switched after years of wearing a pince-nez, he appeared to Allen as "retiring," "bookish," "aloof," and
"almost naïve, with a touch of the ascetic and a spark
of quick, nervous humor." Called "the Abbot" by some,
Cram, with his intense, intelligent features, did resemble a serious clergyman or intellectual. Indeed,
it was his intelligence and erudition which most impressed Allen, who described him as "a phenomenon...
a thoroughly apprised and morally sincere man who
carries his intrepidity of conscience to so tense a
degree that it becomes startling."[3]

Allen was not the only one to be impressed by
Cram's mental abilities and achievements. By the time
of his interview, four colleges and universities--
Princeton, Yale, Notre Dame, and Williams--had conferred honorary degrees on the architect. This recognition pleased Cram immensely, as did the honorary
membership in Phi Beta Kappa presented him by Harvard
on the occasion of an address given in 1921. With regard to lectures and talks, age had done nothing to
diminish his enthusiasm or rhetorical powers.
Throughout the 1920's and early 1930's he continued to
give frequent addresses to professional, collegiate,
and religious groups, sometimes having to decline
speaking engagements for want of time.[4] Some of the
stories surrounding his career as a public speaker are
amusing. One, for example, which may or may not be
apocryphal, has Cram delivering a sermon from an I-
beam of a church he was designing and proudly announcing that no steel was being used for the building's
construction.[5] John Doran relates another story concerning an interview between Cram and Richard Mellon.
The scion of the wealthy banking family had come to
the firm's Boston office to discuss certain aspects
of the East Liberty (Pennsylvania) Presbyterian Church

project. With great interest Mr. Mellon spent the
better part of their meeting listening to the Gothicist's far-ranging discourses.[6] Of course, not all
the clients appreciated Cram's garrulousness. As one
testily remarked: "Mr. Cram would much rather give a
lecture on the structure he is building than inspect
it on the job." The barb struck home, for it was perfectly true that while a master of design, he loathed
the on-site inspections which attended his work.[7]

Despite the good fortune of his family life,
health, professional fulfillment and public recognition, Cram remained a dissatisfied man. Like others,
he had accepted the call-to-arms voiced nearly a century earlier by a fellow New Englander, Ralph Waldo
Emerson: "What is a man born for but to be a Reformer, a Remaker of things...?" In the architect's case,
reform involved nothing less than a re-making of Western society. During the 1920's, as during the war
years, he used his two favorite weapons--the drafting
board and the writer's pen--to crusade against what he
considered an inferior civilization.

While the war was in progress, Cram had attacked
modernism, principally as it manifested itself in
political, economic, and, to a lesser extent, scientific matters. After the publication of Towards the
Great Peace in 1922, however, he increasingly hurled
invectives against the modern spirit in art, architecture, and religion. The change was one of degree
rather than of kind; modernism had become pandemic,
affecting and infecting every aspect of contemporary
society. He was convinced, moreover, as he told his
audience at the Harvard Phi Beta Kappa address, that
beauty and religion were tools for solving fundamental
problems.[8] In redirecting his focus to the fields of
art, architecture, and religion, he was returning to
the scene of the early battles he had fought in the
1880's and 1890's.

Looking back to the years of the Pre-Raphaelite
and Decadent rebellions against the forces of late
nineteenth-century society, he marveled at the changes
they wished to effect, "from paganized architecture to
a new Gothic; from Byron to Francis Thompson; from the
Manchester School to a revived guild system; from
Spencer's Synthetic Philosophy to Sacramentalism; from
'Triumphant Democracy' to a new vision of the kingly
ideal and a vital aristocracy; from a centrifugal and
negative Protestantism to a centripetal and unified
Catholicism." Yet the rebellions had proved abortive:
"Modernism went on to even greater triumphs, while the

specific movements themselves came, some of them, to
an ignominious end."[9]   Failure, in part, had resulted
from superficiality. In a striking analogy, Cram
likened this medievally oriented revival to the Eucha-
ristic concepts of accidents and substance. The revival had been based essentially on accidents (poetry,
pageantry, and an excessively mystical philosophy),
rather than on substance (a scholastic or sacramental
philosophy, Catholic theology, and communal organization). Even in architecture, the earlier Gothic revivals had failed largely because they were guided
more by a shallow antiquarianism than by the dynamic
and imaginative possibilities of the style itself.[10]
Still, neither the Gothic revivals nor the general attempt to restore and rehabilitate medievalism had been
entirely unsuccessful: "As a result of recent revela-
tions, we know both the need and the significance of
a thing that once seemed whimsical and episodic...."[11]
More than a passing fancy, it had been a harbinger of
better things to come. And while modernism had triumphed, its success would prove to be transient.

        Cram, of course, tried to distinguish between
"modern" and "modernism." He did not, for example,
offer a blanket condemnation of all that was novel in
art or architecture. Granted his medieval prepossessions which inclined him to favor the past as superior
to the present, he still found something to admire in
the new artistic forces which erupted in the late
nineteenth century. Frank E. Cleveland, an architect
who knew him since the late 1890's and who became a
partner in his firm in 1926, believed that he accepted
the modern element "as long as it was a creative architecture and art, springing from foundations sure
and accepted as good."[12] Indeed, Cram gladly accepted
innovative structural changes as determining elements
in architectural style and design:

            In an extraordinary way, the forward
        march of architecture and our material
        expansion have been synchronized. What
        we have done in steel and stone can as-
        suredly be said to be the expression of
        the best in us, and may, perhaps, be a
        prophecy of the great things that are
        yet to come. Architecture in this coun-
        try has surpassed the civilization and
        culture of which it is an outgrowth--it
        is immeasurably better than we have a
        right to expect it to be. In the church
        spires and soaring silhouettes of the

buildings that compose our skyline
there is a profound spiritual quality.13
Cram, then, did not object to what was "modern" in the
strictly chronological meaning of the word. "Modernism," in contrast, implying more specific congeries of
ideas, values, and practices, was the object of his
wrath.

Cram condemned modernism in art on a number of
grounds. The great art of the past, he reasoned,
though expressing itself in multifarious ways—from
the pagan Egyptian civilization to the Christian Middle Ages—invariably rested on a certain unity of culture. Art was not divorced from society; ideally, it
was faithfully wed to it. Modern art, however, represented a fragmented human culture whose roots reached
back in time to the breakdown of medievalism. Ironically, precisely because modern art and architecture
were themselves fragmented, they perfectly expressed
the milieu in which they had flourished. Yet because
they had resulted from a centrifugal, noxious society,
though they might on occasions achieve real beauty,
they were incapable of producing on any sustained basis the great art forms which sprang regularly to life
only in times of healthy civilizations. Given the
premises of this argument, the conclusion was as logical as it was inescapable.

But there were other reasons as well for vilify-
ing modernism. For Cram, in theory at least, the
standards of beauty were absolute. Inveighing against
those who championed beauty as relative, he wrote: "I
think there is a difference between beauty and ugliness, and not of degree only but of kind. Beauty is
not something alien to life and hard to come by; it is
not the peculiar possession of the artist, but a sort
of natural right of all men. It is an attribute of
actions, institutions, and beliefs, social, philosophical, and religious, as well as of things natural phenomena."14 He added: "We don't want 'art for
art's sake,' or anything of the kind. We want art because it is beauty, and because beauty is a sign of
right feeling, right thinking and right living. Until
we get it back, as the possession of all the people,
as an instinct, not as the hoarded possessions of a
few hypersensitive and highly trained experts, we
shall have no civilization worth talking about."15

Related to his firm convictions of what did and
what did not constitute art were those concerning the
artist. He admitted: "I have scant sympathy with
that entirely modern view of art which makes the art-

ist a rebel against constituted society, an abnormal
phenomenon feeding upon his inner self, cut off from
the life of his fellows, and issuing his aesthetic
manifestoes in flaming defiance, and in the conviction
of an essential superiority...." [16] (His "scant sympathy" for the alienated artist is remarkable since,
in his own way, he was fully as alienated as those
whom he condemned.) These "megalomaniacs," as he
called them, and their efforts had been woefully
wrongheaded from the beginning. Severing links with
the vital art of the past, modern artists had rejected
the instinctive and communal in favor of the self-
conscious and individualistic. Unwilling or unable to
absorb the wisdom and lessons of the past, they had
committed a sort of aesthetic and spiritual suicide.

Though art and beauty were "natural rights" of
mankind, Cram scarcely approved of mass taste, at
least as it expressed itself during his lifetime. For
all his scorn of contemporary artists, he was delighted that some had been able to impose their views and
ideals on the public between the 1880's and World War
I. In particular, he rejoiced that architecture had
remained "aristocratic," not through public fiat but
as a result of the efforts of the American Institute
of Architects and various schools of architecture. [17]
This view of the relationship which should exist between the artist and the public makes sense only within the larger context of his views on art and society.
In truly organic societies (such as the Middle Ages),
the masses instinctively accept and appreciate fine
art even if they do not rationally and intellectually
understand it. In contemporary superficial and fragmented societies, the masses had become debased by the
institutions and values which they both accepted and
fostered. It was the differnce, in short, between
communal society and mass society, between a society
in which a responsible citizenry deferred to a responsible elite and one in which an irresponsible mass and
an irresponsible few brought out the worst in one another. Viewed in this manner, art was governed by the
same set of assumptions and rules which regulated politics. Cram's Tory leanings in art were as pronounced
as those in politics.

Though the modern movement in the arts had five-
century-old antecedents, it had come of age only in
the years immediately prior to the Great War. As
Morton White discerned a "revolt against formalism" in
the intellectual developments of the early twentieth
century, so Cram, too, recognized a rebellion against

the "stodgy formalism" in the arts.[18] After all, had
he himself not been in the front ranks of those who
had attacked the dominant Victorian tastes of the late
nineteenth century? Justifiable as this rebellion had
been, he lamented that it had been basically one of
form rather than substance, reflecting the vagaries of
an evanescent fashion. The successors to these rebels, moreover, while failing to conserve or re-create
what was good, had managed to develop what was potentially bad. The necessary destruction having been
accomplished, the reconstruction which followed had
been "amazingly absurd."[19]

Cram's specific citations of artists and works of
art which he either liked or disliked demonstrate his
traditionalism and almost complete inability to accept
the avant-garde. In terms of painting and sculpture,
he admired such "modern" traditionalists as Thomas
Hart Benton, Grant Wood, and Augustus Saint-Gaudens,
but deplored Cezanne, Matisse, Rodin. The works of
the former were "healthy" and "inspiring"; those of
the latter, no better than "pathological aberra-
tions."[20] When Marcel Duchamps' controversial Nude
Descending a Staircase appeared in the 1913 New York
Armory Exhibit, Cram joined the ranks of outraged and
alarmed American critics, and with a sneer referred to
it as "a pile of shingles after a cyclone."[21] As for
the various artistic "isms" which mingled with and
rapidly succeeded one another in the first two decades
or so of the twentieth century--cubism, fauvism, primitivism, dadaism, surrealism, and expressionism--he
could scarcely find sufficiently derogatory epithets.
The art produced by these schools seemed "afflicted
with chronic curvature of the spine," reflected only
the artist's "unimportant ego," and represented the
expression of "chronic paranoia." Nevertheless, it
did guarantee to make "two laughs grow where one grew
before."[22] The pity of all this was that the artists
had genuine talent--some of them were geniuses--but
had willfully elected to create the monstrous and de-
basing rather than the beautiful and edifying. With
regard to music, the architect adored Wagner, liked
Debussy and McDowell, but simply loathed Richard
Strauss. What he thought of the atonalists, one can
well imagine. Denouncing both "free verse" and "free
fiction" in literature, he found the Victorian poets,
as well as Amy Lowell, to his taste.[23] He never specifically cited the contemporary writer he most despised, but Gertrude Stein may have been a good bet for
that honor. As he remarked: "If Miss Stein chooses

201

to play dominoes with the component parts of Roget's Thesaurus it is not, I conceive, a matter which calls either for extended comment or lingering embrace."[24]

Cram's specific views on modern painting, sculpture, music, and literature need not be taken very seriously. Possessing no special training or qualifications in these fields, he merely offered highly personal views. In berating others for the subjectivism of their tastes, moreover, he unwittingly but conclusively showed that he was capable of being fully as subjective. About the only things that can be legitimately inferred from the potpourri of his views are that he favored the traditional over the avant-garde, the safe over the daring. On more than one occasion he proved that he could be an unabashed philistine, in the Arnoldian sense of the term. With regard to modernism in architecture, however, his judgments, while fully as opinionated, were based on a genuine knowledge of the subject, are more complex, and, consequently, are more deserving of serious attention.

The advent of Richardson, McKim, and the Gothic Revival, as he never seemed to tire of reiterating, had put an end to the worst fifty years of architecture in the United States and, possibly, in recorded history. The revolt against this ugliness, which was personified by the nation's Centennial Exposition, spread rapidly during the eighties and nineties. While he hardly approved of the triumphant Classicism of the Columbian Exposition ("Imperial Rome reborn in the illusive glory of plaster and pâpier-maché"), he did find a certain beauty in its "White City."[25] Despite its auspicious beginnings, however, the revolt soon took the wrong road and compounded aesthetic woes.

As to what the right road might have been, Cram was suggestive, but not terribly explicit. In his autobiography he lamented that had Halsey Wood's design for the Cathedral of St. John the Divine been accepted, the "vital design" initiated by Louis Sullivan, carried on by Frank Lloyd Wright, and raised to its apex by Bertram Goodhue and his State Capitol at Lincoln, Nebraska, would have come sooner.[26] Unfortunately, he failed to spell out the nature of this "vital design." Moreover, while heartily approving of Wood and Goodhue, he had serious misgivings concerning Sullivan and Wright. Notwithstanding an acknowledgment that his genius was the equal of Wood's and his frank admiration for his Transportation Building at the 1893 World's Fair, Cram regarded Sullivan basically as a representative modernist who destroyed more than he created.[27] Although Wright, Sullivan's pupil and probably the greatest American architect of the twentieth century, admired medieval church building and wished that the Gothic spirit in building could be revived, he met with even more coolness than Sullivan. For all his literary prolificness, Cram apparently referred to Wright on but one occasion, and then only as a "less responsible genius" than Sullivan.[28]

Yet the parallels and contrasts between Wright and Cram are both interesting and illuminating. Admiring Gothic as the "last of architecture as a great style of structure," one which "approached the organic in character," Wright, like Cram, perceived the Renaissance as a period of decline. Like Cram, he also worried that science and the machine might dominate the human spirit, that the nation suffered from too much urbanism, and that standardized education and capitalism had made it difficult, if not nearly impossible, for genius to function. Unlike Cram, however, he saw the medieval example as a cul-de-sac for the modern world: architecturally speaking, the Middle Ages had no place in contemporary life. For Wright, the apprentices of the Middle Ages were little better than slaves; twentieth-century apprentices, in contrast, were self-respecting associates of the master artist, as he had been with Sullivan. Perhaps most important, the future--if there was to be one which was worth having--had to be placed in the hands of the individual genius, and not the masses. Wright, again differing with Cram, had no patience with the medieval concept of talented artists working symbiotically with appreciative masses. The future belonged to the "innate aristocrat." For all his spirited defense of this symbiotic ideal, Cram, of course, despised massman fully as much as Wright.[29]

The ambivalence which Cram felt for Sullivan and Wright was compounded many times over for modern architecture in general. Maintaining to the end of his life that this modernism would not and could not last, at least in the United States, he conceded that it had had positive influences: (1) the honest use of materials, (2) the rediscovery of the value of textures, (3) the rediscovery of color, and (4) the simplicity of its forms and furnishings.[30] This ambivalence was particularly pronounced with regard to skyscrapers. As one might expect, he foamed at the mere thought of the more extravagant ones. The Empire State Building, by disregarding the basic principle of the city as a consistent unity, expressed "the apotheosis of megalomania"; the unfinished Radio City (Cram was writing this in 1931) was a "staircase," in yet another caustic reference to Duchamps' Nude Descending a Staircase. Once Radio City was completed, a contemptible age would end and, so he thought, a new, saner one might begin. Nonetheless, he admitted that as the "soul and essence" of their time, these buildings might justly be considered outstanding architecture.[31] Skycrapers, in fact, held an almost involuntary fascination for him: "In principle, I don't like them at all; for they are quite uneconomic, a fad rather than an intelligent adaptation of needs to reality; while already they are becoming slightly vieux jeu--except in the smaller cities of the Middle West, where they have no excuse at all. They are, however, a new thing, couched in the terms of new materials, and with no stylistic connotations whatever--therefore very fascinating to the imagination."[32] Wishing to build his own skyscraper, he got his opportunity--or almost --when Cram and Ferguson received a government contract for the Boston Federal Building. Since architects who worked for the government repeatedly interposed their designs, he did not consider the building to be his own distinct creation.[33] Ironically, the successors to Cram's firm--Hoyle, Doran and Berry-- have been responsible for two of Boston's largest skyscrapers to date, the New England Mutual Life Insurance Company Building and the John Hancock Building.[34]

Cram's mixed feelings also extended to functionalism, the central precept of the modern movement in architecture. Roughly speaking, this idea, first clearly enunciated by Louis Sullivan, holds that form must follow, not precede, function. At the hands of Walter Gropius and his Bauhaus group, it had become "the Pentecost of ugliness," exuding irreligion relativism, and anti-individualism.[35] While excoriating the development of functionalism in the 1920's, Cram lamented: "This is a great pity because the structural and organic and functional principles are perfectly sound and, sanely applied and expressed might, and still may, redeem a great art from that ignominy which struck it in the nineteenth century."[36] Cram's works, it should be noted, do generally manifest a viable fusion of form and function.

Having granted a certain worth to both functionalism and the skyscraper, having lauded contemporary American architects as superb,[37] Cram remained ada-

mantly opposed to modernism. Stubbornly, he continued
to cling to his dogmatic theory that art, as a true
reflection of the values and institutions of its surrounding society, will be as great or as poor as that
society. Thus, modern art and architecture could not
help but reflect the decadence which had spawned them.
Until the present historical cycle passed, modernism
would remain dominant. In this situation the only recourse for the artist, particularly the architect, was
to safeguard and extend, if possible, true art in
those few areas in which modernism had not as yet triumphed. Leaving commercial and public buildings to
the proponents of modernism, Cram concentrated his
efforts--both artistic and literary--on what could be
salvaged from the wreckage of five centuries of blundering and betrayal: the Church, the school, the
home.[38] He was, in short, preparing his Walled Towns.

One of the reasons which Cram offered for having
relinquished his teaching position at M.I.T. was the
post-World War I building boom. The reason was a
valid one. Whereas Cram and Ferguson employed "in
practical idleness and not without some financial em-
barrassment" only five draftsmen while the nation was
at war, that number rose to forty only a few years
later.[39] In the mid-twenties, three partners--Frank
Cleveland, Chester Godfrey, and Alexander Hoyle--were
added to the firm. All of this correctly suggests
that the 1920's were years of great productivity for
Cram, whose imagination and stamina proved equal to
the task. As Robert Crunden has observed: "In the
years after the war, with Frank Lloyd Wright in
eclipse and the Bauhaus not yet come to America, Cram
could have made an excellent case for himself as the
most distinguished architect in America."[40]

The architectural commissions which Cram received
during this period were diverse.[41] Despite his keen
interest in domestic architecture and the problem of
housing for the lower classes, he did very few private
residences either at this time or, for that matter,
at any time during his nearly half a century as an architect. Nor were commercial and public buildings of
great interest to him. Most of the details concerning
the firm's two major commercial commissions in the
twenties--the National Life Insurance Company Building
in Montpelier, Vermont, and the Provident Mutual Life
Insurance Company Building in Philadelphia--were left
to Alexander Hoyle. For the most part, Cram reserved
his talents for work involving schools and churches.
At this time, for example, work was either started or

continued at Phillips Exeter Academy, Sweet Briar College, Wheaton College, Williams College, and West Point. Regarding ecclesiastical architecture, this was a period of remarkable activity. Some of the churches he built included: the Roman Catholic churches of the Sacred Heart (Jersey City), St. Mary's (Detroit), and Holy Rosary (Pittsburgh); the Second Presbyterian Church (Lexington, Kentucky), as well as the First Presbyterian churches of Tacoma, Washington, and Glens Falls, New York; the Methodist Christ Church (New York), Trinity Methodist Episcopal Church (Durham, North Carolina), the First Evangelical Lutheran Church (Louisville, Kentucky), and the Grace Evangelical Lutheran Church (Fremont, Ohio). Occasionally, he was able to combine the secular with the religious, as when he designed chapels for St. George's School (Newport, Rhode Island), Princeton, Mercersberg Academy (Mercersberg, Pennsylvania), and Rollins College (Winter Park, Florida).

While work on these commissions went smoothly enough, Cram occasionally found himself in a contretemps. In 1917, for example, he was asked to design a Swedenborgian cathedral, along with surrounding studios and workshops for craftsmen, in Bryn Athyn, Pennsylvania. Delighted at the prospect of actually being able to put his theory of medieval guilds to work, he was vexed to find, after the death of the original donor, that his services were no longer wanted. Though his firm's draftsmen were permitted to aid in the construction of the studios and workshops, only the cathedral is properly Cram's.[42] "Only" is deceiving. The Swedenborgian church, done in English Gothic, represents one of his finest architectural achievements.

Another unfinished project involved St. Alban's Cathedral in Washington, D.C. The commission for this edifice initially had been awarded to George F. Bodley and Henry Vaughan, two English Gothicists whom Cram admired and whose disciple he claimed to be. When both died before having completed their work, three architects, two of whom had received training in Cram's office, were chosen to finish the cathedral. Selected as Consulting Architect, Cram believed that he knew exactly what Vaughan, a specialist in fourteenth-century English Gothic, would have done had he lived; those in actual charge of the project disagreed. Cram's services were terminated.[43] The Swedenborgian and Washington undertakings had proved disappointing. Neither, however, was nearly as troublesome and disquieting as the one involving the Cathedral of St. John the Divine. Writing in 1954, one architectural critic noted that while it had taken sixty-two years for the completion of Chartres, seventy-two years for Notre Dame, and one hundred and twenty years for St. Peter's, after sixty-two years St. John's was only sixty per cent finished and had already consumed some fifteen million dollars. It was estimated at this time that it would take an additional fourteen years and twenty million dollars to complete the project.[44] Fourteen years later the revised estimate for the still unfinished cathedral ran to another twelve to twenty-five million dollars in costs. With the building fund hovering around the two-million-dollar mark and with today's inflationary economy, it would seem that the world's largest cathedral (and second largest church) may surpass even St. Peter's in time-of-construction --if, indeed, it is ever completed.[45]

When Cram and Goodhue took over the project from Heins and La Farge in 1911, it is doubtful if they realized the full extent of the difficulties facing them. Ordered to continue in Gothic what the unfortunate Heins and La Farge had begun in Romanesque and Byzantine, Cram--Goodhue had departed in 1913--offered the first major departure from the original design with his plan for a nave of French Gothic, the ground for which was broken in 1916. Though work went slowly--when it went at all--during the war years, he was able to devote a good deal of time to this colossal undertaking during the 1920's and the 1930's with visible results. The nave was redone, and progress was made on the transepts, the west facade, and the roof of the choir. Rejecting English in favor of Spanish and French Gothic, he also completed several buildings adjacent to the cathedral, including the Synod House, Bishop's House, and Deanery. In addition, he designed one of the seven ambulatory chapels for St. John's, with other firms doing the rest.[46] In 1939 the choir was rebuilt. It was to be the last important work done on the Cathedral during Cram's lifetime. World War II occasioned delays, and after some minor work on the crypt in 1948, the project ground to a virtual halt.

More recently, however, there has been some renewed interest in the project, though the program of design has become more modest. 1966 witnessed the decision to scrap the anticipated five-hundred-foot Gothic tower at the crossing of the nave and tran-

septs, and to construct a dome of louvers to alternate
with panes of colored glass. The transepts were to be
modernized, and, eschewing costly cut stone, were to
be constructed of granite-faced concrete. The following year the Reverend Horace W. B. Donegan, Bishop of
New York, announced that no further building funds
were to be raised. Six years later, however, the
Reverend James P. Morton disclosed that work would re-
commence in order to complete the crypt and two en-
trances. The story's ending has yet to be written.[47]
     Though naturally he wished to see St. John's com-
pleted before his death, Cram realized that this probably would not be the case. Aware that his successors
might alter or altogether transform his design, he
reasoned: "After all...why not? A building such as
this does not represent the personal ideas of one man,
or one firm of architects; it is something far larger
than this. In a sense, the architect is only a sort
of amanuensis; through him is expressed something of
far greater magnitude and import than his own personality and that is the creative energy of a time." He
argued that the Cathedral must be completed even
should it cost a possible eight or nine million dollars, as then anticipated. According to experts, he
noted, it could physically endure for two thousand
years and could serve the needs of hundreds of millions of worshippers. A single battleship, in comparison, would cost as much and would offer only death
and destruction. "The parallel," he wrote "should be
conclusive."[48]
     During his lifetime Cram received both plaudits
and abuse regarding his ambitious designs for St.
John's. For Thomas Tallmadge, he had done brilliantly, with the result that there was "not a sham in the
whole cathedral."[49] Others stood less in awe. One of
them, citing the cathedral's lack of unity, snarled:
"The hordes of Attila were not less tinged with humil-
ity, nor less menacing to the peace of a Roman city."
Attacking Cram's "sentimental attachment to form," he
added scoffingly: "We know from the start the intention and the effect and can watch without excitement
the hesitant accretion out of which a new Amiens will
eventually emerge."[50] Sometimes filled with more than
a little self-righteousness, Cram was apologetic in
his reply to the critic. Disclaiming infallibility,
he entreated: "All we can do is to recover what we
can of an old and glorious and expressive art, holding
to its principles in so far as we can detect and understand them, and trying as best we can with our

limited ability to give them some new qualities that will absolve them from archeological archaicism." Something finer would come, he promised, but until that time, like the monks of the Middle Ages, it was necessary to preserve the best of civilization.[51]

Cram's analogy between medieval monks and twentieth-century architects, while strained, was hardly fortuitous. In 1921, in a paean even less unabashed than usual, he exulted: "The startling and anomalous return to Medievalism, in religion, philosophy and the arts, particularly architecture, not to speak of the coincident falling back on the Middle Ages for a criticism of industrial civilization and for a new model of reconstruction, is in actuality the most significant happening of modern times, and a reliable prophecy of the future. It is the Counter-Renaissance in simple fact, the first strivings of what may have ultimate issue in the rejection of the new paganism and a restoration of the Christian polity."[52] So enamored of--one might almost say, besotted with--medievalism was Cram that he began to associate with a small group of scholars who were laboring under the more modest burden of trying to achieve for medieval Latin academic parity with classical Latin. The group wished to establish first a scholarly journal and then ultimately a scholarly organization. Almost single-handedly, the architect convinced these cognoscenti to reverse their priorities. As a result, they formed the Mediaeval Academy of America in 1926 and then began to publish Speculum, the famous journal of medieval studies. Cram served as Secretary to the Academy from its inception until 1933, at which time he was elected president for a one-year term. He also served on the Advisory Board of Speculum during its first years, along with such notable medievalists as Charles Homer Haskins, Lynn Thorndike, and Dana Carlton Munro. Doubtlessly, he must have been pleased by the Announcement in the initial volume of the journal which declared that "a general enthusiasm for Gothic Architecture is perhaps one of the happiest signs of the times."[53]

While Speculum catered to the tastes of medieval scholars, Cram was also concerned that there be a journal for laymen which would "represent the best thought and scholarship, the highest ideals and principles, the most generous temper of the Roman Catholic Church in America." Reading Michael Williams' Priest of the Ideal a few years before World War I, he corresponded with the author. The two men then decided

to publish a journal of Catholic thought, but the outbreak of the war squashed their plans.[54] With the
coming of the Armistice, however, Cram had obtained
nearly half of the two hundred thousand dollars necessary to finance a magazine. Asking his friend General
Hawkins for a donation, he argued that this "Liberal
Review" would offset "the sinister influence of the
'Bad Four'": The Nation, The New Republic, The Dial,
and The Survey. He pleaded: "You realize, of course,
as well as I do, that the world now hangs between two
stools and is very liable to fall to the ground. On
the one hand is the reactionist, status-quo, stand-
patter, ultra imperialist type, on the other the Bol-
shevist-Pacifist type. One is about as bad as the
other. Both are intensely dangerous."[55] It is not
known whether Hawkins obliged. In any case, the magazine was not launched at that time. The dream of Cram
and Michael Williams had to wait until 1924 to become
reality. Nearly fifty years later, The Commonweal remains one of the finest Catholic journals in the country.[56]

Important as was his role vis-à-vis both the Mediaeval Academy and Commonweal, Cram conceived his
most important work with regard to the restoration of
medieval and Catholic principles as lying within the
realm of architecture. He must build as he preached,
and of necessity the style and the gospel were to be
Gothic.

At first glance it seems surprising that Cram
should be reiterating his Gothicism while at the same
time manifesting a new catholicity of expression in
his architectural creations. During the 1920's and
early 1930's he became an eclectic as never before,
employing at various times a modified Byzantine (New
York's Christ Church), Mexican-Spanish Renaissance
(Rollins College Chapel), Colonial (Phillips Exeter
Academy, Williams College, and Wheaton College), Italian Renaissance (the Montpelier and Philadelphia life
insurance buildings), and modern style (Boston Federal
Building). Even his Gothic tastes were broadened. In
addition to his customary English Gothic (Princeton
Chapel, St. George's School Chapel, and Washington
Cathedral) and French Gothic (St. John the Divine)
renderings, he turned to the Spanish variation for
Pittsburgh's Holy Rosary Church and Jersey City's
Church of the Sacred Heart.[57] In reality, there is no
irony or contradiction here since the term "Gothic"
had different denotations for Cram. Architecturally
speaking, there could be two styles of Gothic: one

grounded in actual historical representation, the other implying an organic structural integrity, the particular style notwithstanding. Any one of the several historical styles of architecture which he regarded as valid might be "gothic" if its use resulted in an integrated whole. Or, to rephrase this differentiation: a structure might be "Gothic" and/or "gothic." Earlier in his career Cram was inclined to insist upon the narrower "Gothic" as the legitimate architectural expression of Christianity. By the 1920's, however, he leaned toward the broader concept, "gothic." The difference is more than semantic. He had come to believe that only the restoration of Christian unity could save an imperiled world. For this to transpire it would be necessary for each Christian sect to develop a more latitudinarian spirit. Cram sensed that it could not be otherwise for his own work, due to the affinities that existed between architecture and religion.

The cynosure for the reunification of Christendom was to be the Catholic Church, the repository of true sacramentalism. Insisting that "whether we like it or not, the Catholic Church remains the greatest single fact in human history,"[58] Cram was vitally concerned that its art forms be worthy of its theology. At the turn of the century, Catholic art was neither genuinely "Gothic" nor "gothic," but, instead, "at the lowest level ever achieved in any time or place."[59] Fortunately, the situation had reversed itself dramatically within the next quarter century, so much so that Catholic architecture was equal to the best produced by both the Episcopalian and Presbyterian churches.[60]

It was not sufficient that the Catholic Church had become more receptive to good art; it had to foster it. Overcoming the apathy of modern clerics, the Church had to reassume the role it had enjoyed during the Middle Ages as creator, as well as patron. Though wary of formal training in general, Cram saw no alternative but to have the Church establish schools throughout the United States and Europe expressly for the purpose of teaching various crafts. Until such times as these schools were established, he suggested that seminaries and even secular colleges and universities add courses on Christian art to their curricula.[61] Meanwhile, he advised the Church to launch a crusade against a new heresy, one which had permitted modernism to infiltrate Catholic art, especially in Spain and France. Particularly irate with the sur-

realistic religious art of that Spanish genius Gaudí,
he complained: "To use the forms of Catholic art,
however distorted and desecrated, to express what we
know as modernism, is foolish and illogical, but to
use the forms of modernist art to express the Catholic
faith is not only foolish and illogical, it is sacri-
legious as well."[62]

While exhorting the Catholic Church to develop
and encourage edifying Christian art and to avoid the
snares of modernism, Cram was pleased by the increasingly high level of artistic taste achieved by Protestants. Having overcome his initial reluctance to see
their use of the Gothic, he was encouraged by the
aesthetically and spiritually pleasing houses of worship which Protestant sects were building at the end
of the war. Whether utilizing Gothic or other styles,
their ecclesiastical architecture had reached a new
height. In part this had been the result of his prod-
dings and splendid designs; in part it was due to the
influence of aesthetically minded clergyman like Von
Ogden Vogt. An articulate Congregational minister,
Vogt, besides having been directly responsible for the
fine Gothicism of the First Unitarian Church of Chicago, in 1921 had published an important book, Art &
Religion, in which he lauded (with a few reservations)
the use of Gothic in Protestant art and architecture.
Writing to Vogt from Seville in 1922, Cram praised
the book, but noted that there were crucial differences in their respective points of view:

> What you are trying to do, I
> think, is just this, i.e. get
> back all the richness and beauty
> and symbolic content of a Gothic
> church with nothing of the inform-
> ing force that made it live. That
> is to say, you would get back the
> richness of the ceremonial, the
> opulence of the old liturgies and
> the poignant devotions but without
> the very things they were developed
> to expound, express and enforce, i.e.,
> the Real Presence of God in the
> Blessed Sacrament, the Sacrifice of
> the Mass and the intercession and
> communion of saints with the Mother
> of God as chiefest of these, and
> veritably, Queen of Heaven....A book
> like yours will do...good, and every
> step along the way you have indicated

> is so much clear gain, but the
> end is the Catholic Faith, not
> the plenitude of Catholic worship
> without the Faith.[63]

To have made a major contribution to Protestant churches by bringing to them a greater sense of beauty was not enough for Cram. Religious art without correct religious belief was no better than a picturesque but empty shell. It was insufficient for the various Protestant sects to adopt essentially Catholic art forms; they had to assume its theology as well.[64] Toward this end Cram prove a tireless crusader.

For Cram, the basis for, as well as the greatest barrier to, Christian unity ineluctably was the sacramental system of the Roman Catholic Church.[65] With their disparate views on sacramentalism, all the Christian sects, to one extent or another, had been responsible for maintaining the unnatural rupture occasioned by the Reformation. Nonetheless, the architect placed the onus for reunion on Protestants, who had to embrace the truths of Catholicism. This, he admitted, would be enormously difficult for all of them, with the possible exception of Episopalians, who stood closer to Rome in theological matters.[66]

The general temper of the United States in the 1920's was scarcely conducive to improved Catholic-Protestant relations, let alone Christian unity. Cram was not sure whether a secularized society had led to a secularized religion or vice versa, but he was certain that Protestants were becoming increasingly concerned with mundane considerations.[67] Much more than materialism, however, was hindering religious unity. Bigotry was extraordinarily rife during the decade, and while the architect condemned the vitriolic polemics of both Catholics and Protestants, he considered the latter to be more culpable.[68] Religious prejudice, moreover, was not the special preserve of the lower classes or ill-educated. When John Jay Chapman, patrician and man of letters, viciously denounced the election of a Catholic as a Harvard Fellow in 1924, Cram was furious. He wrote to the one-time urban reformer: "In this letter you take occasion to make some of the most extraordinary and, in my opinion, absurd and unfounded statements and accusations that I have come in contact with outside the lucubrations of the Ku Klux Klan."[69] The culmination of this age of intense intolerance came with the infamous "whispering campaign" against Al Smith in the 1928 presidential election. Though the Catholic governor of New York

213

would have lost in any event to a popular Herbert
Hoover in that year of economic prosperity, his religion did assuredly cost him many votes. One result
of the election was the increased activity of the
Calvert Associates. Financial backers of The Commonweal, this group was zealously striving to implement
the religious toleration of their namesake, George
Calvert, the Catholic Colonial governor of Maryland.
A year after Smith's defeat, five hundred Protestants,
Catholics, and Jews, meeting at Harvard's Fogg Museum,
warmly applauded Cram, who, as Chairman of the Associates, issued an eloquent plea for religious harmony.[70] By this time Cram had begun to achieve a substantial reputation along these lines. In 1928 he received the Cross of Honor of the Order of Sangreal for
his services to the Episcopal Church and to humanity
at large. Somewhat surprisingly, he was also cited in
the "Who's Who Issue" of the American Hebrews as a
friend of Jews.[71]

In all likelihood tolerance per se was not Cram's
ultimate goal, but only a prelude to Christian unity.
Toward that end he joined the American Committee of
the Church Unity Octave Council, which had as its immediate objective the reunion of Catholics and Anglicans. The group had succeeded the Church Unity Octave
of Prayers, an organization which had been founded by
the Anglican Friars of the Atonement in 1908, had been
joined by Catholics in 1910, and had received the
papal blessings of Pius X. Nonetheless, it had failed
to take root in the United States. In 1936 every member of the American Committee signed a manifesto, Ut
Omnes Unum Sint ("That They All May Be One"), calling
for complete unity between the Church of England and
the Church of Rome. The problem was that the Committee's membership totaled a mere twenty-nine, all of
whom, moreover, were Episcopalians: twenty clergymen,
two members of monastic orders, and seven laymen (including Cram).[72] The size and composition of the
group was a good indication of just how tortuously
circuitous lay the road to Christian unity. As early
as 1919, Cram had sighed that only a miracle might
bring about this unification. "The miracle may be
wrought," he averred, "for miracles are now the only
things on which we can rationally count with reasonable assurance."[73]

During the 1930's a number of people were looking
for miracles. The worldwide depression and the rise
of totalitarian regimes, coming only a decade after
the Great War, seemed to indicate that mankind was

teetering on the rim of yet another profound abyss.
Throughout the twenties Cram had focused his attention
largely on aesthetic and religious questions. Now he
was being forced to examine anew the economic and political problems that beset the West. Maybe a miracle
would occur. But, as with Christian unity, one could
not proceed on that assumption. Humanity had no recourse but to work for its salvation.

1. Letter of Mrs. Elizabeth Wall to the author, March 27, 1973. Another vivid recollection of Mrs. Wall, the daughter of Cram's sister, was the glamorous figure her uncle cut when dressed in white tie and tails for a gala evening in Boston.

2. Interview with Ralph Wentworth Cram, August 9, 1972. Mr. Cram recalled how his father not only feared driving a car, but also could be nervous riding in one. The architect had a phobia of bees, and one occasion, when riding with his son, he thrashed about so violently after a bee had flown into the car that a wreck nearly ensued.

3. Ibid.; George H. Allen, "Cram--The Yankee Mediaevalist," The Architectural Forum, LV (July, 1931), 79-80. In terms of his learning, John Doran referred to him as a "walking encyclopedia." Interview with John Doran, August 8, 1972. With regard to Cram as "Abbot," John Kirchmayer, the noted wood-carver who often worked for him, did a statue of the architect standing on a pedestal, attired in a bishop's cloak with a clasp bearing the initials "RAC," and holding a book in hand while in the act of expostulating. The work is entitled: "Ralph Adams Cram Expounding His Faith." For a photograph of this wood carving, see The American Magazine of Art, 20 (February, 1929), 111.

4. For example, he had to forego a series of lectures to be given at Columbia University during the winter of 1931-1932 because of a trip he took to Egypt and the Middle East. Letter of Ralph Adams Cram to Russell Potter, March 6, 1931, Columbia University Library.

5. Allen, "Cram--The Yankee Mediaevalist," 80.

6. Interview with John Doran.

7. Allen, "Cram--The Yankee Mediaevalist," 80.

8. Ralph Adams Cram, "The Test of Beauty," The Harvard Graduates' Magazine, XXX (September, 1921), 4.

9. Ibid., 16. The arts and crafts movement was one such "ignominious" failure for Cram.

10. Ralph Adams Cram, The Substance of Gothic (Boston, 1917), pp. viii-ix.

11. Cram, "The Test of Beauty," 16.

12. Letter of Frank E. Cleveland to Cathedral Age,

[1942?], Hoyle, Doran and Berry Papers, Boston.
13. Virginia Pope, "Architecture of America Molds Beauty Anew," The New York Times Magazine (December 19, 1926), 3.
14. Ralph Adams Cram, My Life in Architecture (Boston, 1936), p. 291.
15. Ralph Adams Cram, The Significance of Gothic Art (Boston, 1918), pp. 29-30.
16. Cram, "The Test of Beauty," 2.
17. Ralph Adams Cram, "The Second Coming of Art," The Atlantic Monthly, 119 (February, 1917), 197; Ralph Adams Cram, "Art and Contemporary Society," The Barnwell Bulletin, 8 (February, 1931), 26.
18. Morton White, Social Thought in America: The Revolt Against Formalism (New York, 1952); Cram, My Life, p. 302. For a most perceptive analysis of the modern attack on Victorian culture and values in America, see also Henry F. May, The End of American Innocence: A Study of the First Years of Our Own Time, 1912-1917 (New York, 1959).
19. Cram, My Life, pp. 268-269; Cram, "The Limits of Modernism in Art," Arts and Decoration, XX (January, 1924), 11.
20. Cram, My Life, p. 271.
21. Cram, "The Limits of Modernism in Art," 11. He was fond of attaching snide titles to works of art which he found repugnant. Choice examples include: (1) "An Egyptian apparently void of any intelligence"; (2) "A fearful example of Brancusi at his 'best'!"; (3) "The Sagrada Familia of Barcelona: A modernist's crime in architecture." Ibid., 12. Theodore Roosevelt claimed that he had a Navajo rug which surpassed Duchamp's work in beauty, but otherwise applauded the quality and innovativeness of the Armory Show. Oliver W. Larkin, Art and Life in America, 2nd ed., rev. (New York, 1960), pp. 363-364.
22. Cram, "The Limits of Modernism in Art," 11-13.
23. Amy Lowell, of course, did write in free verse, but then Cram, despite his earlier attempts at poetry, never claimed any special competency as a judge of it. What does seem surprising, however, is his denunciation of Art Nouveau, a style he had greatly admired in his earlier years. Ibid.; Cram, "The Second Coming of Art," 196-200.
24. Cram, "The Limits of Modernism in Art," 12.
25. Ralph Adams Cram, "Architecture Marches On," The Architectural Forum, 70 (February, 1939), 134. The Columbian Exposition retrospectively seemed

better when Cram compared it to the 1933 World's Fair, which was also held in Chicago and which was a model of "incorrigible ugliness." Ralph Adams Cram, "Retrogression, Ugliness," The Architectural Forum, LIX (July, 1933), 24. In this same issue Frank Lloyd Wright's "Another 'Pseudo'" also condemned the 1933 exhibition.

26. Cram, My Life, pp. 169-170.
27. Cram, "Architecture Marches On," 134; Ralph Adams Cram, "Will This Modernism Last?" The House Beautiful, LXV (January, 1929), 45.
28. Cram, My Life, p. 169.
29. Frank Lloyd Wright, Genius and Mobocracy (New York, 1949), pp. xi-xiii, 14-16, 36, 65, 94. See also Robert C. Twombly, Frank Lloyd Wright: An Interpretive Biography (New York, 1973).
30. Cram, "Will This Modernism Last?" 45, 88. See also, Ralph Adams Cram, "The Rediscovery of Quality in Building," Arts and Decoration, XXI (September, 1924), 16-19.
31. Ralph Adams Cram, Convictions and Controversies (Boston, 1935), pp. 40-44.
32. Cram, My Life, pp. 256-257. Cram was pleased, moreover, that designers of skyscrapers had not followed the example of Cass Gilbert's Woolworth Tower and had not continued to use Gothic ornamentation. Pope, "Architecture of America Molds Beauty Anew," 3.
33. Cram, My Life, p. 257.
34. Though the New England Mutual Life Insurance Company Building was completed (except for an extensive addition in 1962) the year before his death, Cram had taken no active part in its design or implementation.
35. John Burchard and Albert Bush-Brown, The Architecture of America: A Social and Cultural History (Boston, 1961), p. 450.
36. Cram, "Architecture Marches On," 134.
37. Cram, "Art and Contemporary Society," 26; Cram, "Retrogression, Ugliness," 25. Claiming that, with the possible exception of the Scandinavian countries, the United States since 1900 had had the finest domestic architecture anywhere, he noted that this was a result of architects and a judicious fashion imposing their wills on a recalcitrant public. Nonetheless, he thought that resorts, seaside cottages, and suburbs continued to display a striking vulgarity in taste. Ralph Adams Cram, "The Preeminence of Our Own Domestic

Architecture," <u>Arts and Decoration</u>, XXII (April, 25), 21.

38. Cram was very unhappy that functionalism had already made substantial inroads into the architecture of churches, schools, and country houses. Cram, "Architecture Marches On," 134. One hopes for the sake of his peace of mind that he knew nothing of the Princeton Architectural Round Table held in June, 1937. At this conference the famous modernist Ely Jacques Kahn asked some students if Princeton, much of which was Cram's handiwork, were destroyed, would they like it rebuilt by Le Corbusier (whose work Cram despised). They answered in the affirmative. Burchard and Bush-Brown, <u>Architecture</u>, p. 460.

39. Cram, <u>My Life</u>, p. 237.

40. Robert M. Crunden, <u>From Self to Society, 1919-1941</u> (Englewood Cliffs, New Jersey, 1972), p. 164. And perhaps the richest, it should be added, since it has been estimated that in 1925 Cram had five million dollars worth of projects coming into his firm. <u>Boston Sunday Globe</u>, January 14, 1968.

41. For the best illustrated book on Cram's architecture, see <u>Ralph Adams Cram, Cram and Ferguson</u> (New York and London, 1931). For his personal account of the work he did during the 1920's and 1930's, see <u>My Life</u>, pp. 236-258.

42. Cram, <u>My Life</u>, pp. 247-250.

43. Ibid., pp. 250-253. Though the Cathedral was unfinished at the time he wrote his autobiography, Cram approved of it and confessed that the three architects in charge of its design had perhaps been more faithful to Vaughan's intentions than he himself might have been.

44. James M. Fitch, "St. John the Divine," <u>Architectural Forum</u> (December, 1954), 113-114. Fitch argued for its completion in a modern style.

45. "A Dome for the Divine," <u>Time</u>, 88 (December 2, 1966), 78.

46. Despite the overall Gothic design of the Cathedral, Cram convinced the building committee to allow Carrère and Hastings, the firm specified by a donor, to design the Chapel of St. Ambrose in the Italian Renaissance style, the style for which that firm was best known. He was gratified by the results. Cram, <u>My Life</u>, pp. 179-180. For his general recollections of the work on St. John's, see ibid., pp. 167-184.

47. The New York Times, May 21, 1973.
48. Cram, My Life, pp. 176, 184.
49. Thomas E. Tallmadge, The Story of Architecture in America, 2nd Ed., rev. (New York, 1936), p. 304.
50. Joseph Hudnut, "The Romantic Architecture of Morningside Heights," Columbia University Quarterly, XXII, (December, 1930), 401, 403.
51. Ralph Adams Cram, "The Romantic Architecture of Morningside Heights," Columbia University Quarterly, XXIII, (March, 1931), 23-24.
52. Cram, "The Test of Beauty," 13.
53. Cram, My Life, pp. 225-226; John Nicholas Brown et al., "Memoir: Ralph Adams Cram," Speculum: A Journal of Mediaeval Studies, XVIII, (July, 1943), 388-389; Speculum, I (October, 1926), 1.
54. Cram, My Life, p. 224.
55. Letter of Ralph Adams Cram to Rush C. Hawkins, November 21, 1918, in Rush C. Hawkins Papers, Annmary Brown Memorial, Brown University.
56. Although Cram left the editorial responsibilities entirely to Williams, he became a frequent contributor to the journal.
57. It was only on his first visit to Spain in the early 1920's that Cram discovered the beauty of Spanish Gothic, particularly as it found expression in the interior of the Cathedral of Seville. As for Spain itself, he considered that country to be "in the vanguard of real civilization" and the "last stronghold of real Christian civilization." Ralph Adams Cram, "Spanish Notes," The American Architect, CXXV (January 16, 1924), 47-54; Cram, My Life, p. 140; letter of Ralph Adams Cram to Mr. ? White, n.d., Boston Public Library. With the support of the Mediaeval Academy, he visited Palma de Mallorca several years later and made, in his opinion, the first accurate architectural drawings of its extraordinary Cathedral. See Ralph Adams Cram, The Cathedral of Palma de Mallorca: An Architectural Study (Cambridge, Massachusetts, 1932).
58. Cram, Substance of Gothic, p. 43.
59. Ralph Adams Cram, The Catholic Church and Art (New York, 1930), p. 110.
60. Ibid., pp. 110-111. See also Cram's introduction to James McFarlan Baker, American Churches, II (New York, 1915). He noted that while there were very few gifted church builders around 1900, twenty-five years later there were at least fifty such artists. Ralph Adams Cram, Church Building,

3rd ed., rev. (Boston, 1924), p. 290.

61. Ralph Adams Cram, "What Can Be Done for Art?" The Commonweal, X (June 12, 1929), 153-155.

62. Ralph Adams Cram, "Reflections Upon Art," The Commonweal, X (June 5, 1929), 122.

63. Stuart C. Henry (ed.), A Miscellany of American Christianity: Essays in Honor of H. Shelton Smith (Durham, North Carolina, 1963), p. 389.

64. Vogt's position seemed to draw nearer to Cram's when he wrote in the preface to his 1929 edition of Art & Religion: "...a Gothic structure emphasizes primarily religion itself rather than the ideas about it or ethics that flow from it." He added: "There is ample evidence in the most recent developments of the pictorial and plastic arts in churches, that they may intimate new theologies and new ethics caught up into and enlivened by the abiding psychological forms of the religious experience realized in a great building of the Gothic language." Von Ogden Vogt, Art & Religion, 2nd ed., rev. (New Haven, Connecticut, 1929), pp. x-xi.

65. Ralph Adams Cram, Convictions and Controversies, p. 245; Ralph Adams Cram, Towards the Great Peace (Boston, 1922), p. 205.

66. He did not underestimate the general problems presented by Episcopalians, however. In 1913, for example, he found himself denouncing the Lord Bishop of Oxford for having driven from the Church of England several prelates who had abandoned the Anglican form of communion in favor of that of Rome. See Ralph Adams Cram, An Open Letter to the Right Reverend Charles Gore, Lord Bishop of Oxford (1913), pp. 1-21. At the end of 1971, the Anglican-Roman Catholic International Commission announced that it had reached an "essential" agreement on the doctrine of the Eucharist. The New York Times, December 31, 1971.

67. Cram, Great Peace, p. 195; Cram, Convictions and Controversies, p. 67.

68. Cram, Great Peace, p. 202.

69. Richard B. Hovey, John Jay Chapman--An American Mind (New York, 1959), pp. 281-282.

70. "When Men of Good-Will Get Together," The Litererary Digest, 103 (December 14, 1929), 22.

71. This may have been due to an abatement of anti-Semitism on Cram's part and/or to an ignorance of his earlier prejudiced statements on the part of

the editors of <u>American Hebrews</u>.
72. "Protestantism <u>Is Bankrupt</u>," <u>Time</u>, XXVII (January 6, 1936), 32-33. The article features a simply extraordinary picture of Cram, bedecked with wig, cape, cassock, and bishop's staff.
73. Ralph Adams Cram, <u>Gold, Frankincense and Myrrh</u> (Boston, 1919), p. 60. Cram's expressed belief in miracles was very likely a literal one. Always somewhat of a mystic in religious matters, he returned from a trip to Europe in 1910 with a piece of bone from a martyred abbot and the experience of a religious vision. Letter of Ralph Adams Cram to Louise Imogen Guiney, August 17, 1910, Louise Imogen Guiney Papers, Holy Cross College.

CHAPTER IX

THE NEW DEAL AND THE NEW MEDIEVALISM

Throughout the 1930's Cram began to devote less
time to his professional practice. The reason surely
was not one of declining health or stamina. On the
contrary, he remained vigorous during most of these
years. He paid less attention to his firm's business
basically because now, in his twilight years, he wished to give as much time and effort as possible to his
undeclared avocation--writing. On the subject of art
and religion, so important to him in the twenties, he
continued his labors, and within the decade published
several articles and two books, The Catholic Church
and Art (1930) and The Cathedral of Palma de Mallorca
(1932). Increasingly, however, he turned to the critical political, economic, and social questions posed
by the Depression. An abundance of articles, many
collected in Convictions and Controversies (1935), and
a full-length study, The End of Democracy (1937), resulted.[1] These works were to constitute his final and
most searing indictment of modern society.
Cram was not in the least astonished by the coming of the Great Depression. Though somewhat surprised at the relative rapidity with which it had
followed the events of 1914-1918, he had been predicting a breakdown for the capitalist system since
even before World War One. Blaming the ineptitude of
the business community as the immediate cause of the
nation's economic collapse, he reserved his strongest
censure for the interrelated, causative role played by
democracy: "The Great War was to be fought, we were
told, to make the world safe for democracy, but we are
beginning now to realize that it was the wrong sort of
democracy."[2] Throughout the years of the Depression
Cram reiterated many of the complaints he had been
voicing against the democratic system for more than
three decades; he also added new ones. For the in-
tensity of these denunciations he has a reputation as
a virulent foe of democracy.[3] To an extent--but only
to an extent--does this criticism seem justifiable.
Lucubrations notwithstanding, he contineud to regard

himself not as an anti-democrat, but as a dedicated champion of the "right" or "High" democracy. Whatever label one may wish to append to these convictions, the fact remains that his critique of democracy, while at times idiosyncratic and never widely accepted, is by no means devoid of penetrating observations and constructive suggestions. It seems, in short, to involve the ancient and delicate question of separating wheat from chaff.

Any analysis of Cram's later animadversions on democracy must necessarily include his concept of "mass-man," a term which appears with the regularity of a motif in the vast majority of his writings of this period. As far back as his wartime polemics he had shown concern for the blindness and possible tyranny of the majority, hurling his vituperations at the "wrong" democracy, which he more customarily called, "the democracy of method." It was not until 1930, however, that the phrase "mass-man" first appeared in his writings--interestingly enough, in an article based on a commencement address he gave at Rice Institute.[4] The difference between the earlier and later anti-democratic pronouncements is significant. At the time of the war his distrust for the average man was tempered with a certain sympathy, with the bulk of his contempt reserved for leaders; by 1930, however, the distrust had intensified into phobia and the contempt was now directed chiefly at the average man himself.

A pivotal influence in this transformation in his thinking was José Ortega y Gasset's The Revolt of the Masses. Undoubtedly, Cram arrived at his concept of "mass-man" on his own. Though Ortega's widely read book was published in 1930, the year Cram first used his term, it was not translated into English until two years later. Since the architect neither spoke nor read more than a few words of Spanish, he could not have read the Ortega book until 1932 at the earliest, though he may have been aware of its general theme. After 1932, however, there is a reference to the Spaniard to be found in virtually every article that he wrote pertaining to mass-man. The denunciation of mediocrity and the call for rule by an elite, as enunciated by a writer of Ortega's stature, only served to confirm what Cram already believed. Reading Ortega while in his sixties proved no less an influence on him than had the reading of Ruskin while in his teens.

To a significant extent, of course, Cram had always been an elitist. Yet his respect for and belief in great leaders had been somewhat restrained by a parallel conviction that the average man--at least in organic societies such as those in the Middle Ages-- was capable of assuming an integral and, on the whole, beneficent function in the social process. By 1930, however, this conviction had changed dramatically. For Cram, history, no longer the interplay between the individual and the group, had become the achievement of the Carlylean hero. The mass of men, in contra- distinction, remained the "Neolithic type," having changed little, if at all, in their low intelligence and character since the dawn of human life. Moreover, by choosing its leaders "blindly, passionately, and unconsciously," the Neolithic mass had compounded civilization's problems.[5] Occasionally--and this seemed civilization's only real hope--leaders were, in some mysterious way, able to transcend their surround- ing morass. For the most part, however, the Neolith- ic mass, mistaking for its own handiwork the achieve- ments of those few who had been able to transcend Neo- lithic culture, suffered from "delusions of grandeur," aided and abetted, according to Cram, by Protestant theology and democratic ideology. For anyone who doubted that such a thing as Neolithic cutlure actual- ly existed in the United States, the architect sug- gested contemplating such phenomena as the Ku Klux Klan, fundamentalism, the Scopes trial, prohibition, the Methodist Board of Temperance, modern art, and the United States Senate. With the fortune of democracy at a new nadir throughout the West, was it any wonder, he queried, that people were seeking absolutism to re- place parliamentary forms of government?[6]

While it was in "The Limitations of Democracy" that Cram first articulated his concept of mass- or Neolithic man, it was only its elaboration in an article published two years later by The American Mer- cury that brought substantial critical attention to his point of view. The very title of this article-- "Why We Do Not Behave Like Human Beings"--is indic- ative of his growing misanthropy, and its substance reflects (once again) his dubious attempts to place his ideas on a scientific footing.

To begin with, he once more questioned the valid- ity of progressive evolution. If it were true, he ar- gued, each age should reflect greater human capaci- ties, character, and achievement. Prima facie, this was patently and historically absurd; every age had not been superior to its antecedent. The reason for this was not due to any deficiency in human aspira- tions. On the contrary, most people continued blindly to believe in and hope for linear historical progression. The insurmountable difficulty rested in the fact that, despite the progression of time, humans still derived from the same static matrix from which had sprung our Neolithic ancestors. Attacking the Darwinian concept that evolutionary movement was always from lower to higher forms and by way of the accretion of minute differences, he cited the work of the Dutch geneticist Hugo de Vries, who accounted for change by mutations (the "catastrophic process") and warned of atavistic reversions to type. The "great man," for Cram, was thus the fortunate and fortuitous mutant, the person who mysteriously and miraculously rose above the Neolithic mass. "In other words," he argued, "the just line of demarcation should be drawn not between Neolithic mass which was, is now and ever shall be." It was not the difference between a George Washington and the Missing Link which was important; it was the gulf that separated--and here Cram was at his most prejudiced--such persons as St. Francis, the Earl of Strafford, Robert E. Lee, and Thomas A. Edison from John Calvin, Thomas Cromwell, Leon Trotsky and Al Capone. As for the present, he snarled: "I suggest that the cause of comprehensive failure and the bar to recovery is the persistence of the everlasting Neolithic Man and his assumption of universal control."[7] Reconsidering his uncharitable remarks, he apologized in later years to the ghosts of our Neolithic ancestors for having compared them with contemporary mass-men, much as Mark Twain's Mysterious Stranger had offered regrets to animals for their being likened to humans; in both instances, the former were of a superior order.[8]

It seemed fitting that "Why We Do Not Behave Like Human Beings" should appear in The American Mercury. Founded in 1924 by Henry Louis Mencken as a successor to The Smart Set, the Mercury, with its trenchant but witty defense of human values and liberty against the onslaught of the "booboisie," proved to be one of the brightest and most popular journals of the decade. By the early 1930's, however, its celebrated wit seemed inappropriate to the hard times the nation was experiencing. Mutual disenchantment grew between the magazine and its readers, as Mencken's barbs grew outlandishly vitriolic until the time of his resignation as editor in 1933. Mencken, in short, had become fully as alienated from American society as Cram.

Cram and Mencken became acquainted at least as early as 1923. In that year the journalist wrote the architect to suggest that he contribute something for the forthcoming Mercury, perhaps along lines of "another assault on big cities" (a possible reference to Cram's attacks on large cities found in his various wartime writings).[9] Cram, who found himself "stimulated and vastly entertained" by, as well as in general agreement with, what Mencken preached, confessed that he had not written much lately due to his professional preoccupations. He acknowledged, however, that "the necessity for eruption approaches."[10] The "eruption"--at least with regard to writing for the Mercury--did not take place until the thirties. In part, this resulted from his growing aversion to the manner in which Mencken's journal "shamelessly recorded" the antics of the twenties.[11] Equally important, his principal interests during the Jazz Age--art and religion--were not those of the Mercury.

When he received the architect's 1932 article, Mencken privately noted that "Cram's idea that Neanderthal man still survives is anything but new. It has been brought forth at various times by anthropologists." Still, he did not question its validity: "As for me, I believe it fully and point to the United States Senate as proof."[12] Impressed by the article, the irreverent Baltimorean encouraged the Bostonian to continue his work: "It goes without saying that I'll be delighted to print anything that you have to say about American politicians....I believe that relatively few Americans realize the seriousness of the present political situation....We have come to the point where the whole American system seems in grave danger of breaking down."[13] Replying to Mencken's letter, Cram agreed with his observation, but dissented from his concluding implications: "The sooner it breaks down the better. Then there may be a chance of starting afresh."[14] As a result of their generally congruous views, Cram did submit a number of articles during the 1930's to the Mercury. Most of these were published since even after Mencken's resignation as editor in 1933, the journal continued to denigrate the prospects for democracy. In August, 1938, for example, it reprinted Cram's 1932 article, prefacing its inclusion with high praise: "....we have always considered [it] one of the most important contributions ever made to an American magazine." Indeed, as late as 1955, an editor, unaware that Cram had died more than a dozen years earlier, wrote the architect for

227

permission to reprint the article still one more
time.[15]
   Mencken and his associates on the _Mercury_ were obviously highly impressed with "Why We Do Not Behave
Like Human Beings," but Albert Jay Nock (1872 or 1873-
1945), the self-defrocked clergyman and one-time amateur baseball player, was literally overwhelmed.[16]
Nock, a spirited essayist, editor, and biographer, was
a close personal friend of Mencken and avid reader of
the _Mercury_. More than just friendship, the two men
of letters shared a remarkable harmony of views and
tastes, particularly those disparaging to American society during the twenties and thirties. Shortly after
reading Cram's article, Nock wrote to a friend:
"Ralph Cram's piece is remarkable. I have done some
heavy thinking about it, and shall try to get somebody
to publish something--probably Sedgwick--to give his
idea more currency."[17] In addition to urging friends
to read the article, Nock was impelled within the
next few years to write two of his own articles as
favorable critiques of the Cram piece.[18]
   Nock's general political philosophy, clearly posited in _Our Enemy, the State_, might best be described
as that of a radical libertatian. Indeed, his various views strongly resemble an amalgam of those held
by the men whose lives he chronicled--Jefferson, Rabe-
lais, and Henry George. To his many works he brought
the convictions of a Jeffersonian democrat, the zest
for life of a Rabelaisian _bon_ _vivant_, and the modified
capitalistic concerns of a Georgite Single-Taxer. As
a champion of untrammeled individualism and as a neu-
tralist during World War I, he had won a reputation
for radicalism, a reputation further enhanced by his
editorship of the _Freeman_, a short-lived but excellent
journal of the twenties. In the thirties, Nock, like
Mencken, fell victim to changing times. Neither had
changed his basic convictions, but a generation suffering from the woes of the depression now turned a
deaf or hostile ear to their attacks on the New Deal's
enhancement of state power at the expense of the
liberty of the individual. Both, as a result,
achieved new reputations as conservative, if not reactionary, critics, hopelessly out of touch with the
mainstream of the nation's contemporary life. Given
the logic of his convictions, Nock doubtlessly would
have been cast as a "nay-sayer" at any rate. Cram's
seminal article, nevertheless, gave him a strong
push in that direction.
   Actually, Nock had begun to question the desir-

ability of democracy, at least in its current manifestations, for some years before having read the article. Oswald Spengler's The Decline of the West and the Reverend Samuel D. McConnell's Immortability, a work which cast doubt on man's humanity, had shaken his democratic faith, as had even more Ortega's The Revolt of the Masses. Indeed, recognizing that Cram had no special qualifications as a scientist, Nock's "shock of recognition" upon reading "Why We Do Not Behave Like Human Beings" had largely been made possible by these other writings.[19] By 1931 Nock's reservations concerning democracy were becoming increasingly clear. Citing the democratic resentment of natural superiority, he complained: "It must aim at no ideals above those of the average man; that is to say, it must regulate itself by the lowest common denominator of intelligence, taste and character in the society which it represents." And although the false kind of democracy had nothing in common with a true democracy, it boded ill for the future--Cram's exact sentiments.[20]

Encountering Cram's thesis seemed to verify Nock's worst fears. Republicanism, of which he had long been an adherent, now seemed only "a record of continuous, reciprocal and progressive corruption between Homo sapiens and the State. The Neolithic mass corrupts the State, and in turn the State still further corrupts the Neolithic mass; and this brings about a general condition which appears to be increasingly difficult and unsatisfactory, as well as increasingly repulsive and degrading." Until Cram's thesis was conclusively proven, he could remain "a Jeffersonian and Georgite of sorts." He admitted, however: "His [Cram's] history is sound, his logic is airtight, and I have made observations precisely like his."[21]

In Memoirs of a Superfluous Man, his splendid autobiography published the year after Cram's death, Nock continued to cite the importance of his friends's thesis. By drawing attention to the flaws inherent in the democratic, rational, and humane concepts of the Enlightenment, the architect had made it impossible for him to accept any longer his cherished Jeffersonian view of man. As for the idea of human progress, Nock had come, instead, to accept the "periodicity" of historical flux, a periodicity, not incidentally, which he divided into segments of five centuries. Without explicitly stating so, he had also generally accepted Cram's cyclical view of history.[22] If he could find one weakness in Cram's thought, it

was the latter's failure to extend his premises to
their logical conclusions. Having grasped the truth
that the masses were Neolithics in Homo sapiens'
clothing, Cram, so Nock thought, had failed to see the
possibility of revolutionizing the entire field of
genetics by first breeding for spiritual qualities and
then removing the various material obstructions which
might prevent this resultant elite from reaching dominant positions in society.[23]   Cram had not overlooked
this possibility, however. Nock was simply unaware of
how strongly Cram, for all his prejudices and elitism,
detested eugenics and the Nietzschean concept of the
Superman.

As for Cram, the effect of his thesis concerning
mass- or Neolithic man served not to negate but to
reinforce long-held convictions that the seeming breakdown of civilization in the twentieth century was the
result of the various nefarious developments which had
been systematically weakening the West over the past
five centuries. With the malady apparently in its
terminal stages, what now had to be decided was
whether to perform radical surgery and extend the life
of society, though without any real hope for recovery,
or to practice a sort of societal euthanasia. Cram
opted for the latter, but with certain critical stipu-
lations. The present five-hundred-year cycle was
drawing to its inevitable and inglorious end. Nothing
or no one could change that. Yet the dominant character of the next cycle would depend, to a large extent,
on what forces, institutions, and spirit survived the
present epoch. Despite the determinism of his cyclical theory of history, Cram was, at heart, a Pelagian
Christian. That is to say, he believed that man possessed free will and could seek and, to a degree, earn
his own salvation in this world, as well as in the
hereafter. Indeed, since the technological and scientific advances of the past one hundred and fifty years
had brought unparalleled material prosperity, it seemed reasonable, possibly likely, that the West, particularly the United States, might reach unprecedented
heights in the next historical cycle if it acted with
wisdom.[24]   The title of one of his articles written in
1934, "Recovery or Regeneration?" serves as the fundamental question he posed to his contemporaries. While
both recovery and regeneration seemed possible for
Cram, only the latter was desirable. For total regeneration to be achieved, however, it would first be
necessary to change drastically the existing structure
and thinking of society.

When the Great Depression set in shortly after
the Wall Street debacle of "Black Friday," 1929, Cram
correctly noted that overproduction, masked by an emphasis on consumerism, had brought technological and
industrial society to a cul-de-sac. Nor did he find
any basis for optimistically believing that the system could easily engineer an avenue of escape from
this position.[25] The immediate problem, however,
seemed primarily a political one. Agonizing over the
failure of President Hoover and Congress even to
abate, much less solve, the worst effects of the crisis, he reserved his special wrath for the lawmakers.
Though having long ago concluded that modern democratic legislative bodies were worse than useless, he
thought that the present one was "marked by a more
exaggerated state of imbecility and incapacity than
has been recorded thus far in the history of the nation."[26] Complaining that the Chief Executive could
not dissolve the legislature--one of the few ways in
which he deemed European constitutions superior to the
American one--he suggested in July, 1932, that Hoover
act extra-constitutionally by dissolving Congress,
calling in the various state governors to form an interim government, and then governing by fiat. Since
the governors (who, he believed, generally had more
character and ability than congressmen) would have to
approve of the president's edicts, Hoover would not
be analogous to a Hitler or a Mussolini. Meanwhile,
this newly formed "council of State" could perform
such vitally needed services as reorganizing the government, reducing the budget, repealing the Eighteenth
Amendment in order to make further excise taxes possible, enacting a revenue-producing tariff, and dealing
with reparations, war debts and, of paramount concern,
assistance to the unemployed. The nation, moreover,
would hold its scheduled elections in November for
President, Vice-President, and Congress, with Hoover
having announced beforehand that he would abide by the
results.[27]
    The excoriation of Congress and the appeal for
Hoover to rule, however temporarily, by decree offer
a clear indication of Cram's thinking on how to combat
the Depression: he wanted a dictator to rule the
country. When Franklin D. Roosevelt succeeded to
the presidency, Cram thought that he had found his
dictator. The point was moot.
    For a man who had come to espouse a "great man"
theory of history, Cram found remarkably few American
statesmen to idolize. Hamilton, of course, he had ad-

mired from his early years;[28] Jefferson, whom formerly he had invidiously compared to Hamilton, now, too, had become a statesman in his eyes, thanks largely to the influence of Nock. Lincoln also was of heroic stature, as were two early twentieth-century figures, Theodore Roosevelt and William Jay Gaynor.[29] With the advent of Franklin Roosevelt to power, one more hero was added to his small but distinguished pantheon of national statesmen.

For Cram, Roosevelt, the "one supreme politician since Lincoln," was a man of "high principles, integrity of character, and a wider breadth of vision than most politicians."[30] He was, moreover, the symbolic man on horseback, for the nation, as Cram predicted, was reverting back to Caesarism:

> Historically this course is strictly in accordance with precedent while from a practical standpoint it is not only wise but apparently the only thing to do. Neolithic Man, being in the preponderant majority, having chosen its own kind, with a strong infusion of Paleolithic elements, to make, interpret and enforce such laws as commend themselves to his grade of intelligence, discovers, or is convincingly told, that they have rather made a mess of things.... Either he calls stertorously for a man to take over and perform anew the function of Hercules in the Augean stables, or the man himself, and of his own motion assumes this function, is gratefully accepted and has the plenary powers he has assumed obediently ratified.[31]

It is of more than passing interest to note Cram's general admiration for Roosevelt. As two historians of the period have noted: "For those who would be critics of Roosevelt and the New Deal there was something for everybody."[32] Traditionally, critics of that president--both then and now--have divided in their reasons for censure. Those on the Left have attacked him for shoring up a decadent capitalism; those on the Right have fumed over his "anti-capitalism" and expansion of governmental powers. Though he was invariably labeled a conservative, Cram's stand more closely approximated that of the Left. While he assuredly did not want Marxian communism to replace capitalism, he did espouse a form of communal socialism. Moreover, by lauding FDR's extensive use of executive power, a desideratum generally professed by most leftist critics, he parted company with the Right, including his otherwise ideologically sympathetic friends, Nock and Mencken.[33]

But if the architect expected miracles from Roosevelt he was soon sorely disappointed. Writing in 1934, he cited the president's efforts as having been "magnificent" but only "palliative." Necessary as they were in this time of crisis, they would end in a few years, and the nation would still have to face the harder, more important question of recovery or regeneration. Should it choose the former, it would be insufficient, "and the danger of economic and social collapse, with chaos and revolution just beyond, remains as it was before." Coming to the end of its historical cycle, the United States, as part of the West, had the alternatives of falling into a new Dark Age or achieving a genuine rebirth. Should Roosevelt and the nation, on the other hand, opt for regeneration rather than mere recovery, "then the events of the next few years may send the middle decades of this century into the records of history as constituting one of the great creative revolutions of all time ...."[34] It was becoming increasingly clear to Cram, however, that, for all his abilities and good intentions, Roosevelt was able to lead the country only so far along the road to regeneration. Though a statesman, he was like Daniel in the lion's den, only this time surrounded by a pride of politicians and the "collegiate schools of sociology and economics." Agreeing with Nock, particularly with his visceral Our Enemy, the State, Cram indicted politicians as massmen, who, despite their education, could not rise above their troglodytic status. As for the "Brains Trust," they had been responsible for such incredibly poor laws as the Agricultural Adjustment Act, which he dubbed a creation of "the surrealist school of economics."[35]

It seems anomalous, to say the very least, that Cram, the perfervid extoller of the liberty of the Middle Ages, should advocate dictatorship. In fact, the Gothicist, who despite his undeniable dogmatism could be pragmatic to the point of rashness (his suggestion that Hoover rule by decree being a case in point), had advanced dictatorship only as a temporary and emergency measure. Permanent dictatorships were disastrous, undermining liberty by confirming the "omnipotent secular State."[36] Having originally approved of Mussolini's dictatorship (until his aggres-

233

sive foray into Ethiopia) and having called for a similar form of government for his particular bête noire, France, he had concluded by the mid-1930's that: "Fascism, Bolshevism, Nazism, have produced substitutes [for parliamentary democracy], but day by day and in every way it begins to look as though the last state would be worse than the first, though such a result staggers the imagination."[37] Meanwhile, Roosevelt, even as a temporary "dictator," had failed to live up to Cram's expectations. In 1938, the year most historians consider as signifying the end of the New Deal's forward thrust, the architect was able to discern only a "bureaucracy touched with Messianic vision" at work. The United States had but an "incipient dictatorship tempered by a smile and periodically obstructed by partisan politics."[38]

Cram's dalliance with dictatorship was, in reality, more of a mild flirtation than an amorous affair. Beneath the frustrated appeals for an autocrat lay the stronger hopes for a democratic solution to the crisis. Admitting that "the record of democratic failure is monotonous,"[39] he sincerely believed that only a radical return to the right kind of democracy could reverse the nation's ill-starred course. His suggestions along this line were, as usual, a provocative blend of the far-fetched and the possible.

Whereas during World War I Cram had differentiated between "the democracy of the ideal" and "the democracy of method," he now contrasted "High Democracy" with "Low Democracy," terms which were more euphonious but reflected basically the same content of his earlier dichotomy. High Democracy had been achieved as the "Monarchical Feudalism" of the Middle Ages and reconfirmed by the "Aristocratic Republic" of America's Founding Fathers; Low Democracy, "the bastard form of an originally sane and fine idea," was insolently ushered in by the French Revolution and subsequently came to dominate throughout the West (except possibly in Switzerland and the Scandinavian countries) until the present when "it has had to be abolished as a public nuisance in most of the countries of Europe."[40] Cram by no means totally denied the validity of the aspirations of democratic revolutions. Indeed, they sometimes—but not often—achieved very real successes such as overthrowing or diminishing the powers of a decadent and effete dynasty or aristocracy and, to some degree, returning land to a dispossessed peasantry. Yet he added:

The point is, however, that these laudable ends obtained, the revolutionists should have stopped there. The moment they tried to set up a new and democratic form of government, they exceeded their mandate, fabricated a democratic device which had no reasonable relation to reality and, indeed, guaranteed the return of the old ills against which they had contended, only at other hands and in somewhat different forms. The power that wins a war should never organize the victory, for the mental and character requirements for the several tasks are different in their nature. [41]

This general condemnation was not meant to apply to the American Revolution, which, in Cram's opinion, was not really a revolution at all, but the legitimate attempt by oppressed landed and commercial interests to secure their due rights as Englishmen. [42] Further, he insisted that the Constitution was the work of "statesmen and gentlemen." [43] Indeed, during the Early National period the nation was graced with a natural aristocracy comprised of New York landed gentry, Boston Brahmins and China traders, and Souther planters. [44] With the advent of Jacksonian Democracy, however, national development went astray. "When universal suffrage came in," moaned Cram, "democracy went out as a practical proposition." The Founding Fathers simply had been unable to foresee that power would be placed "in the hands of a propertyless, unfree proletariat, organized, directed and exploited by a caste of professional politicians deriving directly from this same class of men." Seeing the Democratic party invoking the names of Jefferson and Jackson simultaneously, as if they stood for identical philosophies, he complained, "is to gauge with some accuracy the mental calibre of the general run of human beings." [45]

The post-Civil War problems of Reconstruction, urbanization, mass immigration, the rise of corporations and labor unions, technological innovations, and Darwinism might have been resolved more favorably, he argued, had better men been in responsible positions. By the late nineteenth century, unfortunately, the pernicious interplay of power based on science and technology and liberalism had triumphed and had exalted the mass-man. The sheer strength of money and corporate organization had completely dislodged the natural aristocracy of character, land, or status, and liberals had joined forces with do-gooders. As a result, "with the best intentions in the world, the

paving of hell went on apace," as did the transition
from High to Low Democracy. Working on the mistaken
assumption that "the cure for Democracy is more Democracy," the nation's leaders had achieved a dubious
success. Or as Cram put it: "The operation was successful, but the patient died."[46]

The patient may have been dead for some time, but
Dr. Cram was not beyond attempting a bit of resuscitation. The first two operations pursuant to this end
involved the use of a scalpel (or perhaps "hatchet"
would be more appropriate) to remove abcesses which
had formed on the Constitution and the Supreme Court.
For Cram, there was nothing wrong with the Constitution of 1787. In fact, with its "aristocratic-repub-
lican form of organic law with no salient democratic
features," it was a masterpiece.[47] Yet with the exception of the Thirteenth Amendment, every amendment
subsequent to the Bill of Rights had, to one degree
or another, militated against the intent of the docu-
ment's framers. The Twelfth had put the election of
the President in popular hands; the Fourteenth and
Fifteenth had given the suffrage to a not-yet qualified group; the Sixteenth had led to too much government and had become confiscatory; the Seventeenth, the
worst of the lot, had negated the bicameral system by
destroying indirect elelctions and had been indirectly
responsible for the rise of such ruthless demagogues
as Huey Long; the Eighteenth was totally absurd.[48]
He would have been delighted to see all these amendments abrogated, but confessed that he would be satisfied with nullifying or at least curbing the effects
of the Twelfth, Sixteenth, and Seventeenth.[49]

One might assume that, like virtually all conservatives of the period, Cram would have rallied to the
defense of the beleaguered Supreme Court, as it struck
down a host of popular laws passed by Congress. Quite
the contrary. In a statement reminiscent of Justice
Oliver Wendell Holmes' famous dictum that the life of
the law was based on experience and not logic, he denounced the parochialism of the Court, insisting that
"life is of greater moment than juridical formulae."[50]
At times the medievalist's hard-headed pragmatism and
realism could be downright astounding. "Whether we
like it or not," he insisted, "and approve or not, it
is pretty clear that State power is coming in to assume wider and wider control of certain individual and
corporate activities. Our destiny, like that of other
peoples, is inescapable, and before long the major
part of our natural resources are coming under govern-

236

ment control and administration." Hence, it was imperative to revise the Constitution "to bring it into a relationship of reality with the new social, economic and industrial conditions that, in less than a century, have made a new world as diametrically different from that of 1787 as this, in its turn, diverged from the world of St. Louis and Innocent III."[51] The Constitution, as then interpreted by the majority of the Court, clearly took little cognizance of either these vast changes or the popular will. Moreover, Cram believed that by invalidating legislative enactments the "Nine Old Men" were continuing to exert the nefarious usurpation of constitutional power initiated by Chief Justice John Marshall. Clearly, the Court had to be curbed, but how to achieve this troubled him. A constitutional convention or further amendments might work, but given the capacity of the nation's legislators, he was dubious. Instead, he proposed that Congress act: (1) to permit the Court to void legislation only by unanimous vote, and/or (2) to allow the President, in cases of split opinions, to refer the matter to the people through the state governments. When Cram rhetorically asked, "Back to What Constitution?" he answered quite simply: the Constitution of 1787.[52]

If, in a sense, Cram took a scalpel or hatchet to the Constitution and Court, he turned a howitzer on certain other ingredients of the political process such as the party-system, the lawmakers, and the electorate. As for political parties, he was pleased to quote the cynical Albert Jay Nock: "What is a party? It is an aggregation formed around the nucleus of individual politicians; that is to say, a nucleus of men who are interested in jobs. They are interested in so-called issues or principles only so far as these may be made contributing to their interest in jobs. The only actual differentiation among them is that one is a party of job-holders, and the others are parties of job-seekers."[53] By and large, parties, for Cram, were collections of mass-men, who, in their ineptitude and selfishness, had helped to make the parliamentary system "probably the worst system of government ever devised by man."[54] As with the various amendments to the Constitution, he would have liked to have seen them abolished.

Cram had denounced the various levels of legislative branches of government as early as the 1920's. "Democracies always govern too much," he complained, "that is one of their great weaknesses." Since, in his opinion, legislatures were most culpable in this respect, he proposed that the executive branches take the initiative in introducing bills. Legislators thus would be reduced to introducing supplementary legislation.[55] Meanwhile, for the national government he envisioned (though admitting it probably would not be feasible) something akin to the British system, whereby the President would serve for life or during good behavior. In turn, his appointed cabinet would also be responsible to Congress.[56] Relating to this general problem of executive versus legislative power, he called for an overall decentralization of government and proposed that the various states, to be more easily governable, be regrouped into a few regional units, a proposal which currently finds numerous supporters.[57]

With regard to the electorate, Cram considered many--too many--unfit to exercise the privilege of suffrage. As mass-men, they did not govern, but, instead, were governed by the more clever of their own ilk and never voted for policies or candidates, but merely against them. The various recommendations for restricting the suffrage which he volunteered over the years allow his anti-democratic convictions to stand out in high relief. For example, he wished to withhold the franchise from those convicted of crimes or misdemeanors involving "moral turpitude," a term which in his definition included such heinous offenses as cruelty to animals and libel, and from those who could neither speak, read, nor write English. Pursuant to the latter, he called for even more restrictive immigration laws. Harkening back a century to the days of Chancellor Kent, he also wished to reinstate property qualifications in order to reduce the size of the electorate, though "property" was to be construed broadly so as to include a man's profession or ownership of tools, as well as the more tangible commodities of land or money.[58] While he realized that the reduction of the suffrage was highly unrealistic, it did not deter him from an unswerving conviction that the cure for democracy was less democracy.

When the mass of voters, refusing to heed the editorial advice proffered by the heavy majority of the nation's newspapers, reelected Roosevelt as president in 1936, Cram apologized for his scurrilous denunciation of their intellectual capacities.[59] Even before this, however, he seems to have been taking a somewhat more generous view of their abilities. Although he never actually renounced his theory of Neolithic man--indeed, he claimed that he had become even more convinced of its veracity--there is a good deal of evidence to indicate his feeling that mass-man was not altogether beyond redemption. One might not have unreasonably thought that before 1936 Cram considered virtually everyone--with only himself and possibly Nock, Mencken, President Roosevelt, and a fortunate few others excepted--to be mass-men. With the publication of "The Forgotten Class" in the spring of 1936, however, one can definitely sense a new direction in his thinking.[60] For all his likely protestations to the contrary, "mass-man" had been metamorphosized into "class-man."

The "Forgotten Class" described by Cram was closely related not to Roosevelt's downtrodden, impoverished "forgotten man," but to William Graham Sumner's "forgotten man," that member of society who quietly went along doing life's business without asking quarter from any other man, let alone the government. According to Cram, this motley group included: farmers, small shopkeepers, tradesmen, craftsmen, artisans, most of the professional classes, artists, teachers, "pure," as opposed to "applied" scientists, writers, clergymen, small <u>rentiers</u>, clerks, college students, and the preponderant number of unorganized skilled and unskilled laborers. In other words, it comprised "a good working majority." Despite its majority status, however, the group was finding itself increasingly crushed between the two extreme classes: the rich and the proletariat. In truth, wealth did not constitute the principal criterion for delineating all the classes. While the rich did include only the rich, the proletariat, by the architect's definition, contained organized labor, veterans' groups, and a variety of farmers ranging from the well-to-do to the lowly sharecroppers; members of the Forgotten Class might be wealthy, poor, or in-between. What he seems to have had in mind when referring to these three orders was more their attitudes and usefulness than relative wealth or occupation. Both extreme classes, for example, were characterized by inordinate self-interest and a selfish spirit of "let the devil take the hindmost." Whatever their precise definition, these disparate classes had acted in harmony to create "the technocratic, finance-capitalistic State." For T. S. Eliot, they might be the "hollow men"; for Cram, they, and not the Forgotten Class, had become the mass-men.

Though the Forgotten Class was, for all intent and purpose, the middle class, Cram hesitated to use the latter term, feeling that it had become one of opprobrium. In part, the scorn was deserved since the middle class virtues of independence, self-reliance, sociability, and patriotism, so much in evidence in the nineteenth century, had yielded in the twentieth to its vices so well described by Mencken and Sinclair Lewis. In more recent times, he acknowledged, "its vision was exceedingly circumscribed, its scheme of life earth-bound and pedestrian, its morals conspicuous but stodgy, its religion very largely compacted of the bean-supper, a degenerate Protestant superstition, and ballyhoo."

Despite this lugubrious state of affairs, Cram thought it very important to change the middle class "into a name of honor and of power rather than of disparagement." Moreover, it had been recently winning some excellent new members. Strikingly prefiguring the work done in the 1950's and the 1960's by American historians such as Richard Hofstadter and George Mowry, Cram noted that a loss of status in the old middle class (an elite in its own right) relative to the well-to-do had made them likely allies of the newer middle class. This "saving remnant"--and here he was wittingly or unwittingly using the phrase of that other elitist, Irving Babbitt--could prove the salvation of the Forgotten Class, which, assuredly, could not look to the nation's legislators, who had "forgotten" them in favor of mass-men like themselves. What they could do, however, was to recognize the commonness of their various interests. Once their class consciousness was aroused, they had only to find and accept proper leadership in the form of the "saving remnant." After all, argued a seemingly converted Cram, "mass-man is just as susceptible to good influences as well as to bad."

While he was discovering the virtues of the Forgotten Class, Cram simultaneously was writing what he sincerely hoped would be the final epitaph for Low Democracy:

> Democracy, the new democracy, both socially and politically has failed because, under the impact of mistaken philosophies and at the hands of the unfit, it has taken insufficient cognizance of the real nature of life itself and of the biological and anthropological facts. It has brought universal society to the very edge of that final abyss to which it was, in its last five-hundred-year-old phase, evidently des-

240

tined. Their destiny now being practically accomplished, it is necessary to look
forward to the new era and to make preparation for it in so far as this is humanly
possible.[61]

Cram made his theoretical preparations, and the result
was a rather fantastic alloy of fascism and medievalism.

During the twenties and thirties fascism appealed
to diverse segments of the American population. Rac-
ists, some businessmen, and a number of persons concerned with that period's law-and-order issue found
that ideology, particularly in its Italian emanation,
attractive. So did a number of conservative and
right-wing intellectuals. As John P. Diggins has
noted, the Right found in Mussolini's rule "a remedy
for America's amorphous culture and its atomistic individualism."[62] From the New Humanist Irving Babbitt
to the Southern Agrarian Stark Young, from the naturalist George Santayana to the elitist Lawrence Dennis,
intellectuals of varying conservative persuasion took
a close look at the revolutionary phenomenon to see
whether or not it held out the promise of salvation
for a damned society. A few--like Ezra Pound and
George Sylvester Viereck--either looked too closely or
did more than just look and were subsequently tried
for treason in the forties.

It is completely misleading to refer to Cram as a
fascist, in any real meaning of that term, for he ultimately found it "antipathetic and unpromising" in
terms of holding out any true hope for a troubled
world.[63] Nonetheless, during the early 1930's he did
seem to be hovering in the wings with a bouquet of
roses, not quite sure whether the drama would be a
succès de scandale or a fiasco. In part, one tends to
place him on the periphery of fascism if for no other
reason--and here one does not intend to imply any
guilt by association--than he contributed so frequently to Seward Collins' fascist-leaning American Review.[64] In part, it was also that he found the corporate state, though still in its experimental stage of
development in Europe, to be "the only sane and logical system now in process," and praised Il Duce for
his reorganization of Italian life, "though the methods and regulations thus far adopted seem appallingly
and unnecessarily complicated."[65] Most important,
however, was the fact that he drew on and wholeheartedly embraced one particular component of the fascist
credo: functional organization.

241

For Cram, functional organization or representation appeared immeasurably more reasonable and fecund than did representation by either geography or party. Or to give a hypothetical American example: a bricklayer who is a registered Democrat living in New York City is best served through the political efforts of another bricklayer who is not necessarily either a Democrat or a fellow Gothamite. Extend this example further, and one has an apolitical and vertical rather than horizontal structure of society à la fascism. Besides, reasoned Cram, "there is no valid reason why the affairs of human society should be directed by politicians anyway."[66] Following the Italian pattern, he wished to see established twenty-two such groups in the United States which would replace or at least partially offset the traditional congressional and party systems. These groups might well be responsible for the selection of both the President and the governors.[67] In any event, they would remember the Forgotten Class.

Fascism, then, may have held a certain limited appeal for the architect, but if human society were to undergo any lasting reconstruction and regeneration, it would have to look to medievalism for its primary model. Not that the features of fascism and medievalism were altogether mutually exclusive, of course. For Cram, there were a few marked similarities between the two, notably the emphasis on function and hierarchy. Yet fascism, whose actual practice was becoming increasingly repugnant to him, was, without the guiding spirit of religion, merely a secular credo, while medievalism, in contrast, represented nothing less than an organic polity permeated by the spirit of true religion and offering the highest form of civilization.

During these years Cram had been digesting the works of the Russian philosopher Nikolai Berdyaev, particularly The End of Our Time and Christianity and the Class War. In a way, Berdyaev was as important an influence on him as had been Ruskin, Spengler, and Ortega y Gasset.[68] By predicting the coming of a new Middle Ages, the Russian existentialist had helped to keep alive the aging architect's dreams of a revivified medievalism. Like his use of the Gothic in architecture, however, Cram's New Medievalism was intended to be inspirational and dynamic rather than literal and static. As he warned when delivering his Presidential Address to the Mediaeval Academy of America: "New Mediaevalism can mean neither retrogression nor archeological restoration. Not forms but ideals and governing principles are what we are to recover and use."69

For Cram, the "New Medievalism" consisted pretty much of the old medievalism he had been preaching indefatigably for nearly half a century. There were, however, emendations, elaborations, and certain new ideas. Of the last, some were jejune, others presented reasonable, occasionally highly attractive alternatives to the status quo. Whether feckless or fruitful, all evinced the sincerity and moral fervor which had been his trademark.

One aspect of this New Medievalism was a greater emphasis placed on the concept of a hierarchical society. "'Vox populi vox Dei,'" he wrote "was... a gross non sequitur that lies pretty close to the roots of the troubles that have beset the body politic (and the social body as well) during the last five centuries."70 Having lost by the mid-nineteenth century the limited aristocracy it had produced, the nation had been deprived completely of the leadership it so badly needed for guidance on public issues, as well as for models of social conduct. What passed for an elite in current times was merely a skillful group of mass-men, who had engineered their ascent by cleverly exploiting the weaknesses and credulity of their peers. Like Nock, Cram longed for the emergence of a vital and forceful <u>aristoi</u> based on the Jeffersonian criteria of birth, wealth, and talent. Towards this end he suggested the establishment of non-hereditary Orders of Knighthood, which would recognize the natural elite and reward them with the honorific title of "sir."71

That the great mass of people during the 1930's were starved for leadership, Cram entertained no doubt. In Europe, Turkey, China, even the United States, they had demonstrated repeatedly that they preferred a strong man to the chaos of anarchy. Whether he be an unabashed dictator like Hitler, Mussolini, or Stalin, or a lesser demagogue along the lines of a Huey Long or Father Coughlin, it made little difference. The important point was that he was generally accepted.72 The New Medievalism would provide the better, more genuine leadership that people sought, partly as a result of its natural aristocracy, partly--and Cram was in absolute earnest--as a result of the resurrection, in slightly disguised form, of the theory and practice of kingship.

When Cram first proudly promulgated his monarchism towards the end of the nineteenth century, he

did not, he confessed, expect to be taken seriously.
At that time, monarchism, overshadowed by democratic
forces which appeared irresistible, was nothing more
than a "pious aspiration," a "sentimental and decora-
tive" fantasy, and not a "critical" and "philosophical" credo.[73] After fifty years of painfully stumbling through its "democratic-parliamentary-represen-
tative adolescence," however, the nation, in his view,
was amenable to drastic change.[74] Moreover, it now
seemed necessary to accept a benevolent monarchism in
order to forestall a malevolent totalitarianism: "Unless we recognize conditions as they have come to be,
accept an aggrandized, directing, coordinating Executive as a political necessity, and give the Chief of
State this new status through Constitutional modifi-
cations, we may find ourselves in the same box with
Italy, Germany, the U.S.S.R. and the many other dictatorships in Europe, Asia and South America."[75]
Though accepting the legitimacy of dictatorship as a
desperate measure, he could not believe that anyone
could possibly enjoy living constanly under that form
of government. Besides, once having had dictatorship,
a nation could not revert back to a democracy even if
it so desired. Convinced of this historically as well
as theoretically fallacious argument, he posed the alternatives: dictatorship or monarchy, the "Renaissance despot" or the "patriot king."[76]

Cram's argument for monarchy did not rest entirely on his faulty assumption that, once burdened with
dictatorship, the would-be democrat could not go home
again. Even if the United States and Europe were able
to maintain or return to their present form of democracy, the Low Democracy, it would mean settling for
not the Lincolnian dream of government of, by, and for
the people, but instead, "a government of the people,
by the politicians, for the party."[77] To his way of
thinking, the West could opt either for the false democracy, which had brought it very nearly to the point
of ruin, or a new form of monarchy resting on the medieval principles of justice, order, and liberty.

The New Monarch of the New Medievalism, at least
in the United States, was to possess both the trap-
pings and substance of power. Having been chosen by
some form of indirect election (the original plan for
the Electoral College or a variation thereof), he
would hold office for good behavior or life. Among
his sweeping powers would be the right to initiate
legislation and to dismiss the legislative body if a
government bill failed to pass, a contingency which

would be followed by general elections and a new government should the incumbent one be defeated in the referendum.[78] So far, the New Monarch appears as a hybrid form of English monarch and English prime minister. While this is what he did indeed envision, Cram underscored the monarchical more than ministerial element. A debilitating weakness of the American presidency had been the obligations imposed on the Chief Executive to act, on the one hand, as guardian of the people's interests and, on the other, to preside as head of a political party. The two ineluctably worked at cross-purposes. It was imperative, therefore, that the New Monarch be totally above partisan considerations so that he might devote himself exclusively to the welfare of his people. To emphasize the richness and majesty of his position, as well as symbolically to set him further apart from the politicians, suitable regal ceremonies and rituals would be devised. Fully realizing, however, that Americans, inured to the language of republicanism, would have difficulty in accepting the title of "King," he suggested using the term "Regent." Indeed, Cram thought that the nation actually would remain a republic even if governed by "His Highness the Regent of the Republic of the United States."[79] If people gagged on this awkward appellation, it was a very small price to pay for a giant step in the direction of High Democracy.

The New Monarch and the New Aristocracy formed only part, and if practicality is to be used as a criterion, only the least important part, of the New Medievalism. By far, the most significant and constructive element in Cram's blueprint for society was what might be called the New Decentralization. Based on his long-held assumption that society ought to function on the "human scale," its sine qua non was a return to the land, a proposition held in high esteem by a number of dissident intellectuals and groups during the Depression.

The "back to the land" movement in its Anglo-American context was first coherently articulated as the Distributist movement by the English Catholic writers, Hilaire Belloc and G. K. Chesterton.[80] By the 1930's, a number of Americans, critical of the capitalist-industrial system which had produced the worst depression in the nation's history, had established a similar movement on this side of the Atlantic. Groups as diverse as the Southern Agrarians and the Catholic rural life movement, as well as prominent individuals such as Herbert Agar and Ralph Borsodi, supported it with the special zeal reserved for occasions of crisis.[81]

Cram had reached the conclusion that American society must reverse its accelerating trend toward urbanization long before the Depression intellectuals had. In his wartime works (particularly Walled Towns) and, more notably, in Towards the Great Peace, published in 1922, he had appealed for this transvaluation of values as one of the primary steps needed to undermine the dominance of the acquisitive society. Encouraged by newly found support in the 1930's, he stepped up his appeals. To return to the proper "human scale" of social cohabitation meant a drastic restructuring of society and the several social classes:

> The proletariat--that is the landless, wage-earning class, bound to industrial plants or dwelling in non-producing cities--must be drastically reduced in numbers. The same is true of the bourgeoisie, also largely unproductive of real values, subsisting on trade or administrative processes--a class that ranges form the wealthy, pseudo-aristocratic rentier to the bond salesman, the life insurance solicitor and the high-powered salesman. The new society must become predominantly self-supporting, and from the land, supplemented by part-time factory or craft work.[82]

If, he added, big business and finace, as well as the "red in tooth and claw" competition of trade, were reduced in size, cities would shrink and people concomitantly would move to rural areas, thus diminishing prospects for social disintegration and ultimate revolution or communism.

In 1933 Roosevelt and Congress began to give some substance to the dreams of the American Distributists with the establishment of subsistence homesteads under the National Industrial Recovery Act, an act which Cram described as a "tentative essay," but, at the same time, the president's "greatest constructive measure."[83] With an initial twenty-five million dollars appropriated to relocate rurally some twenty-five thousand families and the speculation that several billion dollars more would be forthcoming, this seemed, for once, a regenerative rather than palliative measure. Yet Cram remained concerned that Roosevelt, far from viewing the project as a step toward the destruction of capitalistic industrialism, had intended

it as a prop for the system itself. The president,
he feared, had merely established these homesteads as
adjuncts to the ensconced factory system, in which
case the plan would prove ameliorative at best. He
warned: "They [the workers] would still be millhands.
The mills would be there and they would still be oper-
ating to produce dividends on invested capital and by
the methods of mass-production. This is not good
enough, for it preserves the old and bad qualities of
segregation of labor, specialization of industry, and
by mass methods, the preservation in the social organism of the unit of un-human scale. In other words,
capitalistic industry..."84
     In 1934 he publicized his own version of the
communitarian ideal, an ideal which he hoped and
thought would be the "social organism of the future,"
and for which he suggested that the federal government
initially lend those interested some three and one-
half million dollars to organize a community of five
hundred persons.85 Ultimately, he predicted, this
utopian venture would consist of two thousand inhabitants per commune and would include some five hundred
private homes, each with gardens of roughly two acres.
Deploring the "rugged individualism" which had corrod-
ed the economy, society, and even the arts,86 he envisioned farmlands which would be cultivated in common
by the community's denizens, with all farming imple-
ments held mutually and with produce distributed on a
prorated basis. The community, naturally, to be self-
sufficient would need to develop more than agricultural pursuits. The old medieval arts of craftsmanship
and weaving would therefore be restored, as would such
necessary and practical modern-day "arts" as plumbing,
housebuilding, and electrical expertise.87
     While politically appended to an existing town-
ship, the community would develop its own self-govern-
ing practices. The inhabitants, urban-oriented but
trained for their new labors, would at first come
under a certain amount of control by technical mana-
gers, but, as the community progressed, would become
democratic shareholders in the corporation. If anyone
wished to leave the commune, he or she could do so and
would receive a prorated cash payment. The original
indebtedness to the government could be paid off, he
reckoned, in twenty years, after which the individuals
would become householders. Once the debt was liquidat-
ed, moreover, the individuals, as farmers, workers,
or shopkeepers, could retain the profits which their
work had made possible. This is one of the major ways

in which Cram's ideal differed from the hated forced collectivism of the Bolsheviks.[88] While he deplored Bolshevism, however, he did fully agree with the Marxist slogan--"From each according to his ability. To each according to his needs"--and believed that a person's wages should be based on the quality of his work, a rule, incidentally, he assumed would assist considerably in expunging the communal debt. With a division of labor based on both individual aptitude and seasonal considerations, all of this could be done with the worker's efforts reduced to a thirty-hour week and a thirty-week year. Hence, there would be a good deal of surplus time for the individual to develop his or her personal interests and tastes.[89]

By 1935, however, the "back-to-the-land" movement was in dire straits. The Supreme Court, having struck down the NIRA, had reduced prospects of additional billions in revenue for the scheme to a visionary's pipe-dream. An equally bitter blow to proponents of the movement came that same year when the homestead program passed under the control of Rexford Guy Tugwell's Resettlement Administration. Tugwell, of course, was a collectivist at heart who generally disliked movements which smacked of too much individualism. The Distributists now feared--and correctly--that the New Deal was about to discard the policy "that will transform the family-farm operator into a farm owner instead of transforming owners into tenants or day laborers on a corporation farm."[90]

While agreeing that Roosevelt's program seemed to be breaking down, Cram continued to advocate the Distributist policy: "There never was, and never will be, any just and sane and wholesome basis for society except land, land held by a family, worked by the owners, and used as a primary means of support. To this basis we must return."[91] Further, he now began to call his ideal communes "Cities of Refuge," a term which in spirit, if not fully in substance, echoed his "Walled Towns" of the World War One period. Though he fully accepted--indeed, welcomed--various religious denominations to these new communities, he believed that Catholics should take the lead in their formation since they best knew the weaknesses of capitalistic industrialism. The government, apparently, could be counted on for little real assistance since it persisted in emphasizing the factory over the farm and profits over communal interests. Cram foresaw three social groups seeking the shelter of his "Cities of Refuge": (1) those who were unemployed but who

were or could be trained and would enjoy their new
lives; (2) those whom automation and "improved" tech-
niques of management would soon leave jobless; and (3)
those who were seeking a better life for themselves
and their families. Fully five per cent of the current population, he estimated, fell into these catego-
ries, and twice as many would be included in the foreseeable future.[92] Denying that he was promoting Bolshevism, he replied to a critic: "The plan I suggest
is conceived for the purpose of averting Communism."
Though its viability was not an assured fact, "it
couldn't make a worse failure than the one we now enjoy."[93]

Cram had concluded that the abandonment of the
land may have been at the very root of the nation's
social and economic problems. Far from viewing agrarian toil as degrading, he believed a "basic and well-
tempered peasantry," filled with dignity and self-respect, provided society's vital stability. "Strength,"
he concluded, as had the Luddites a few centuries earlier, "comes from the earth, weakness from the machine."[94] A full-fledged return to the land, he now
reasoned, might destroy an iniquitous economic system,
as well as restore Christian unity, which was, ultimately, "the only salvation of human society."[95] For
all its undeniable assistance to the rural poor--
sharecroppers, tenant farmers, day laborers--the New
Deal, in the end, failed to solve the problems of the
countryside or even to foster any enduring subsistence
homestead movement. "There is almost no talk of rural
reconstruction. These things will become important
only when a series of technical catastrophes and fis-
cal bankruptcies have occured in the cities, as they
will." These words were not Cram's, though well they
might have been; they belonged to a more recent proph-
et-like critic of the capitalist system, the late Paul
Goodman.[96] Whether called the "New Medievalism" or
"New Reformation," human dreams and visions have their
own way of staying alive.

1. He also wrote his autobiography <u>My Life in Archi-tecture</u> during this decade.
2. Ralph Adams Cram, <u>The End of Democracy</u> (Boston, 1937), pp. 9, 26.
3. For a particularly sharp attack on Cram's position, see David Spitz, <u>Patterns of Anti-Democrat-ic Thought</u>, 2nd ed., rev. (New York, 1965), passim.
4. Ralph Adams Cram, "The Limitations of Democracy," <u>The Rice Institute Pamphlet</u>, 17 (July, 1930), 180.
5. Ibid., 187, 193.
6. Ibid., 183-185, 194.
7. Ralph Adams Cram, "Why We Do Not Behave Like Human Beings," <u>The American Mercury</u>, XXVII (September, 1932), 41-48, passim.
8. Ralph Adams Cram, "The Mass-Man Takes Over," <u>The American Mercury</u>, XLV (October, 1938), 166.
9. Letter of Ralph Adams Cram to Henry L. Mencken, August 14, 1923, Henry L. Mencken Papers, New York Public Library.
10. Letter of Ralph Adams Cram to Henry L. Mencken, August 8, 1923, Mencken Papers. In his letter of August 14, 1923, Cram informed Mencken that he might write an article on physiognomy, "as applied to social and political potentiality." He explained: "After all, there is something in physiognomy if not phrenology, and I am not sure that choice of individuals for legislative and executive purposes could not better be made on this basis than on the one we at present pursue." Apparently, he never wrote or at least did not publish any such article.
11. Cram, "The Limitations of Democracy," 194.
12. Letter of Henry L. Mencken to Albert Jay Nock, September 14, 1932, Mencken Papers.
13. Letter of Henry L. Mencken to Ralph Adams Cram, February 9, 1933, Mencken Papers.
14. Letter of Ralph Adams Cram to Henry L. Mencken, February 7, 1933, Mencken Papers. Cram took the occasion to ask Mencken for extra copies of "Why We Do Not Behave Like Human Beings"in response to a barrage of requests he had received for the article.
15. Letter of Natasha Boissevian to Ralph Adams Cram,

October 25, 1955, Hoyle, Doran and Berry Papers, Boston.

16. For two perceptive studies of Nock, see Robert M. Crunden, The Mind and Art of Albert Jay Nock (Chicago, 1964) and Michael Wreszin, The Superfluous Anarchist: Albert Jay Nock (Providence, R.I., 1972). Wreszin devotes an entire thoughtful chapter, "The Revelation of Cram," (pp. 105-125) to the architect's influence on Nock.

17. Letter of Albert Jay Nock to Henry L. Mencken, September 12, 1932, Mencken Papers. "Sedgwick" was Ellery Sedgwick, then editor of The Atlantic Monthly. While the Atlantic did publish several of Cram's articles during the 1930's, none were nearly as provocative as the one Nock had lauded.

18. The two articles were: "Are All Men Human?" Harper's Magazine (January, 1933), 240-246, and "The Quest of the Missing Link," The Atlantic Monthly, 155 (April, 1935), 399-408.

19. Nock, "Are All Men Human?" 240; Letter of Albert Jay Nock to "My dear friend" (either Mrs. Edmund C. Evans or Ellen Winsor), June 2, 1940, Frank W. Garrison (ed.), Letters from Albert Jay Nock, 1924-1945 (Caldwell, Idaho, 1949), p. 123; Nock, "The Quest of the Missing Link," 399.

20. Albert Jay Nock, The Theory of Education in the United States (New York, 1932), pp. 38-39.

21. Nock, "The Quest of the Missing Link," 403-404, 408. Nock's admiration for Cram continued to grow. Though rather disappointed with the latter's The End of Democracy, an introduction for which he had declined to write, he wished to collaborate with the architect on a collection of the John Adams-Thomas Jefferson correspondence, but feared Cram was too old for the undertaking. More interesting, he wished to publish his correspondence with Cram but--and this idea came only a very short while before Cram died--realized that his friend was becoming frail and nearly blind. Letters from Albert Jay Nock to Mrs. Edmund C. Evans, March 12, 1937; to "My dear friend" (Mrs. Evans or Ellen Winsor), February 15, 1938; to Mrs. Edmund C. Evans, August 7, 1942, Garrison (ed.), Letters from Albert Jay Nock, pp. 88, 101, 158-159.

22. Albert Jay Nock, Memoirs of a Superfluous Man (New York, 1943), pp. 136-137, 311, 317.

23. Letter of Albert Jay Nock to Ellen Winsor, June 2, 1942, Garrison (ed.), Letters from Albert Jay

Nock, p. 154.

24. Cram, "The Limitations of Democracy," 189.

25. Ibid., 185-186.

26. Ralph Adams Cram, "How Shall We Govern?" The Commonweal, XVI (July 13, 1932), 287.

27. Ibid., 287-288. The editors of Commonweal did not agree with his proposals, but thought they would serve to stimulate useful discussion. Cram, they noted (pp. 277-278), "has been a prohpet crying aloud and insistently in the ears of a people that paid scant attention to either his warnings or his visions of a better order of things."

28. Ralph Adams Cram, The Gothic Quest (New York, 1907) p. 19.

29. Cram, in an undated letter to Mencken, called Gaynor, the patrician mayor of New York (1909-1913) who died in office, "the last of our great men in public office." Mencken and Nock concurred in this judgment. As the Mercury's editor noted: "I have believed for some years that·he was the best man ever heard of in public affairs in America." Letter of Henry L. Mencken to Albert Jay Nock, September 9, 1932, Mencken Papers. for the most recent and extensive biography of Gaynor, see Lately Thomas, The Mayor Who Mastered New York: The Life and Opinions of William Jay Gaynor (New York, 1969).

30. Ralph Adams Cram, The End of Democracy (Boston, 1937), p. 74; Ralph Adams Cram, "The Forgotten Class," Part II, The American Review, VII (May, 1936), 186.

31. Ralph Adams Cram, Convictions and Controversies (Boston, 1935), p. 163. For a concurring but more concerned view that Europe and the United States were reembracing Caesarism, see Amaury de Riencourt, The Coming Caesars (New York, 1957).

32. George Wofskill and John A. Hudson, All But the People: Franklin D. Roosevelt and His Critics, 1933-1939 (New York, 1969), p. 342.

33. Preferring to dwell upon the general similarity of their views, neither Nock nor Mencken seems to have made any reference to Cram's different perception of Roosevelt and the New Deal.

34. Ralph Adams Cram, "Recovery or Regeneration," Part I, The Commonweal, XXI (November 2, 1934), 7-8.

35. Cram, End of Democracy, pp. 117-119; Ralph Adams Cram, "The Forgotten Class," Part I, The American

Review, VII (April, 1936), 183. Cram felt particularly hostile towards the Columbia professors (Tugwell, Moley, and Berle) and Roosevelt's friend and adviser, James Farley (p. 186).

36. Cram, Convictions, pp. 163-164.
37. Ralph Adams Cram, "The End of Democracy," The American Mercury, XXXIX (September, 1936), 28.
38. Cram, "The Mass-Man Takes Over," 170-171.
39. Cram, End of Democracy, p. 57.
40. Ibid., pp. 19-22; Cram, "The Mass-Man Takes Over," 170-171. Cram also thought that England approximated the High Democracy, while France might have been the most egregious example of the Low Democracy.
41. Cram, End of Democracy, pp. 57-58.
42. Ibid., p. 59. Whether or not Cram has succeeded in freeing himself from charges of inconsistency by having praised the "landed and commercial interests" while condemning capitalists in general is debatable. He is by no means unique, however, in differentiating between the businessmen of the eighteenth and early nineteenth centuries, on the one hand, and the entrepeneurs who have flourished since the Civil War, on the other.
43. Ibid., p. 68.
44. Ibid., p. 213.
45. Ibid., pp. 144-145, 42.
46. Cram, "The Mass-Man Takes Over," 168-170, 172.
47. Ralph Adams Cram, "Back to What Constitution?" The American Mercury, XXXVI (December, 1935), 388.
48. Ibid., 386; 388-391. For some reason, he dodged taking a firm stand on the Nineteenth Amendment by saying merely that female suffrage was a social rather than political issue. Perhaps his medieval sense of chivalry induced a certain reticence.
49. Ibid., p. 392. At the heart of Cram's dislike for the Twelfth and Seventeenth Amendments was his belief that the suffrage should be restricted since it was "a privilege and a duty and not a right inherent in man by virtue of his inclusion in that debatable genus, Homo Sapiens."
50. Cram, End of Democracy, pp. 12-13.
51. Ibid., pp. 74-75.
52. Ibid., pp. 194-199, passim. Cram scored those, particularly the American Liberty Leaguers, who protested that they were defenders of the Constitution. He noted that those screaming the loud-

est for the Constitution were the ones who least wished to return to the spirit of 1787. As Senator Edgar Borah once sarcastically noted of the Liberty League: "They were deeply moved about the Constitution of the United States. They had just discovered it."

53. Ibid., p. 73. Cram, incidentally, avowed that he was a Cleveland Mugwump, but "with scant respect for either political party." Why he considered himself such, with all its implications of laissez-faire, is not easy to fathom. It may, however, be the result of Cleveland's unquestioned public probity. Ralph Adams Cram, My Life in Architecture (Boston, 1936), p. 118.

54. Letter of Ralph Adams Cram to Henry L. Mencken, February 7, 1933, Mencken Papers.

55. Ralph Adams Cram, Towards the Great Peace (Boston, 1922), pp. 137-143, passim.

56. Ibid., pp. 131-134. By the 1930's, however, he had become so distrustful of legislative bodies that he was leaning toward the selection of a president by a special convention. Ralph Adams Cram, "The Nemesis of Democracy," The American Review, VIII (December, 1936), 138.

57. Ibid., 131-134; Cram, End of Democracy, pp. 201-203.

58. Cram, "The Nemesis of Democracy," 133-134; Cram, Great Peace, pp. 134-137.

59. Cram, End of Democracy, p. 26.

60. Ralph Adams Cram, "The Forgotten Class," Part I, The American Review, VII (April, 1936), 32-46; Part II, The American Review, VII (May, 1936), 179-191. The information on the "Forgotten Class" presented in the following three paragraphs is derived from these articles.

61. Cram, End of Democracy, pp. 14-15.

62. John P. Diggins, Mussolini and Fascism: The View from America (Princeton, N.J., 1972), p. 213.

63. Cram, "The Mass-Man Takes Over," 176. For a further condemnation of fascism, see Cram, "The Forgotten Class," Part II, passim.

64. The avowed purpose of Collins and his provocative but short-lived journal (1933-1937), however, was to publicize and promote the Distributist or Proprietary State movement and its two most articulate English advocates, Hilaire Belloc and G. K. Chesterton. One of the journal's contributors, sympathetic to fascism, explicitly stated that Cram was anti-fascist though, at the same

time, "one of that small body of men who are try-
ing to think out our problems in the light of
what history has shown man to be." Geoffrey
Stone, "The End of Democracy: Ralph Adams Cram's
Plea for a New Order," The American Review, IX
(September, 1937), 376, 379.

65. Cram, "The Forgotten Class," Part II, 190; Cram,
End of Democracy, p. 299.

66. Cram, "The Forgotten Class," Part II, 188.

67. Cram, "The Nemesis of Democracy," 137-138.

68. In 1935 the Boston Public Library asked Cram for
a list of books which he considered vitally important. Restricting himself to ten "recently
published" works which pertained to the contemporary situation, he listed Berdyaev's The End of
Our Time and Ortega's The Revolt of the Masses.
Some of the others included: Spengler's The Hour
of Decision ("with reservations"), Adams' Mont-
St.-Michel and Chartres, Lewis Mumford's Technics
and Civilization, and Christopher Dawson's, The
Making of Europe. Letter of Ralph Adams Cram to
Edith Guerrier, May 3, 1935, Boston Public Librar-
y.

69. Cram, Convictions, p. 272.

70. Cram, End of Democracy, p. 207.

71. Cram, "The Mass-Man Takes Over," 175; Cram, End
of Democracy, p. 211.

72. Ralph Adams Cram, "The Return to Feudalism," The
American Review, VIII (January, 1937), 343, 348.

73. Ralph Adams Cram, "Invitation to Monarchy," The
American Mercury, XXXVII (April, 1936), 479-480.

74. Cram, End of Democracy, p. 171.

75. Ibid.

76. Cram, "Invitation to Monarchy," 482-483.

77. Cram, End of Democracy, p. 177.

78. Cram, "Invitation to Monarchy," 484-486.

79. Cram, End of Democracy, p. 187.

80. Cram seems to have been particularly impressed
with Belloc's The Servile State, which, along
with such other anti-capitalist works as William
Morris' The Dream of John Ball and R. H. Tawney's
The Acquisitive Society, he suggested as collateral reading for his own Towards the Great Peace.
Cram, Great Peace, p. 264. By the 1930's he had
come to include Chesterton as one of the most important modern writers. Ralph Adams Cram, Review
of Herbert Agar's Land of the Free, The American
Review, VII (May, 1936), 215.

81. For an analysis of the "back to the land" move-

ment, see Edward S. Shapiro, "The American Distributists and the New Deal," unpublished doctoral
dissertation, Harvard University, 1968, and his
article, "Decentralist Intellectuals and the New
Deal," The Journal of American History, LVIII
(March, 1972), 938-957.

82. Cram, My Life, pp. 297-298.
83. Cram, Convictions, p. 169.
84. Cram, "Recovery or Regeneration," Part I, 9-10.
85. Ralph Adams Cram, "Recovery or Regeneration,"
    Part II, The Commonweal, XXI (November 9, 1934),
    56-57.
86. Ralph Adams Cram, "The Unity of the Arts, Land-
    scape Architecture, XXIII (April, 1933), 159.
87. Cram, "Recovery or Regeneration," Part II, 56.
88. Andrew Hacker has noted some further differences
    between radical and conservative communities.
    While the former tend to be ahistorical and often
    the direct result of violent revolutions, the
    latter, as the sociologist Robert Nisbet insists,
    tend to rely on tradition, hierarchy, and defe-
    rence. These characteristics certainly apply to
    the communes envisioned by the medieval-minded
    Cram. A further conservative attribute (though
    not cited by Hacker) would be the emphasis placed
    on religion. Andrew Hacker, "On Original Sin and
    Conservatives," The New York Times Magazine
    (February 25, 1973), 68, 70.
89. Cram, "Recovery or Regeneration," Part II, 57-58;
    Cram, End of Democracy, p. 64.
90. Shapiro, "Decentralist Intellectuals and the New
    Deal," 948-949.
91. Ralph Adams Cram, "Cities of Refuge," The Common-
    weal, XXII (August 16, 1935), 379-380.
92. Ibid., 380; Cram, "Recovery or Regeneration,"
    Part II, 56. Professor Shapiro has pointed out
    that Catholic ruralists feared that urbanization
    had been responsible for, among other things, a
    growing secularism among Catholics and a decline
    in the number of persons entering the priesthood.
    "Decentralist Intellectuals and the New Deal,"
    940.
93. Ralph Adams Cram, Letter in The Commonweal,
    XXIII (November 1, 1935), 21.
94. Cram, My Life, p. 230. At least one critic has
    doubted the sincerity of Cram's agrarianism. As
    Robert Crunden, Nock's biographer, notes: "The
    whole dream really must have seemed charming to
    a man who escaped the farm at his first opportu-

nity and lived his life amid the bottled milk and delivered eggs on Beacon Hill."Robert M. Crunden, _From Self to Society, 1919-1941_ (Englewood Cliffs, N.J., 1972), p. 167. Though having read _My Life in Architecture_, Crunden, one of Cram's most hostile critics, fails to cite the architect's profound love for the pastoral life he led at Whitehall.

95. Cram, _My Life_, p. 224.
96. Paul Goodman, _New Reformation: Notes of a Neolithic Conservative_ (New York, 1970), pp. 184-185. See also Goodman's _Like a Conquered Province_ (New York, 1967), passim.

CHAPTER X

THE LAST YEARS: "HE BUILT HIS OWN MONUMENTS"

By 1938 the New Deal, having lost its forward momentum, was in a kind of stasis. Undeniably, the nation found itself far better off midway through Roosevelt's second term of office than it had in 1933. Yet as Cram had feared, the President and his policies had largely succeeded in producing recovery but not regeneration. A new, graver menace was threatening meanwhile in the form of European and Asiatic totalitarian states bent on expansion. Munich had quieted the fears of some, but others, like Cram, were under no illusion that peace had come in their time.

Correctly interpreting the reality of the threat to world peace, Cram assumed a stance quite different from the one he had adopted in 1914 when, almost immediately after the Great War erupted, he called for the nation to join the Allies. As the pall of war descended in the late thirties, in contrast, he urged, at least privately, his countrymen to remain aloof from the coming martial confrontation. Less than a month before World War II broke out he wrote to his friend and at that time editor of The American Mercury, Paul Palmer: "Europe is finished, and I fear the ending will be rather nasty. If we keep out of war we may help the United States preserve some vestiges of an old and sound culture." He added: "This will be done just as ignorantly as the monks of the Middle Ages preserved the vestiges of classical culture, but somebody has got to save something, and there is no one else that I know of who can do this now except ourselves. In my darker moments, I despair of even our doing this, 'but my hopes are better.'"[1]

In the face of this menace even capitalism was beginning to take on if not bright, at least less gloomy hues. "I believe in capitalism (as opposed to communism and totalitarianism)," he confessed to Palmer, but as always, his brand of capitalism was of a species so exotic that it was questionable whether it belonged to the genus:

I am pronouncedly an agrarian, a cooper-

ativist, and incidentally a monarchist.
So far as our present administration is
concerned, I look upon "pump priming" in
all its forms as worse than useless.
There are more unemployed now than there
were when the New Deal took over. With
technological invention going steadily on,
this number of unemployed is bound to
increase, and as this process advances,
taxation will be magnified in order to
take care of the ever-increasing number
of those who are out of work. The issue
of this process is, of course, Revolution.
The capitalist society does nothing to
avert this catastrophe, and the substitutes that are offered by totalitarianism
and communism are worse still.[2]
Cram's badly mistaken assumption that unemployment had
actually increased heavily underscores his total disillusionment with the New Deal's early promise. Subsistence homesteads, a new guild system, government
along lines of functional organiztion--all had been
plowed under by an administration dedicated to the
preservation of capitalism and liberal democracy. He
now frankly admitted that in his more pessimistic moments he was "inclined to hold that a complete collapse of modern civilization (following the line of
that which overtook the Roman Empire) is about the
best we can hope for. It would mean another Dark Age,
but nowadays where everything is streamlined, it might
be only for a decade or two, and then we can start
afresh."[3]
     Yet Cram was not really content to sit by and
wait for the advent of a new Dark Ages. Shortly after
Hitler's army had blitzkrieged its way across the
Polish border, he wrote an article, "The Change Beyond," which appeared in Commonweal and which repeated
his familiar plea for a cooperativist "back to the
land" movement. Strangely, he also took the occasion
to voice his general optimism, even as "war and rumors
of war" starkly proliferated.[4] For once, he was unwilling or unable to believe the worst. With the publication of this article, however, the architect, who
had published relatively little since 1937, seemed on
the verge of redonning his prophet's robes as the
world attempted to muddle through still another monu-
mental crisis. As he had written to Palmer a few
weeks before the war broke out: "There is plenty of
work today to do along literary lines, especially

where these deal with politics, social organization and cultural as well as ethical regeneration. If this work is going to be done, it had better be begun and carried on here. We need it as much as anyone else, and I still optimistically believe there is a faint possibility for us, whereas I see none whatever on the other side of the Atlantic."[5] The article for Common-weal proved to be the last work he was ever to publish.

Long blessed with familial happiness, Cram had been struck by personal misfortune in early 1938 when his wife Elizabeth became seriously ill. Elected a member of the American Academy of Arts and Letters two years later, it was a saddened Cram who made the lonely, late autumn trip from Boston to New York without his wife in order to attend the initiation ceremony and luncheon for new members.[6] Shortly after returning home, he was encouraged by hopes held out by doctors that Elizabeth would ultimately recover. Indeed, he then began to believe that she might be sufficiently improved to accompany him that winter to Haiti, which he described as "the most delightful place I know."[7] He did visit that tropical island in the winter--but alone. Although he never abandoned hope, Elizabeth, who died in 1943, was never again to regain her health. With great effort Cram continued to welcome friends and acquaintances to his Boston and Sudbury homes and to carry on life's daily routine, but it was simply not the same without his wife of more than forty years.[8]

Grieved by her lamentable illness and suffering from glaucoma and what he called "nicotine poisoning," Cram felt his zest for living perceptibly decline by 1940. During the previous year he had found it difficult to absent himself from his office "even where there is nothing much for me to do"; now he went only "once or twice a week just to keep up appearances."[9] Beset as he had always been by individuals and groups who wanted him to lecture or attend various meetings, he began to refuse. "A week or two ago," he wrote Palmer, "I spoke before the Grange in Vermont and that was the last time." He admitted that he still maintained "a certain interest in agrarianism and all the 'back to the land movements,'" but termed it "more or less academic," though "the only thing in which I see any real help." He also informed his friend that he currently was writing nothing and probably never again would write, but, in good Candidean fashion, would literally and figuratively cultivate his gardens at

Whitehall. "I associate with Socrates," he explained,
"who, if you remember, 'stood aside under the wall
while the storm of dust and dead leaves goes by.'"[10]
     The silence and withdrawal were not total, how-
ever. Though he did end his active career as a writer
and speaker, he continued to send to sympathetic re-
cipients like Palmer letters in which he still evinced
a marked intellectual curiosity and concern for the
world's future. Inquiring about the health of the
Mercury, extolling recently read books such as Eugen
Rosenstock-Huessy's Out of Revolution (1938), Cram
opened his mind to Palmer. When the latter asked for
a list of worthwhile books pertaining to Egypt, the
architect, a long-time student of Egyptian art, culture, and history, was at no loss and recommended
James Henry Breasted's The Dawn of Conscience (1933)
and Earl Baldwin Smith's Egyptian Architecture (1938),
promising to send more titles as soon as he was able
to go through his extensive personal library with more
care. In turn, he requested the Mercury's editor, who
was about to visit Europe, to provide him with the
latest developments in Scandinavian architecture. Of
course, Cram could not restrict his epistolary topics
to art or literature; he kept bringing up old themes.
Denouncing, for example, "what is humorously termed
'democracy,'" he again lashed out at the Low Democracy
of the West which was "as much a pagan 'religion' as
the worship of Stalin and Hitler." "I am not sure,"
he added bitterly, that "it is not a greater danger."
Not surprisingly, he concluded his peroration by reminding Palmer that the Catholic Church remained "our
one hope."[11]
     As 1941 wore on, the outlook failed to improve
for either the West or for Cram personally. Hitler
was consolidating his acquisitions to the Third Reich,
invading Russia, and still threatening England; the
architect was visiting a sick daughter in New Mexico,
fighting off bouts of depression, and still suffering
from glaucoma and "nicotine poisoning."[12] On December
7th of that year the fortunes of both the West and
Cram reached a new low. The latter, who had maintained his admiration for Japan--its people and civi-
lization--since his visit to that country some forty
years before, was disturbed by her ruthless expansion
in the 1930's, but stubbornly believed that, unlike
Germany, she would soon become sated and peaceful.
Ralph Wentworth Cram was with his father when the
radio carried the electrifying news of Pearl Harbor to
homes throughout the nation. Stunned, the old archi-

tect shook his head in utter disbelief. According to
his son, his physical decline accelerated and became
increasingly evident after this event.[13] Ill during
most of that winter, he seemed a little improved during the spring and early months of 1942. In early
August, however, now nearly seventy-nine years old,
he was stricken with pneumonia and rushed to Boston's
Peter Bent Brigham Hospital. Despite the drugs and
intensive care he received, his condition gradually
worsened. Shortly before the end he told Frank Cleveland that he had lived too long, but hoped that he
could live yet long enough "to witness the triumph of
Democracy over Nazism, Fascism, and... Japanese
aggression and duplicity." As enemies of the Christian world, the various dictators, so he told his
visitor, must be destroyed."[14] Death came quietly for
Cram on September 22nd. A few days later, following a
Requiem Mass at the Episcopalian Church of St. John
the Evangelist in Boston, the high priest of American
Gothicism was interred just outside his chapel at
Whitehall.

Personal friends and professional colleagues paid
the deceased architect tributes which were as lavish
as they were manifold. The architect Samuel R. T.
Very, who had been one of the last persons to speak
with the dying Cram, later told Cleveland: "I had not
before noticed the pleasant and human and gracious
phases of his character."[15] The Reverend Andrew L.
Drummond, a Scottish minister from Ava, Clackman-
nashire, who had last seen Cram in 1929 on the occasion of a visit to the United States, wrote to the
architectural firm and recounted the kindness and hos-
pitality of his host: "I cannot say I had any sympathy with his theological, ecclesiastical, or 'Jacobite' views," he tartly observed, "but I always admired his enthusiasm, and he was undoubtedly a personality." The Reverend Drummond ended his letter by re-
questing copies of obituary notices.[16]

A number of the encomiums, as might be expected,
were couched in terms of praise for his professional
achievements. Charles D. Maginnis, Cram's fellow
Gothicist, thought it particularly sad that he had not
lived to see the "stupendous task" of St. John the
Divine completed, but was confident that "the objective nobility of his memorials will linger to chal-
lenge the resources of modern realism."[17] William
Ward Watkin, a professor of architecture at Rice Institute, concurred in Maginnis' high praise. "No man
I have ever known," he wrote, "possessed such a true

love of masonry." More than that, "in his ever exuberant way, he carried on, almost alone, a crusade for
Christian art as symbolic of the powers and ideals
which are needed to recreate a more perfect state in
which to live."[18] The internationally famous art
critic Herbert Read judged at this time that Cram
and Frederick Bligh Bond, the fine British medievalist, "were identical in one respect and unique in the
capacity of appreciating ecclesiastical gothic, especially woodcarving."[19]

While most of the tributes concentrated on either
his character and forceful personality or on his ac-
complishments as an architect, some went beyond and
recognized the social philosophy he had been proclaim-
ing over the years. Sympathetic to his point of view,
Maginnis insisted that "it was the identification of a
passionate and romantic thesis with his professional
product which made him so piquant and even provocative
a figure in the national life."[20] The Mediaeval Academy was still more effusive in praising his achievements. As an architect, writer, and concerned citizen, Cram was, "as will become increasingly evident as
the years go by, one of the truly great men of our
country." "He remains," continued the eulogists from
the Academy, "_primus_ _inter_ _pares_, or better, in
Horace's phrase, the moon amongst the lesser stars.
He was the initiator of an epoch."[21]

Ralph Adams Cram, through no fault of his own,
failed to initiate any epoch, but his contributions as
an architect and social critic could not be overlooked. Preoccupied with "the war to end all wars,"
President Roosevelt, himself the recipient of some
choice abuse from the Gothicist, took time to send a
letter of condolence to the family.[22] The tributes
had come from near and far, from the famous and not-so
famous. But an unidentified person offered perhaps
the most fitting of all: "He built his own monuments."[23]

NOTES

1. Letter of Ralph Adams Cram to Paul Palmer, August 11, 1939, Paul Palmer Papers, Yale University Library.
2. Ibid. So alarmed by communism was Cram that he suggested to Palmer that he persuade either Albert Jay Nock or someone else "to write a scathing article on the 'Red Menace' of the Writers Guild, newspaper reporters, and most newspaper editors." It was "ominous" that "most writers" and "all young journalists" were left-wing in their convictions. Letter of Ralph Adams Cram to Paul Palmer, February 4, 1939, Palmer Papers.
3. Letter of Ralph Adams Cram, to Paul Palmer, August 11, 1939, ibid.
4. Ralph Adams Cram, "The Change Beyond," The Commonweal, XXXI (November 3, 1939), 35.
5. Letter of Ralph Adams Cram to Paul Palmer, August 11, 1939, Palmer Papers.
6. Letter of Ralph Adams Cram to Mrs. William Vanamee, November 12, 1940, in the American Academy and Institute of Arts and Letters, New York. Two of the five members of the Academy who nominated him for membership were his friend from fifty years before, Bernard Berenson, and Booth Tarkington. On an earlier occasion Hamlin Garland had unsuccessfully nominated him. Untitled and undated manuscript, ibid.
7. Letter of Ralph Adams Cram to Mrs. William Vanamee, November 26, 1940, ibid.
8. Letter of Ralph Adams Cram to Mr. (?) Peck, May 13, 1941, Boston Public Library.
9. Letters of Ralph Adams Cram to Paul Palmer, August 11, 1939, and August 16, 1940, Palmer Papers.
10. Letter of Ralph Adams Cram to Paul Palmer, August 16, 1940, ibid.
11. Letters of Ralph Adams Cram to Paul Palmer, February 22, and March 10, 1941, ibid.
12. Letter of Ralph Adams Cram to Paul Palmer, March 10, 1941, ibid. He complained to Palmer: "This year is just one damned thing after another." The shaky handwriting of the letters he wrote during 1941 contrasts sharply with the strong penmanship of previous letters, even those written only a year earlier.

13. Interview with Ralph Wentworth Cram, August 9, 1972.
14. Letter of Frank E Cleveland to Charles J. Connick, November 2, 1942, Hoyle, Doran and Berry Papers, Boston. According to Cleveland, Cram, in denouncing the Japanese, did "something he [Cleveland] could not have believed possible only a few years ago...."
15. Letter of Samuel R. T. Very to Frank E. Cleveland, October 4, 1942, ibid.
16. Letter of the Reverend Andrew L. Drummond to Cram and Ferguson, (?), 1942, ibid.
17. Charles D. Maginnis, "Ralph Adams Cram," The Octagon, 15 (February, 1943), 14; Charles D. Maginnis, Editorial in Liturgical Arts, XI (November, 1942), 1.
18. William Ward Watkin, "I Knew Him Well," The New Pencil Points (October, 1942), 8.
19. Letter of Samuel R. T. Very to Frank E. Cleveland, October 4, 1942, Hoyle, Doran and Berry Papers. Cram held Bond in high regard both as an architect and friend, though he did consider him to be an "extremely simple-minded man." Letter of Ralph Adams Cram to Dr. Herman T. Radin, July 23, 1918, Herman T. Radin Papers, New York Public Library.
20. Maginnis, "Ralph Adams Cram," 13.
21. John Nicholas Brown, George Raleigh Coffman, and Edward Kennard Rand, "Memoir: Ralph Adams Cram," Speculum: A Journal of Mediaeval Studies, XVIII (July, 1943), 388-389.
22. Letter of Frank E. Cleveland to Mrs. Edward Nicholas, December 29, 1942, Hoyle, Doran and Berry Papers.
23. Letter of Frank E. Cleveland to Charles J. Connick, n.d., ibid.

Already having lost a good deal of popular favor
in the 1930's, the Gothic movement in American architecture received its coup de grâce with the advent of
World War II as the building of barracks and various
military installations came to dominate over the construction of churches and schools. In the postwar
years prohibitive costs of labor and materials, an accelerating secularism and preoccupation with modernism, and the weight of public taste rendered the movement a thing of the past. Given the cyclical nature
and vagaries of popular taste, of course, there is no
guarantee that yet another Gothic revival will not
transpire. Already there are strong signs of dissatisfaction with the geometric abstractions of modern
architecture and a renewed call for greater ornamentation. Nevertheless, until or unless it comes to pass,
the Gothic creations--of Cram and of others--stand
Ozymandias-like in the deserts of modernism as reminders of past splendors.

The architect from Hampton Falls would have been
sorely disappointed had he lived to witness this decline. For the better part of half a century it had
been his works and polemics which had nurtured and
sustained the Gothic as a dynamic force in the nation's artistic life. Yet he doubtlessly would have
understood the reasons for its decline. Gothicism can
flourish only in a suitable environment, and the environment from the 1930's onward could scarcely have
been less amenable. As Oliver Larkin has observed:
"To the modern critic, Cram's distinction lies in his
insistence that only a sound community can build noble
architecture, and in his lifelong refusal to accept an
easier ideal."[1] And though today he is best remembered for his buildings, it may well be that his social
philosophy and efforts to achieve this "sound community" will engage increasing interest in the future.

The architect tended, unfortunately, to weaken
his position by incorporating a host of contradictions
and paradoxes. A staunch communitarian, he was an
elitist and firm believer that the masses could not
govern themselves; a decentralist, he flirted with
dictatorship, as well as the centralizing forces of
the New Deal; an anti-capitalist, he was decidedly
Goodhue's "well-fed genius"; an anti-Social Darwinist
and anti-eugenicist, he was a proponent of the view

267

that genetic differences count for more than environmental factors; a foe of scientism, he appealed to science in defense of his cyclical theory of history and theory of mass-man; a believer in free will, he posited a deterministic view of history; more than a bit of an anti-intellectual, he wrote and lectured incessantly; an advocate for the Catholic Church, he never converted; a critic of the Catholic Church's reluctance to become involved in mundane matters, he complained of the growing secularization of religion.

If consistency were to serve as the ultimate yardstick, Cram's ideas clearly would not detain us for very long. Yet as George Santayana once observed, consistency is like a jewel, and as such, one can only marvel at the high price some are willing to pay for it. Were even the most seminal minds in history to be judged principally in this manner, civilization would be so much the poorer. Nor is popularity an infallible criterion for assessing the true value of an idea. Most ideas, it has been said, have their time; some of those that do not, should. For all their inconsistencies, fallacies, and general lack of popularity, Cram's views do deserve consideration. Cloaked in strange medieval garb, some speak very clearly to modern man and his problems.

By persistently offering invidious comparisons between modern political processes and those of the Middle Ages, Cram won a reputation as a reactionary. His agitation for a quasi-monarchy and nobility seemed so bizarre that one of his critics tartly observed that artists should perhaps limit themselves to writing only about art.[2] Certainly these views were quaint at best. Yet the Gothicist always maintained that he was primarily interested in the spirit, not the actual forms of medievalism. In essence, the Middle Ages was to be a symbolic rather than literal model. If the facts did not support the model, the latter was not necessarily vitiated, but remained an ideal, a vision. His warnings concerning mass democracy and irresponsible leadership, moreover, were scarcely the special preserve of medievalists or reactionaries. Similar caveats have had widespread historical reverberations. For Americans to dismiss the authors of these warnings would mean writing off possibly the better part of their statesmen and critics, from Hamilton and Jefferson to the contemporary figure who defends the electoral college in the face of a proposed more democratic, one-man, one-vote method of electing presidents. The following diatribe sounds like one of Cram's: "Masses are rude, lame, unmade, pernicious in their demands and influences, and need not be flattered but to be schooled.... The worst of charity is that the lives you are asked to preserve are not worth preserving. Masses! The calamity is the masses.... Away with this hurrah of masses, and let us have the considerate vote of single men spoken on their honor and their conscience." It was that of Ralph Waldo Emerson, a lustrous figure in the nation's pantheon of heroes.[3] As long as democracy exists, it seems likely that there will be a corresponding (and necessary) attempt to differentiate between, as Cram did, its "high" and "low" forms.[4] To make this differentiation does not deserve the simple, almost reflexive label, "anti-democrat."

Another view which merits attention by our contemporary age was his advocacy of a decentralized government and society. Again, one need not be a medievalist to cry out against bigness--in government, industry, and society--and to wish to restore the "human scale" of value. As Lewis Mumford has observed: "Once such initiatives [toward decentralization] become widespread, as they at last show signs of becoming, it will restore power and confident authority to its proper source: the human personality and the small face-to-face community."[5] Mumford may not have been enamored of all of Cram's beliefs, but he heartily concurred that that government governs best which governs on a decentralized basis. Related to this were Cram's warnings concerning imperialism. Concerned with the extension and abuse of power by any government, he was particularly fearful of the appetites of democratic states. Like Count Mirabeau who witnessed the expansive drives of the French Revolution, he correctly sensed that a democratic government could be fully as imperialistic as an authoritarian one, and that only constant and critical self-examination could avoid this miscarriage of civilization.

Cram's economic views do not seem less pertinent to contemporary problems than his political ones. One need not succumb to medievalism or, for that matter, to communism to be critical of the malfunctions of the capitalist system. The presence of poverty and substandard living conditions in the midst of plenty tends to make critics of us all. Nor must one go to the extreme of the Luddites to be aware of the problems wrought by technology and the machine. It has become commonplace to speak of the deleterious effects of automation on workers and to seek to devise ways by which the worker can attain some satisfaction, if not joy, from his toil. Craft guilds themselves may be far-fetched in a modern world, but certainly not their overarching values of craftsmanship and corporate self-sufficiency.

It has also become commonplace to note the congestion and other assorted ills of urban life. Suburbia, however, has not only failed to provide a panacea, but appears to be rapidly becoming prey to most of the same ailments as cities. Even should the nation's population fall below the astonishing figure of nearly three hundred million some predict for the year 2000, it is difficult for many to see any possible future "good life" for either cities or suburbs. Some foresee the only solution as resting with the development of exurban life, or, as it was formerly called, the "back to the land" movement, a movement which Cram was advocating more than fifty years ago.

Another of Cram's more important beliefs, communitarianism, increasingly forms an integral part of contemporary thought and action. It is not likely that he would have appreciated "hippie" communes because it is all but impossible to conceive of him, conservative in taste and demeanor, approving of hippies. Prejudiced in favor of hierarchy and elitism, he also would have grave doubts concerning communal associations. Nevertheless, with their inherent smallness and decentralized features, communes might be more apt and able to select, formally or informally, gifted leaders. In any event, the communal idea--the idea that the individual is part of something greater than himself, that he is not merely an isolated unit in an atomized society--always seemed more important to him than any one particular form it might take. Call it Paul Goodman's "communitas," Thorstein Veblen's "parental bent," or Cram's medieval communism, the concept remains very much alive today.

Though not of that faith, Cram was one of the most articulate twentieth-century secular spokesmen for the validity of the Catholic religion. Had he read--and there is no evidence that he had--George Bernanos' The Diary of a Country Priest, he would have discovered the mutual sympathy of their views concerning the vital work which Catholicism had to undertake. As one of Bernanos' clerics noted: "We preserve. No doubt. But we only preserve in order to save, and the world can never realize that, for the world asks only to survive. And mere survival suffices no longer."[6] The desirability of a Catholic-dominated unified

Christendom, of course, remains a highly moot point.
While the Anglo-Catholicism which Cram had espoused
in the late nineteenth century has made some gains toward Christian unity, as well as some remarkable converts (one need go no further than the example of T.S.
Eliot), that unity, even if desirable, seems distant.
Yet to deny the presence of spiritual needs and aspirations, underscored as they are in an age of dominant
secularism, would be fatuous. The architect, moreover, like countless numbers of persons who preceded
and followed, sought a moral basis for human conduct,
as well as a means of transcendent salvation. Like
Dostoyevsky, he perceived that without God everything
is possible.

Taken separately, Cram's views present a curious
amalgam of the conservative, the reactionary, the
radical, the utopian, the communitarian, and the
Christian. In toto, they represent the convictions
of a medievalist in a modern setting. Precisely because of this condition he appears as a latter-day
knight-errant tilting with the windmills of modernism,
trying to rescue religion and society from the
clutches of evil, and toiling to restore a world long
lost. He may even have appreciated the analogy. Yet
the refusal to countenance imperialism, the quest for
a form of labor to satisfy the instinct of workmanship, the wish for a more decentralized society, the
appreciation of rural living as an alternative to life
presented by the megalopolis--none belong only to the
Don Quixotes of the world. Or if they do, a good number of moderns have already mounted their Rosinantes
and can be seen, lance in hand, charging the enemy.
As Cram himself once observed: "Man is the animal
that tries--but seldom succeeds, and the real man is
found in his ideals and his aspirations and his
struggles, rather than in his definite accomplish-
ments."[7] Like other honest critics of society, Cram
ultimately should be judged in terms of the questions
that he posed and the efforts that he exerted to find
answers.

NOTES

1. Oliver Larkin, <u>Art and Life in America</u>, 2nd. ed.,
   rev. (New York, 1960), p. 340.
2. Robert M. Crunden, <u>From Self to Society, 1919-1941</u>
   (Englewood Cliffs, New Jersey, 1972), p. 167. Re-
   viewing his autobiography, one unidentified critic
   complained: "Mr. Cram does not merely turn the
   clock hands backward. He denies them any consecu-
   tive movement at all." Review of <u>My Life in Ar-
   chitecture</u>, in Supplement to <u>The Architectural
   Record</u>, Volume 79, Number (March, 1936), p. 12.
3. Ralph Waldo Emerson, <u>The Conduct of Life</u> (Boston,
   1888), p. 237.
4. For enthusiastic support given to Cram's differentiation between High and Low Democracy, see
   Donald Atwell Zoll, <u>Twentieth Century Mind:
   Essays on Contemporary Thought</u> (Baton Rouge,
   Louisiana, 1967). According to Zoll (p. 9):
   "High democracy exalts man; low democracy exalts
   myths about man." High democracy, he further
   argued (p. 10), is possible only when an elite
   governs: "...if one concedes that wisdom and
   virtue are commendable characteristics of an entire society, then that society's leadership
   should reflect the highest level of those social
   and civilized attainments." He concluded (p. 14):
   "All humane leadership is at base paternal and
   benevolent; this man shares with his fellow animals."
5. Lewis Mumford, <u>The Myth of the Machine</u> (New York,
   1970), p. 408. He also agreed with Cram's castigation of the Enlightenment for having considered
   the Middle Ages as "a neo-Gothic horror story."
   "This anti-Gothic obsession," he wrote, "resulted
   not only in the devaluation of medieval achievements but also in the wholesale destruction of
   buildings and institutions that, if preserved and
   renewed, might have helped to humanize the rising
   power system." Ibid., p. 6.
6. George Bernanos, <u>The Diary of a Country Priest</u>,
   trans. Pamela Morris (New York, 1937), p. 46.
7. Ralph Adams Cram, <u>Architecture in Its Relation to
   Civilization</u> (Boston, 1918), p. 3.

BIBLIOGRAPHY

I. WORKS BY CRAM

    A. BOOKS

        (ed.) <u>American Church Building of Today</u>. New
            York: Architectural Book Publishing Com-
            pany, 1929.
        <u>Black Spirits and White</u>. Chicago: Stone & Kim-
            ball, 1895.
        <u>Church Building</u>. 3rd ed., rev. Boston: Mar-
            shall Jones Company, 1924.
        <u>Convictions and Controversies</u>. Boston: Mar-
            shall Jones Company, 1935.
        <u>English Country Churches: One Hundred Views
            Selected by Ralph Adams Cram</u>. Boston:
            Bates & Guild Company, 1898.
        <u>Farm Houses, Manor Houses, Minor Chateaux and
            Small Churches from the Eleventh to the
            Sixteenth Centuries in Normandy, Brittany
            and Other Parts of France</u>. New York: Ar-
            chitectural Book Publishing Company, 1917.
        <u>Gold, Frankincense and Myrrh</u>. Boston: Marshall
            Jones Company, 1919.
        <u>Heart of Europe</u>. New York: Charles Scribner's
            Sons, 1919.
        <u>Impressions of Japanese Architecture and the
            Allied Arts</u>. 2nd ed., rev. Boston: Mar-
            shall Jones Company, 1930.
        <u>My Life in Architecture</u>. Boston: Little, Brown
            and Company, 1936.
        (et al.) <u>Six Lectures on Architecture</u>. Chicago:
            University of Chicago Press, 1917.
        <u>The Cathedral of Palma de Mallorca: An Archi-
            tectural Study</u>. Cambridge, Massachusetts:
            The Mediaeval Academy of America, 1932.
        <u>The Catholic Church and Art</u>. New York: The
            Macmillan Company, 1930.
        <u>The Decadent: Being the Gospel of Inaction:
            Wherein Are Set Forth in Romance Form
            Certain Reflections Touching the Curious
            Characteristics of These Ultimate Years,
            and the Divers Causes Thereof</u>. Boston:
            By the Author, 1893.
        <u>The End of Democracy</u>. Boston: Marshall Jones
            Company, 1937.

273

The Gothic Quest. New York: Baker and Taylor
    Company, 1907.
The Great Thousand Years. Boston: Marshall
    Jones Company, 1918.
The Ministry of Art. Boston: Houghton Mifflin
    Company, 1914.
The Nemesis of Mediocrity. Boston: Marshall
    Jones Company, 1919.
The Ruined Abbeys of Great Britain. New York:
    Churchman Co., 1905.
The Sins of the Fathers. Boston: Marshall
    Jones Company, 1919.
The Substance of Gothic. Boston: Marshall
    Jones Company, 1917.
Towards the Great Peace. Boston: Marshall
    Jones Company, 1922.
Walled Towns. Boston: Marshall Jones Company,
    1919.

B. ARTICLES

"Architecture As an Expression of Religion,"
    The American Architect, XCVIII (December
    28, 1910), 209-214, 216-220.
"Architecture Marches On," The Architectural
    Forum (February, 1939), 134.
"Art and Contemporary Society," The Barnwell
    Bulletin, 8 (February, 1931), 17-29.
"Back to What Constitution?" The American
    Mercury, XXXVI (December, 1935), 385-392.
"Cathedrals Under the War Cloud," Everybody's
    Magazine, 31 (December, 1914), 782-793.
"Cities of Refuge," The Commonweal, XXII
    (August 16, 1935), 379-381.
"Education and the Qualitative Standard," Edu-
    cational Review LVII (April, 1919), 304-311.
"Fulfillment," The American Review, IV (March,
    1935), 513-528.
"Good and Bad Modern Gothic," The Architectur-
    al Review, VI (August, 1899), 115-119.
"How Shall We Govern?" The Commonweal, XVI
    (July 13, 1932), 287-288.
"Invitation to Monarchy," The American Mercury,
    XXXVII (April, 1926), 479-486.
"On the Religious Aspect of Architecture,"
    The Architectural Record, II (January-
    March, 1893), 351-356.
"Princeton Architecture," The American Archi-

tect, XCVI (July 21, 1909), 21-30.

"Recovery or Regeneration," Part I, The Commonweal, XXI (November 2, 1934), 7-10.

"Recovery or Regeneration," Part II, The Commonweal, XXI (November 9, 1934), 56-58.

"Reflections Upon Art," The Commonweal, X (June 5, 1929), 120-122.

"Retrogression, Ugliness," The Architectural Forum, LIX (July, 1933), 24-25.

"Scrapping the Slums," The American Architect, CXIV (December 25, 1918), 761-763.

"Spanish Notes," The American Architect, CXXV (January 16, 1924), 47-54.

"Style in American Architecture," The Architectural Record, XXXIV (September, 1913), 233-239.

"The Change Beyond," The Commonweal, XXXI (November 3, 1939), 33-35.

"The End of Democracy," The American Mercury, XXXIX (September, 1936), 23-31.

"The Forgotten Class," Part I, The American Review, VII (April, 1936), 32-46.

"The Forgotten Class," Part II, The American Review, VII (May, 1936), 179-191.

"The Influence of the French School on American Architecture," The American Architect and Building News, LXVI (November 25, 1899), 65-66.

"The Last of the Squires," The Atlantic Monthly, CLXV (January, 1930), 80-85.

"The Limitations of Democracy," The Rice Institute Pamphlet, 17 (July, 1930), 175-199.

"The Limits of Modernism in Art," Arts and Decoration, XX (January, 1924), 11-13.

"The Mass-Man Takes Over," The American Mercury, XLV (October, 1938), 166-176.

"The Nemesis of Democracy," The American Review, VIII (December, 1936), 129-141.

"The Pre-eminence of Our Own Domestic Architecture," Arts and Decoration, XXII (April, 1925), 21-23, 73.

"The Rediscovery of Quality in Building," Arts and Decoration, XXI (September, 1924), 16-19.

"The Relation of Architecture to the People," Supplement to Art and Progress, I (July, 1910), 16-22.

"The Return to Feudalism," The American Re-

<u>view</u>, VIII (January, 1937), 336-352.
"The <u>Romantic Architecture of Morningside</u>
   <u>Heights</u>," <u>Columbia University Quarterly</u>,
   XXIII (March, 1931), 19-24.
"The Second Coming of Art," <u>The Atlantic</u>
   <u>Monthly</u>, 119 (February, 1917), 193-203.
"The Test of Beauty," <u>The Harvard Graduates'</u>
   <u>Magazine</u>, XXX (September, 1921), 1-20.
"The Unity of the Arts," <u>Landscape Architec-</u>
   <u>ture</u>, XXIII (April, 1933), 159-163.
"What Can Be Done for Art?" <u>The Commonweal</u>, X
   (June 12, 1929), 153-155.
"Why We Do Not Behave Like Human Beings," <u>The</u>
   <u>American Mercury</u>, XXVII (September, 1932),
   41-48.
"Will This Modernism Last?" <u>The House Beauti-</u>
   <u>ful</u>, LXV (January, 1929), 45,88.

C. OTHER PUBLISHED WORKS

<u>A Plan for the Settlement of Middle Europe on</u>
   <u>the Principle of Partition Without Annex-</u>
   <u>ation</u>. Boston: Marshall Jones Company,
   1918.
<u>An Open Letter to the Right Reverend Charles</u>
   <u>Gore, Lord Bishop of Oxford</u>. [Boston?],
   1913.
<u>Architecture in Its Relation to Civilization</u>.
   Boston: Marshall Jones Company, 1918.
Editorials in <u>Christian Art</u>, I (April, 1907),
   19; I (August, 1907), 235; II (October,
   1907), 54; II (January, 1908), 209; II
   (March, 1908), 305-306.
<u>Excalibur: An Arthurian Drama</u>. Boston: R.G.
   Badger, 1909.
Introduction to Henry Adams, <u>Mont-Saint-Michel</u>
   <u>and Chartres</u>. Boston: Houghton Mifflin
   Company, 1913.
Introduction to <u>Historia Calamitatum, The</u>
   <u>Story of My Misfortunes, an Autobiography</u>
   <u>by Peter Abelard</u>, trans. Henry Adams
   Bellows. St. Paul, Minnesota: T.A. Boyd,
   1922.
Letter in <u>The Commonweal</u>, XXIII (November 1,
   1935), 21.
Review of <u>Land of the Free</u>, by Herbert Agar,
   <u>The American Review</u>, VIII (May, 1936),
   214-216.

The Boat of Love: A Masque for Music, in Poet
Lore, XLVI (Summer, 1940), 165-177.
The Significance of Gothic Art. Boston: Mar-
shall Jones Company, 1918.
The Significance of the Great War. Boston:
Victorian Club, 1914.

D. UNPUBLISHED MATERIAL

Journal, 1881-1885. Department of Rare Books
& MSS., Boston Public Library.
Lecture Notes and Examinations. Rotch Library,
MIT Libraries, Cambridge, Massachusetts.

II. PRIMARY SOURCES

A. MANUSCRIPT COLLECTIONS

American Academy and Institute of Arts and
Letters Papers. New York.
The Century Collection. New York Public Li-
brary.
Louise Imogen Guiney Papers. College of the
Holy Cross.
Rush C. Hawkins Papers. Annmary Brown Memorial,
Brown University.
Hoyle, Doran and Berry Papers. Boston.
Henry L. Mencken Papers. New York Public Li-
brary.
MIT. Office of the President. Institute Ar-
chives and Special Collections, MIT Li-
braries, Cambridge, Massachusetts.
Paul Palmer Papers. Yale University Library.
Herman T. Radin Papers. New York Public Li-
brary.
S. C. Watkins Collection. Yale University Li-
brary.

B. REPORTS

Bulletin of the M.I.T.: Reports of the Presi-
dent and Treasurer, 50 (January, 1915).
East Boston, A Survey and a Comprehensive Plan.
Report of the City Planning Board of Bos-
ton, Massachusetts. Boston, 1915.
The North End, A Survey and a Comprehensive
Plan. Report of the City Planning Board

277

of Boston, Massachusetts. Boston, 1919.
"Technology Pageant," 1916 Papers. Institute
Archives and Special Collections, MIT
Libraries, Cambridge, Massachusetts.

C. NEWSPAPERS

Boston Sunday Globe. January 14, 1968.
The New York Times. September 23, 1942; December 31, 1971; May 21, 1973.

D. LETTERS TO AUTHOR

John T. Doran, March 8, 1973.
Shirley Gustavson, April 17, 1973.
Elizabeth Wall, March 27, 1973.

E. INTERVIEWS WITH AUTHOR

Ralph Wentworth Cram, August 9, 1972.
John T. Doran, August 8, 1972.

III. WORKS BY OTHERS

A. BOOKS

Adams, Henry. Mont-Saint-Michel and Chartres.
Boston: Houghton Mifflin Company, 1913.
_____. The Degradation of the Democratic
Dogma. New York: Harper & Row, Harper
Torchbooks, 1969.
Addison, Agnes. Romanticism and the Gothic
Revival. New York: R.R. Smith, 1938.
Ambrose, Stephen, E. Duty, Honor, Country:
A History of West Point. Baltimore:
Johns Hopkins Press, 1966.
Andrews, Wayne, Architecture, Ambition and
Americans. New York: Harper & Row, 1947.
Baker, Ray Stannard. Woodrow Wilson: Life
and Letters. Vol. II. Garden City, New
York: Doubleday, Page & Co., 1927.
Becker, Carl. The Heavenly City of the Eigh-
teenth-Century Philosophers. New Haven,
Connecticut: Yale University Press,
1932.

Bernanos, George. The Diary of a Country
    Priest, trans. Pamela Morris. New York:
    The Macmillan Company, 1937.
Bragdon, Henry Wilkinson. Woodrow Wilson: The
    Academic Years. Cambridge, Massachu-
    setts: Harvard University Press, 1967.
Brooks, Van Wyck. Scenes and Portraits:
    Memories of Childhood and Youth. New
    York: E.P. Dutton, 1954.
Burchard, John, and Bush-Brown, Albert. The
    Architecture of America: A Social and
    Cultural History. Boston: Little, Brown
    and Company, 1961.
Cater, Harold Dean, ed. Henry Adams and His
    Friends: A Collection of His Unpublish-
    ed Letters. Boston: Houghton Mifflin
    Company, 1947.
Chandler, Alice. A Dream of Order: The Medi-
    eval Ideal in Nineteenth-Century
    English Literature. Lincoln, Nebraska:
    University of Nebraska Press, 1970.
Coulborn, Rushton, ed. Feudalism in History.
    Princeton, New Jersey: Princeton Uni-
    versity Press, 1956.
Cram, Charles M. Genealogical Outline of the
    Cram, Walker, and Weekes Families.
    Boston, 1934.
Cram, William Everett. Time and Change.
    Boston: Marshall Jones Company, 1927.
Crane, Walter. An Artist's Reminiscences.
    New York: The Macmillan Company, 1907.
Crunden, Robert M. From Self to Society,
    1919-1941. Englewood Cliffs, New Jersey:
    Prentice-Hall, 1972.
_____. The Mind and Art of Albert Jay Nock.
    Chicago: Henry Regnery Company, 1964.
Dickason, David Howard. The Daring Young
    Men: The Story of the American Pre-
    Raphaelites. Bloomington, Indiana: In-
    diana University Press, 1953.
Diggins, John P. Mussolini and Fascism: The
    View from America. Princeton, New
    Jersey: Princeton University Press,
    1972.
Emerson, Ralph Waldo. The Conduct of Life.
    Boston: Houghton Mifflin and Co., 1898.
Fitch, James Marston. American Building: I:
    The Historical Forces That Shaped It.
    Boston: 2nd ed., rev. Houghton Mifflin

Company, 1948

Fleming, Thomas J. West Point: The Men and Times of the United States Military Academy. New York: William Morrow, 1969.

Ford, Worthington Chauncey, ed. Letters of Henry Adams, Vol. II. Boston: Houghton Mifflin Company, 1938.

Ford, Ford Madox. The Pre-Raphaelite Brotherhood. London: Duckworth & Co., 1907.

Garrison, Frank W., ed. Letters from Albert Jay Nock, 1924-1945. Caldwell, Idaho: Caxton Printers, 1949.

George, Alexander L., and George, Juliette L. Woodrow Wilson and Colonel House: A Personality Study. New York: J. Day Co., 1956.

Goodman, Paul. Like a Conquered Province. New York: Random House, 1967.

_____. New Reformation: Notes of a Neolithic Conservative. New York: Random House, 1970.

_____. The Community of Scholars. New York: Random House, 1962.

Gourmont, Remy de. Decadence and Other Essays on the Culture of Ideas, trans. William Aspenwall Bradley. New York: Harcourt, Brace and Company, 1921.

Granger, Alfred Hoyt. Charles Follen McKim. Boston: Houghton Mifflin Company, 1913.

Grant, Madison. The Passing of the Great Race. New York: Charles Scribner's Sons, 1916.

Guiney, Grace, ed. Letters of Louise Imogen Guiney. 2 Vols. New York: Harper & Brothers, 1926.

Guttmann, Allen. The Conservative Tradition in America. New York: Oxford University Press, 1967.

Hamlin, Talbot Faulkner. The American Spirit in Architecture. New Haven, Connecticut: Yale University Press, 1926.

Hartz, Louis. The Liberal Tradition in America: An Interpretation of American Political Thought Since the Revolution. New York: Harcourt, Brace and Company, 1955.

Hawthorne, Nathaniel. The Marble Faun, Vol. IV, The Centenary Edition of the Works of Nathaniel Hawthorne, William Charvat

et al., ed. Columbus, Ohio: Ohio State
University Press, 1968.
Henry, Stuart C., ed. A Miscellany of Amer-
ican Christianity: Essays in Honor of
H. Shelton Smith. Durham, North Caroli-
na: Duke University Press, 1963.
Hitchcock, Henry-Russell. Architecture,
Nineteenth and Twentieth Centuries.
Middlesex, England: Penguin Books, 1958.
_____. The Architecture of H.H. Richardson
and His Times, rev. ed. Hamden,
Connecticut: Archon Books, 1961.
Hovey, Richard B. John Jay Chapman--An Amer-
ican Mind. New York: Columbia Universi-
ty Press, 1959.
Howe, Helen. The Gentle Americans, 1864-1960:
Biography of a Breed. New York: Harper
& Row, 1965.
Hunt, William Holman. Pre-Raphaelitism and
the Pre-Raphaelite Brotherhood. 2 Vols.
New York: The Macmillan Company, 1905.
Jackson, Holbrook. The Eighteen Nineties.
New York: Alfred A. Knopf, 1922.
Jacobs, Jane. The Death and Life of Great
American Cities. New York: Random House,
1961.
Jordy, William H. American Buildings and
Their Architects: Progressive and Aca-
demic Ideals at the Turn of the Twen-
tieth Century. Garden City, New York:
Doubleday, 1972.
_____. Henry Adams: Scientific Historian.
New Haven, Connecticut: Yale University
Press, 1952.
_____, and Coe, Ralph, ed. American Archi-
tecture and Other Writings by Montgom-
ery Schuyler. 2 Vols. Cambridge,
Massachusetts: Harvard University Press,
1961.
Kazin, Alfred. On Native Grounds. New York:
Reynal and Hitchcock, 1942.
Kimball, Fiske. American Architecture. New
York: AMS Press, 1970.
Kirk, Russell. The Conservative Mind: From
Burke to Santayana. Chicago: Henry
Regnery Company, 1953.
La Farge, John, S.J. The Manner is Ordinary.
New York: Harcourt, Brace Company, 1954.
La Follette, Suzanne. Art in America. New

281

York: Harper & Brothers, 1929.

Larkin, Oliver W. Art and Life in America, 2nd ed., rev. New York: Holt, Rinehart and Winston, 1960.

Levine, George, ed. The Emergence of Victorian Consciousness: The Spirit of an Age. New York: Free Press, 1967.

Link, Arthur S., ed. The Papers of Woodrow Wilson, Vols. XVII-XX, XXII. Princeton, New Jersey: Princeton University Press, 1974-1976.

_____. Wilson: The Road to the White House. Princeton, New Jersey: Princeton University Press, 1947.

Lora, Ronald. Conservative Minds in America. New York: Rand McNally & Company, 1971.

Lynes, Russell. The Art-Makers of Nineteenth-Century America. New York: Atheneum, 1970.

_____. The Tastemakers. New York: Harper & Row, 1954.

Macdonald, Allan Houston. Richard Hovey, Man & Craftsman. Durham, North Carolina: Duke University Press, 1957.

Maginnis, Charles. Introduction to The Work of Cram and Ferguson, Architects. New York: The Pencil Points Press, 1929.

Marx, Leo. The Machine in the Garden: Technology and the Pastoral Ideal in America. New York: Oxford University Press, 1964.

Massa, Anna. Vachel Lindsay: Fieldworker for the American Dream. Bloomington, Indiana: Indiana University Press, 1970.

May, Henry F. The End of American Innocence: A Study of the First Years of Our Own Time, 1912-1917. New York: Alfred A. Knopf, 1959.

Moore, Charles. Daniel H. Burnham: Architect Planner of Cities. Vol. I. Boston: Houghton Mifflin Company, 1921.

_____. The Life and Times of Charles Follen McKim. Boston: Houghton Mifflin Company, 1929.

Morris, William. Collected Works, Vol. XXIII. New York: Russell & Russell, 1966.

Mumford, Lewis. Sticks and Stones: A Study of American Architecture & Civilization. New York: W.W. Norton & Company, 1924.

_____. The Brown Decades. New York: Harcourt, Brace and Company, 1931.

_____. The Myth of the Machine. New York: Harcourt Brace Jovanovich, 1970.

Nash, George H. The Conservative Intellectual Movement in America: Since 1945. New York: Basic Books, 1979.

Nock, Albert Jay. Memoirs of a Superfluous Man. New York: Harper & Brothers, 1943.

_____. The Theory of Education in the United States. New York: Harcourt, Brace Company, 1932.

North, Arthur Tappan. Foreword to Ralph Adams Cram, Cram and Ferguson. New York and London: Whittlesey House, McGraw-Hill, 1931.

Noyes, John Humphrey. History of American Socialisms. Philadelphia: J.B. Lippincott, 1870.

Pater, Walter. Marius the Epicurean. New York: The Macmillan Company, 1898.

Pierson, William H. Jr., American Buildings and Their Architects: Technology and the Picturesque, the Corporate and the Early Gothic Styles. Garden City, New York: Doubleday, 1978.

Riencourt, Amaury de. The Coming Caesars. New York: Coward-McCann, 1957.

Rossiter, Clinton. Conservatism in America. New York: Alfred A. Knopf, 1955.

Roth, Leland M. The Architecture of McKim, Mead & White. New York: Garland Publishers, 1973.

Spitz, David. Patterns of Anti-Democratic Thought. 2nd ed., rev. New York: Free Press, 1965.

Stein, Roger B. John Ruskin and Aesthetic Thought in America, 1840-1900. Cambridge, Massachusetts: Harvard University Press, 1967.

Stoddard, Theodore Lothrop. Clashing Tides of Colour. New York and London: Charles Scribner's Sons, 1935.

_____. The Rising Tide of Color Against White World-Supremacy. New York: Charles Scribner's Sons, 1920.

Sullivan, Louis H. Democracy: A Man-Search. Detroit: Wayne State University Press, 1961.

283

Tallmadge, Thomas E. The Story of Architecture in America. 2nd ed., rev. New York: W.W. Norton and Company, 1936.

Tenison, E.M. Louise Imogen Guiney: Her Life and Works, 1861-1920. London: Macmillan and Company, 1923.

Thomas, Lately. The Mayor Who Mastered New York: The Life and Opinions of William Jay Gaynor. New York: William Morrow & Company, 1969.

Twombly, Robert C. Frank Lloyd Wright: An Interpretive Biography. New York: Harper & Row, 1973.

Tucci, Douglass Shand. All Saints' Church: An Introduction to the Architecture of Ralph Adams Cram. Boston: Dorchester Savings Bank, 1973.

_____. Church Building in Boston, 1720-1970. Concord, Massachusetts: The Rumford Press, 1974.

_____. The Gothic Churches of Dorchester: Readings in Modern Boston History. Tribune Publishing Company, 1972.

Tyler, Alice Felt. Freedom's Ferment: Phases of American Social History to 1860. Minneapolis, Minnesota: University of Minnesota Press, 1944.

Van Roosbroeck, Gustave L. The Legend of the Decadents. New York: Columbia University Press, 1927.

Vanderbilt, Kermit. Charles Eliot Norton: Apostle of Culture in a Democracy. Cambridge, Massachusetts: Harvard University Press, 1959.

Veblen, Thorstein. Imperial Germany and the Industrial Revolution. New York: The Macmillan Company, 1915.

_____. The Engineers and the Price System. New York: B.W. Huebsch, 1921

_____. The Higher Learning in America: A Memorandum on the Conduct of Universities by Business Men. New York: B.W. Huebsch, 1918.

_____. The Theory of the Leisure Class. New York: The Macmillan Company, 1899.

Vogt, Von Ogden. Art & Religion. 2nd ed., rev. New Haven, Connecticut: Yale University Press, 1929.

Welland, Dennis. The Pre-Raphaelites in Lit-

erature and Art. London: Harrap, 1953.
West, Andrew Fleming. The Graduate College of
Princeton. Princeton, New Jersey:
Princeton University Press, 1913.
Whiffen, Marcus. American Architecture Since
1780. Cambridge, Massachusetts: M.I.T.
Press, 1969.
Whitaker, Charles Harris, ed. Bertram Gros-
venor Goodhue--Architect and Master of
Many Arts. New York: Press of the Ameri-
can Institute of Architects, 1925.
White, Morton. Social Thought in America: The
Revolt Against Formalism. New York:
Viking Press, 1952.
White, Morton, and White, Lucia. The Intel-
lectual Versus the City: From Jefferson
to Frank Lloyd Wright. Cambridge, Massa-
chusetts: Harvard University Press, 1962.
Wolfskill, George, and Hudson, John A. All
But the People: Franklin D. Roosevelt
and His Critics, 1933-1939. New York:
The Macmillan Company, 1969.
Wood, Esther. Dante Rossetti and the Pre-
Raphaelite Movement. New York: Charles
Scribner's Sons, 1894.
Wreszin, Michael. The Superfluous Anarchist:
Albert Jay Nock. Providence, Rhode Is-
land: Brown University Press, 1972.
Wright, Frank Lloyd. Genius and Mobocracy.
New York: Duell, Sloan and Pearce, 1949.
Ziff, Larzer. The American 1890's: Life and
Times of a Lost Generation. New York:
Viking Press, 1966.
Zoll, Donald Atwell. The Twentieth Century
Mind: Essays on Contemporary Thought.
Baton Rouge, Louisiana: Louisiana State
University Press, 1967.

B. ARTICLES

"A Dome for the Divine," Time, 88 (December
2, 1966), 78.
Allen, George H. "Cram--The Yankee Mediae-
valist," The Architectural Forum, LV
(July, 1931), 79-80.
Brown, John Nicholas; Coffman, George
Raleigh; and Rand, Edward Kennard.
"Memoir: Ralph Adams Cram," Speculum: A

Journal of Mediaeval Studies, XVIII
(July, 1943), 388-389.
[Candidus]. "The Cathedral of St. John the
Divine: A Criticism," The American Ar-
chitect, XCI (May 18, 1907), 203-204.
"Cross Currents," The Architectural Record,
II (October-December, 1892), 216-220.
Fitch, James M. "St. John the Divine," Archi-
tectural Forum (December, 1954), 113-117.
Hacker, Andrew. "On Original Sin and Conser-
vatives," The New York Times Magazine
(February 25, 1973), 13,65-66, 68, 70-72.
Hamlin, A.D.F. "Gothic Architecture and Its
Critics: Part I, The Lure of Gothic,"
The Architectural Record, XXXIX (April,
1916), 338-354.
Hudnut, Joseph. "The Romantic Architecture of
Morningside Heights," Columbia Universi-
ty Quarterly, XXII (December, 1930),
397-406.
Johnson, James F. "Ralph Adams Cram: Ideal-
ist, Scholar, Architect, Christian
Property Administration, 8 (January-
February, 1944), 9-14, 41-43.
La Farge, Grant. "St. John the Divine,"
Scribner's Magazine, XLI (April, 1907),
385-401.
Leffert, Henry. "Richard Hovey," in Dumas
Malone, ed., The Dictionary of American
Biography, V (New York, 1932), pp. 273-
274.
Maginnis, Charles D. "Ralph Adams Cram," The
Octagon, 15 (February, 1943), 13-15.
Nock, Albert Jay. "Are All Men Human?"
Harper's Magazine (January, 1933), 240-
246.
_____. "The Quest of the Missing Link," The
Atlantic Monthly, 155 (April, 1935),
399-408.
Pope, Virginia. "Architecture of America
Molds Beauty Anew," The New York Times
Magazine (December 19, 1926), 3, 21.
"Protestantism Is Bankrupt," Time, XXVII
(January 6, 1936), 32-33.
"R.A. Cram, Professor of Architecture at
Boston 'Tech,'" The Architectural Record,
XXXVI, (August, 1914), 175-176.
Schuyler, Montgomery. "The Architecture of
West Point," The Architectural Record,

XIV (December, 1903), 463-492.

_____. "The New St. Thomas's Church, New
York," Scribner's Magazine, LIV (December, 1913), 791-794.

_____. "The Works of Cram, Goodhue & Fergu-
son," The Architectural Record, XXXIX
(January, 1911), 1-112.

Shapiro, Edward S. "Decentralist Intellectuals and the New Deal," The Journal of
American History, LVIII (March, 1972),
938-957.

Stone, Geoffrey. "The End of Democracy: Ralph
Adams Cram's Plea for a New Order," The
American Review, IX (September, 1937),
365-379.

Watkin, William Ward. "I Knew Him Well," The
New Pencil Points (October, 1942), 8.

"When Men of Good-Will Get Together," The
Literary Digest, 103 (December 14, 1929),
22-23.

C. OTHER SOURCES

Letter of Robert Tappan to The American Architect, CXXXIX (January, 1931), 66.

Maginnis, Charles D. Editorial in Liturgical
Arts, XI (November, 1942), 1.

Review of My Life in Architecture. Supplement
to The Architectural Record, 79 (March,
1936), 12.

Sinnett, Reverend Charles N. "Ancestor John
Cram and His Descendants." Typescript.
Fertile, Minnesota, 1925 (?)

Stansky, Peter. Review of William Morris:
Romantic to Revolutionary, by E.P.
Thompson, in The New York Times Book Re-
view (May 15, 1977), 7, 48.

[Stevens, Frederick W.] Observations by an
Obscure Mediocrity, on a Recently Pub-
lished Brochure Entitled "The Nemesis of
Mediocrity." Ann Arbor, Michigan: G.
Wahr, 1918.

INDEX

Cook, Walter, 81
Cope and Stewardson, 89, 96n
Cram, Elizabeth Carrington (Read), 80, 261
Cram, John, 8-9, 20n
Cram, Ludolf von, 8
Cram, Marion, 10, 21n
Cram, Mary Carrington, 80
Cram, Ralph Adams, fame of, 1; conservatism of, 2-3; birth, 7; childhood, 11-13, settles in Boston and begins apprenticeship with Rotch and Tilden, 14-16; wins competition for Suffolk County Courthouse, 16; trips to Europe, 16-19; religious conversion, 18; attitudes toward evolution and science, 28-30; and Aesthetic Movement, 30 ff.; and *Knight Errant*, 33; and *Black Spirits* and White, 35; as poet and lyricist, 36-37; and *The Decadent*, 37-39; early socialism and monarchism of, 39-40; and Order of the White Rose, 40-41; admiration for McKim and Richardson, 56-57; partnership with Charles Francis Wentworth, 58; on Gothic architecture, 56-66; early commissions, 73-77; takes Bertram Grosvenor Goodhue into firm, 77-78; trip to Japan, 79-80; marriage, 80; and West Point, 80-83; and St. Thomas', 83-85; and Goodhue end partnership, 85-86; and Rice Institute, 86-87; and Princeton University, 87-90; and Cathedral of St. John the Divine

90-92; medievalism of, 116 ff.; on Gothic style for Christianity, 117-120; theory of history 121-123; denounces Renaissance and Reformation, 130-131 ff.; on Japanese civilization, 133-134; and Henry Adams, 135-137; domestic life, 145-147; and city planning, 147-149; teaching at Massachusetts Institute of Technology, 149-159; and World War I, 165 ff.; on Social Darwinism and races, 177-179; on Bolshevism and radicals, 179-180; and Walled Towns, 183-185; on modern art and architecture, 198-205; commissions and firm during 1920's, 205-208; continues to work on Cathedral of St. John the Divine, 207-209; and Mediaeval Academy of America, 209; and *Commonweal*, 210; and Christian art, 211-213; and "massman," 224-230 ff.; and Henry L. Mencken, 226-228; and Albert Jay Nock, 228-230; and the New Deal, 231 ff.; and "Forgotten Class," 239-240; and fascism, 241-242; and New Medievalism, 242-249; and World War II, 259-263; wife's illness, 261; death, 263; estimate of, 267-271
Cram, Ralph Wentworth, 139n, 216n, 263
Cram, Sara (Blake), 9-13
Cram, Thomas Jefferson, 9
Cram, William Augustine, 8-14
Cram, William Everett, 10, 20-21n

290